THE SPARROW AND THE HAWK

THE SPARROW AND THE HAWK

Costa Rica and the United States during the Rise of José Figueres

Kyle Longley

The University of Alabama Press

Tuscaloosa

Manufactured in the United States of America

∞

The paper on which this book is printed meets the minimum requirements of American National Standard for Information Science-Permanence of Paper for Printed Library Materials, ANSI Z39.48-1984.

Library of Congress Cataloging-in-Publication Data

Longley, Kyle.
The sparrow and the hawk : Costa Rica and the United States during the rise of José Figueres / Kyle Longley.
p. cm.
Includes bibliographical references and index.
ISBN 0-8173-0831-8 (pbk. : alk. paper)
1. United States—Foreign relations—Costa Rica. 2. Costa Rica—Foreign relations—United States. 3. Figueres Ferrer, José, 1906– . I. Title.
E183.8.C8L66 1997
327.7286073—dc20 96-19042

British Library Cataloguing-in-Publication Data available

The following articles were previously published and have been reused with permission:

“Resistance and Accommodation: The United States and the Nationalism of José Figueres, 1953–1957,” from *Diplomatic History* 18 (Winter 1994): 1–28.

“Peaceful Costa Rica, the First Battleground: the United States and the Costa Rican Revolution of 1948,” from *The Americas* (issue, volume, dates unknown).

For Betty Pettit

CONTENTS

PREFACE

Numerous relationships between species exist in the animal kingdom. Some are cooperative while others are antagonistic, but in all cases the instinct to survive dominates. One such association has developed between the hawk and the sparrow. The former is larger, stronger, and faster, a merciless predator that roams the skies with few equals. On the other hand, the sparrow is comparatively weak and powerless. Yet, when the hawk enters the sparrow's nesting area, the smaller bird viciously attacks the intruder, exploiting its maneuverability to sweep down and strike. Although the hawk really faces no physical threat, it usually retreats. Despite its victory, the sparrow rarely pursues the hawk outside its domain.

While the militant response of the sparrow to the hawk is fascinating, it is only a small part of the struggle. The sparrow relies on violence rarely and only as a last resort. To review only this part of the relationship ignores the larger story. Before attacking the hawk, the sparrow employs other, more cautious tactics to deal with the stronger power because it recognizes the hawk's superiority. Some methods include hiding its nests in areas rarely frequented by predators, decoying the stronger bird away from the nest, and a number of seemingly small acts that, taken together, form the bulk of the sparrow's response to the hawk.

In many ways, the relationship between the hawk and the sparrow resembles that of the United States and the nonindustrialized world.[1] Washington possesses military, economic, and diplomatic superiority, often exerting its power over weaker nations. Some countries vigorously resist U.S. domination. One need only walk through bookstores or the stacks of libraries to find that many works emphasize violence in U.S. relations with the nonindustrialized world, especially when the latter successfully repels U.S. attempts to establish hegemony.[2] The titles on topics such as Vietnam and Cuba greatly outnumber those characterized by more routine responses to the United States. This trend extends into textbooks and broader surveys of U.S. foreign relations where historians emphasize either violent or collaborative relationship.

A number of reasons for this phenomenon exist. The historical community has always been interested in learning lessons from U.S. commitments in the world, a process accelerated by the U.S. defeat in Vietnam. In addition, wars of national liberation fascinated many Americans. Some left-wing intellectuals identified with Marxism, while others saw similarities between the U.S. experience of the eighteenth century and the struggles of other countries of the twentieth century. Finally, the clashes seemed like heroic contests between the weak and the powerful, a story that appeals to many Americans' identification with the underdog. As a result, much of the literature of the U.S. experience in the nonindustrialized world focuses more on crisis points than normal relations.

While all the studies of violent responses are important, this pattern leads to a gap in the historiography of U.S. relations with the nonindustrialized world. A goal of this book is to suggest that historians should examine carefully the more routine and orderly forms of peripheral resistance and accommodation. The majority of countries do not employ radical or violent responses, relying instead on "working the system . . . to their minimum disadvantage," to borrow Eric Hobsbawm's phrase.[3] Weak nations often respond to a stronger state within the established framework, learning to manipulate the process for their own gain without provoking a violent response from the core power. In almost every case, the nonindustrialized world has not been passive, although the specific responses have differed from culture to culture. It is necessary to review the development and implementation of these more orthodox actions; otherwise the historian misses or downplays a significant segment of international relations.

An interesting case study in U.S. relations with the nonindustrialized world distinguished by nonviolent resistance and accommodation exists in Central America, one of the most volatile and unstable regions in the world. In this environment, Costa Rica has evolved differently from its neighbors, a country observers often characterize as "The Switzerland of the Americas," "The Land of Eternal Spring," and "The Gem of the American Republics." Although a country not without problems, it boasts a good health care system and much higher rates of literacy, life expectancy, and political participation than its Central American neighbors. From the nineteenth century forward, Costa Rican society evolved with strong democratic political institutions and less social stratification than its neighbors. When disputes arose, Costa Ricans rarely resorted to violence to settle their differences, allowing their democratic tradition to become one of the most respected in Latin America.

Costa Rica's development helped shape its relations with metropole powers such as the United States when it achieved independence from Spain in the 1820s. The Costa Rican experience has been one of the rare cases in which the United States and one of its Central American neighbors have maintained essentially good relations. A pattern involving resistance and accommodation by the smaller, less powerful Costa Rica matured throughout the nineteenth century. From the 1830s onward, U.S. officials and American citizens recognized Costa Rica's "exceptionalism," noting its democratic and progressive traditions. Its internal stability gave the United States no need to intervene to protect U.S. business interests and citizens or to prevent foreign domination. In addition, the Costa Ricans typically supported Washington's policies on major international issues. Differences did sometimes arise over such regional matters as U.S. interventionism in the Caribbean Basin and control of the Nicaraguan canal route. Despite these disputes, the United States rarely viewed the actions of San José as directly threatening its national security. As a result, it allowed the Costa Ricans greater autonomy in political, diplomatic, and economic affairs than other nations in the region. This model has continued comparatively uninterrupted until today.

Unfortunately, U.S.–Costa Rican relations have received very little attention. Most English-language materials focus on the United States and the more unstable societies in the region, primarily Nicaragua, El Salvador, Panama, and Guatemala. Historians have concentrated on other nations where the United States directly intervened, often militarily, or collaborated with *comprador* élites, such as that led by Anastasio Somoza-García. While there are several dissertations and a few Spanish-language books and journal articles, most of the information on U.S.–Costa Rican relations can be found in general studies of the region by Walter LaFeber, Thomas Leonard, and John E. Findling.[4]

To better illustrate the importance of U.S.–Costa Rican relations at the national, regional, and international levels, this book will examine the very explosive period from 1942 to 1957. This era provides an opportunity to understand the dynamics of the traditional pattern because it coincides with the early career of one of the most controversial and flamboyant figures in Costa Rican history, José "Don Pepe" Figueres. Specifically,

I will analyze his rise to power and his interaction with his opponents and allies to demonstrate how he and his party resisted U.S. political and economic domination during the tumultuous period following World War II. Unlike some nationalists during the same period, Figueres avoided provoking the United States insofar as no direct intervention occurred. Nevertheless, his programs differed more in degree than in form from those implemented by others throughout the world, a point stressed by conservatives when they attacked him in Washington during the 1950s. The essential question this work will address is why the United States tolerated Figueres's economic and political nationalism when it rejected comparable policies in other parts of the nonindustrialized world.

The most significant factor in maintaining the successful relationship between Costa Rica and the United States was Figueres and his associates. They possessed both a keen dedication to their principles and a realistic comprehension of a hemispheric system in which the United States clearly dominated. While the United States possessed economic, military, and diplomatic superiority, the *figueristas* utilized a variety of "weapons" to allow them to promote their country's interests within the existing framework. These tools included playing upon the long-standing history of amicable relations, developing strong ties with democratic liberal groups in the United States, invoking common symbolism and ideologies, and understanding American views toward economic and social issues. Finally, they benefited from a willingness to accommodate Washington, comprehending that compromise is an essential ingredient of any political relationship.

Most important, they recognized the significance of the issue of communism in the rapidly expanding cold war. The *figueristas* shared the U.S. aversion to communism, a point reinforced by their actions and statements. They also recognized the domestic and international constraints that U.S. leaders encountered after World War II, supporting U.S. actions on major international questions while often challenging regional policies. This keen understanding of geopolitical conditions allowed Figueres and his advisers to make informed decisions that both resisted and accommodated Washington. This response reduced the potential for conflict and allowed cordial relations to continue in a period characterized by Washington's overreaction to most forms of nationalism in the nonindustrialized world.

The record of U.S.–Costa Rican relations during the rise of José

Figueres will highlight an admittedly unusual case in which the United States had a comparatively good relationship with a peripheral nation. Essentially friendly relations based for the most part on mutual respect and cooperation have distinguished the interchanges between the two nations. This study will try to uncover some of the complex factors that have allowed this relationship to develop and flourish, mainly the role of the developing world in the evolution and implementation of policies. Finally, it suggests that the United States can have good relations with a nation in the nonindustrialized world when both countries work toward a mutually acceptable exchange.

Many people have assisted my efforts to answer the questions posed in this study. I must thank all the people in the archives and libraries I have visited in the last three years, especially those at the National Archives, the Nettie Benson Latin American Collection, and the Roosevelt, Truman, and Eisenhower presidential libraries. I owe special thanks to the archivists at the Archivo Nacional in San José, especially Christian Kandler-Rodríguez for his patience in helping me search for my materials as well as for proving to be an important guide to finding other sources during my two visits to his country. Finally, I must praise the librarians at the University of Kentucky for helping me secure a seemingly endless number of books, microfilms, and periodicals.

I also owe special thanks to several institutions for providing financial support for my endeavors. The University of Kentucky Graduate Council and the Department of History awarded significant travel funds and a dissertation-year fellowship that allowed me to finish my work in a timely fashion. I also received much needed financial assistance from the Franklin D. Roosevelt and Harry S. Truman libraries to facilitate my research in their archives. Finally, I would like to thank the Society for Historians of American Foreign Relations for the generous grant provided by the W. Stull Holt Fellowship. Each of the aforementioned sources made my task significantly easier.

There is also a long list of people I must thank for helping me in my search for materials and for reading my manuscript, conference papers, and journal articles. Thanks go to John P. Bell, Robert Brigham, Francie Chassen-López, Eric Christianson, Charles Davis, Mark Gilderhus, James Harper, Robert Hayes, Ann Heiss, David Hamilton, Richard Immerman, Michael Krenn, Thomas Leonard, Stephen Rabe, Daniel Reedy, Greg Stanley, Charles Stansifer, Stephen Streeter, Roger Trask, William Walker,

Jeffrey Wasserstrom, Stephen Webre, and Thomas Zoumaras. I must extend special thanks to George Herring for the endless hours he spent reading my work and for acting as both a critical editor and friend simultaneously. He helped me clear some very imposing hurdles. I cannot say enough about all the assistance he gave me.

Malcolm MacDonald and the staff of The University of Alabama Press deserve special praise for guiding me through the often daunting task of moving the project from manuscript to final product. I must also acknowledge the assistance of free-lance editor Anders L. Thompson, who provided helpful suggestions for improving the form and prose of the book. They have made the task of publishing this work a much easier one.

I also must underscore my gratitude to my friends and family. My parents, Joe and Chan, deserve special thanks for all the sacrifices that they made ensuring I received a good education and providing a nurturing environment for my development. They have kept me going and served as the inspiration in all areas of my life.

I owe special appreciation to my wife, Tracy. She has endured the long hours of my work and, more important, my mood swings. During the entire time she was there to listen, and, although she is a biologist, she proved a good critic and a strong supporter of my study.

In conclusion, I would like to dedicate this work to my wife's maternal grandmother, Betty Pettit. She should serve as an inspiration to all students, young and old. She returned to school to study anthropology after raising a family. Her thirst for knowledge has rarely been matched. If all people had her attitude about learning, then my job as a writer and teacher would be infinitely easier. We will always remember her with the fondest of memories.

THE SPARROW AND THE HAWK

1

THE SWITZERLAND OF THE AMERICAS
Costa Rica and the Foundations of Cordial Relations with the United States

"Of all the Central American republics," Charles Howland of the American Council of the Institute of Pacific Relations declared in 1929, "Costa Rica has been the most tranquil and progressive." "The government is the most stable and democratic," and "popular elections, although sometimes corrupted, represent in the main the desires of the people. . . . Opinion finds free expression in the public press, and graft and bribery are less common than in neighboring states." Howland also noted that "the population is predominantly white, the number of small agricultural proprietors is unusually large, and the Republic prides itself on spending more money on her schools than on her army, and on having more school teachers than soldiers."[1]

Positive perceptions of Costa Rica prevailed throughout the nineteenth and twentieth centuries in the United States at a time when negative stereotypes dominated Americans' views of Latin America. A major factor contributing to this unique development was Costa Rica's evolution toward a democratic-capitalist nation. The colonial era laid the foundation for a society to mature in the postindependence period, a period characterized by a relative absence of infighting and foreign control of domestic industries. The movement toward a comparatively stable society continued into the twentieth century as suffrage, education, and the respect for basic civil liberties expanded. By World War II and the rise of José Figueres, many Americans extolled Costa Rica as a model for Latin America.

The myths and realities of the historical development of Costa Rica strongly affected U.S.–Costa Rican relations. The domestic stability and lack of foreign influence prevented the United States from intervening in

Costa Rica's affairs. Common concepts of government and society also prevented misunderstanding between the two countries. A pattern of relations evolved characterized by San José's support for Washington in major international crises. In regional affairs, however, the Costa Ricans sought to maintain some independence of action. Disputes arose occasionally, but they never undermined Washington's belief that Costa Rica was a solid ally in a region where the United States often relied on tyrannical dictators to support its policies. This relationship was important because Figueres and his associates would benefit from the legacy of amicable exchanges.

The realities of Costa Rica's evolution toward a democratic-capitalist society included the comparative lack of development of repressive and divisive Spanish colonial institutions. Costa Rica's geography was important, establishing its economic potential, strategic importance, and demographic patterns.[2] The discovery of gold initially sparked interest among the Spanish, but early attempts to find additional minerals failed. Subsequent explorers searched vainly for gold and silver, suffering heavy losses in the inhospitable jungles and high mountains. Discouraged, most conquistadors turned their attention elsewhere, although a few Spaniards continued to believe that Costa Rica possessed wealth. In 1564, Juan Vásquez de Coronado established the first permanent city at Cartago. Like his predecessors, he uncovered no riches, and the isolation and poverty of Costa Rica caused Spanish officials to show little interest in the colony throughout the colonial period.[3]

The absence of an exploitable labor force caused further disinterest among potential settlers and the Crown. The indigenous peoples violently resisted subjugation by the Spanish. Destroyed by wars, disease, and miscegenation, native Americans had virtually disappeared by the turn of the nineteenth century.[4] As a result, the *encomienda* system remained underdeveloped in Costa Rica. Instead, the Spanish relied on *reducciones* (small settlements) to pacify the Indians and provide a work force. This form was relatively ineffective, depriving them of the cheap labor they found in Mexico, Peru, and Guatemala.[5]

The lack of wealth attracted few settlers, and those who did settle typically relied on subsistence farming. Even in the early eighteenth century, the bishop of Nicaragua observed that Costa Rican colonists lived "in naked paganism because of their abundance in the countryside. They go out to live there, leaving the cities and pueblos like desert."[6] Trading occasionally occurred, with mule trains crossing the isthmus, and in several areas the harvesting of cacao and tobacco permitted some capital accumulation.[7] Throughout the era, most colonists survived by growing their own foods and bartering for other necessities. Hard currency remained so scarce that in 1719 the Costa Rican governor, Diego de la Haya Fernández, complained that "the current money is the cacao bean, the silver real not being known at all at the present time anywhere." "In fact," he added, "the province has become so exceedingly impoverished that no one has been able to discover whence the country got the designation and title 'Costa Rica.' "[8]

Economic conditions and the geographic isolation of the colonial era created the foundations for the establishment of a more democratic social and political order during the republican era. The shortage of labor and the land tenure system helped blur class lines. Many Costa Ricans owned some land (although often very small parcels) and manifested the pride associated with private ownership. In Costa Rica, unlike other parts of the empire, the economic system caused citizens to emphasize individualism over a group orientation, leading to a greater tolerance of others and an aversion to extremes in social and political affairs.[9]

Costa Rica's poverty and isolation also undermined conservative Spanish institutions such as the Catholic Church. In many areas of the Spanish empire, the Church acted as a repressive force, fostering inequitable land distribution and social stratification. The Church remained weak throughout the colonial era because of Costa Rica's isolation from ecclesiastical power centers. Under the guidance of the archbishop of Nicaragua, parish priests were the only Church officials. The archbishop exerted little control, visiting only eleven times in the three hundred years of the colonial period, sometimes at intervals as long as thirty-three years.[10] Local Church representatives never accumulated wealth or land and participated sparingly in political matters. Interchanges occurred typically when the colonists failed to remit their tithes. This pattern continued until 1850, when the Holy See finally created a diocese in Costa Rica.[11] This absence of powerful religious institutions removed an issue that caused strife between conservatives and liberals in other Latin American nations during the postindependence era.

In addition to the realities of the Costa Rican experience, several myths developed regarding Costa Rica's social and economic development, myths that strongly influenced perceptions among Costa Ricans and foreigners. Some Costa Ricans clearly have exaggerated the notion that during the colonial era, small farmers with Jeffersonian republican values dominated. They have argued that the presence of this group made Costa Rica's evolution toward a democracy easier, although the dislocations caused by the coffee boom dissipated the impact. Recent research, however, underscores the idea that certain families gained more power in the colonial period, many descended from the original conquistadors.[12] Nevertheless, the myth of a country of middle-class farmers remained an influential one in the nineteenth and twentieth centuries, affecting domestic and foreign perceptions.

Another important myth from the colonial era was the *leyenda blanca* (white legend). The absence of a significant Indian population fostered a belief that Costa Rica was a racially homogeneous society, almost exclusively white.[13] While census figures did not correspond with the concept, the notion of a dual society (one native, the other Europeanized) never developed, helping mitigate class and social conflicts that arose in other Central American states in the nineteenth century.[14] The myth of the white legend also influenced foreign observers, who stressed the whiteness of the Costa Ricans, attributing much of Costa Rica's progress to the absence of an Indian population. In many ways, this idea and others increased the belief in the country's exceptionalism among Costa Ricans and foreigners.

The realities and myths of Costa Rica's colonial economic and social evolution directly influenced the development of its political culture.[15] Poverty and remoteness undermined the authoritarian concepts and institutions that often accompanied Spanish rule. In Costa Rica, governmental service ensured few advantages. "Exercising power," Samuel Stone has noted, "did not endow its members with a sense of identity as a ruling class, for their status conferred little authority."[16] The political structure remained relatively weak and nonintrusive. Although élites dominated, they possessed an ill-defined ideology and exerted only limited control.[17]

The small ruling class of the original conquistadors and Spanish officials dominated the weak political structure during the colonial period, but some forms of mass participation evolved. Colonial representatives occasionally called an "open cabildo" to discuss important public matters, laying the foundation for civic interest in the republican period. When combined with other factors such as the *leyenda blanca,* the participatory rule helped place in Costa Rica's political consciousness a preference for consensus over conflict.[18]

In the colonial era, poverty and the lack of strong political controls also undermined the development of the military, another institution that stymied democratic growth in other Latin American nations. The lack of mineral wealth and the small Indian population offered few enticements to soldiers to settle in the impoverished colony. On several occasions, the Spanish Crown tried organizing a military force to combat piracy and British interventions on the Atlantic coast, but the Costa Ricans resisted. Most of them lived in the *meseta central* safe from foreign incursions, and they wanted to avoid the heavy financial burden of an army. This absence of a military tradition significantly affected Costa Rica's political institutions. Although the military assumed more prominence in the republican era, it remained relatively unimportant as a political actor throughout most of the country's history, virtually disappearing after 1948.[19]

Besides the local disinterest in the political system, the Spanish Crown devoted very limited attention to Costa Rica. The Audiencia of Guatemala periodically tried exercising dominion over the colony, especially in fiscal matters, but the country's isolation and the tendency of local Spanish officials to side with the Costa Ricans undermined centralized rule. Occasionally Costa Ricans demonstrated against Spanish rule, primarily in response to policies handed down by the leaders in Guatemala, but these acts were relatively few. Overall, the Costa Ricans readily accepted the "salutary neglect."[20]

Costa Rica's political culture also influenced its interaction with other colonies and countries. In dealing with the Spanish Crown, the Costa Ricans deferred on most issues. Independence was thrust upon them, not actively sought. In regional and domestic affairs, however, they maintained positions that best served their interests. They voiced their concerns about matters that directly affected them, resisting attempts by Spanish officials in Guatemala to interfere in their lives. This pattern of relations carried over into the postindependence era, when Costa Rica continued yielding to stronger powers, primarily the United States, on major international questions, while retaining relative freedom of action in the region.[21]

The colonial experience implanted into the country's political culture an aversion to centralized government and an emphasis on negotiation and consensus over conflict.[22] Costa Ricans viewed government less as a vehicle for personal gain and power than was common elsewhere in Central America. Some people gained more power from advantages of birth or from their wealth, but the political system remained comparatively impotent. The relative weakness of the conservative political institutions of the Spanish colonial era, including the military and the Church, allowed democratic institutions to develop in the late nineteenth and twentieth centuries.

Costa Rica's historical development during the colonial period influenced its evolution after independence in 1823. The basic forms of political, economic, and social institutions were in place, allowing the evolution toward a capitalist democracy in the nineteenth and twentieth centuries. There were problems of race, economic disparity, and social stratification, but they were relatively finite when compared to other parts of Central America. While unresolved dilemmas of the era caused the country to take a slow, winding path toward a stable society, the foundations for democratic development existed in the 1820s.

Political disputes were commonplace during the early republican period as Costa Ricans struggled to decide their political, economic, and social paths. Costa Rican élites constructed a limited democracy, but the class stratification of the colonial era and the rise of the coffee oligarchy undermined democratic development. The government held elections frequently, but few presidents finished their terms because of constant pressure from competing groups. The upheavals typically consisted of coups and remained relatively bloodless because of an absence of public interest in politics.[23] The long and destructive struggles that plagued other Latin American countries never afflicted Costa Rica, allowing democratic evolution to continue throughout the nineteenth century and reducing the core powers' rationale for intervention.

Domestic politics and economic expansion preoccupied the country from midcentury to 1900. Some additional political instability accompanied the appearance of the coffee oligarchy in the 1850s.[24] Many coffee barons were descendants of the original conquistadors who had accumulated some capital during the colonial era. They strengthened their position on the revenues generated by coffee exports to Europe, successfully promoting government policies such as low tariffs and the construction of transportation and communication facilities that guaranteed the success of their crop. Well into the twentieth century, the coffee oligarchy played a crucial role in Costa Rican society, although the rapidly expanding farmers on the peripheries and the emerging merchant and finance sectors began counterbalancing the coffee élites.[25]

The expanded reliance on export agriculture and the subsequent concentration of land and production facilities generated some discontent. Economically, however, a shortage of labor sustained relatively high wages. The displaced farmers and smaller producers who needed supplemental income became comparatively well-remunerated laborers on the larger coffee plantations.[26] To sustain a stable work force, most *patróns* maintained good relations with their laborers. The landowners stayed closer to their lands, and absentee landlords were few. They knew the names of their workers and attended community functions such as weddings and festivals. In contract disputes, management dealt directly with the laborers and rarely utilized force.[27] All these factors reduced militancy among the workers, limiting the conflict and repression that later exploded into social warfare in other Central American states during the twentieth century.

An increased foreign presence also accompanied the growth of the coffee industry. British bankers provided the capital to support the expansion of the industry and brokered a large percentage of the Costa Rican crop. The oldest commercial bank in Costa Rica was the *Banco Anglo Costarricense,* chartered in 1863.[28] Although the British played an important role, Costa Ricans retained control of many of the production facilities. When combined with the domestic tranquillity of Costa Rica, the relatively small foreign influence limited international meddling in domestic affairs. Competition between the major powers never developed as it did in Cuba, Haiti, the Dominican Republic, and other Caribbean Basin nations. When U.S. industries became more prominent at the turn of the century with the arrival of Minor Keith and the United Fruit Company (UFCO), Costa Rica was politically and socially stable and relatively free of outside domination, reducing Washington's rationale for intervening.

The rise of the coffee oligarchy failed to derail Costa Rica's democratic evolution. New forces developed in the 1860s and 1870s to promote change.[29] Influenced by nineteenth-century liberalism, the leaders of the oligarchy promoted many of their ideas in the Constitution of 1871. It created a strong executive department. Elected by the congress, the president possessed broad powers to appoint and remove governors, cabinet ministers, public employees, and army officers. The constitution also mandated a unicameral congress (the Legislative Assembly) to propose budgets, levy taxes, and limit the military. It also could override a presidential veto by a two-thirds majority, amend the constitution, and impeach the president. The Supreme Court constituted the third branch of government. Selected by the assembly, the justices monitored the lower courts and acted independently of executive controls.[30] Although some presidents dominated the country through force, the Constitution of 1871 accelerated political maturation by providing the vehicle for firmly rooting democratic principles into Costa Rican culture.

A desire to implement a more republican form of government united the new leaders in the 1870s. They shared a commitment to expanded educational and political opportunities and the separation of church and state. Taking power in 1882, they expelled the Jesuits, secularized cemeteries and education, and closed the Catholic-controlled University of Santo Tomás. They also created a tolerance for non-Catholic religions that allowed evangelical Protestant missionaries to enter the country.[31] Catholicism remained the dominant faith, but Costa Ricans tolerated other religions, creating favorable impressions among foreign religious leaders.

Educational opportunities also grew during the late nineteenth and early twentieth centuries. Although Costa Rica's first president was a schoolteacher and its early constitutions provided some support for education, opportunities remained limited because of a lack of funds and an absence of ecclesiastical institutions.[32] The new leaders believed education was the cornerstone of democracy, and they passed laws that provided funding for more teachers and buildings. In 1886, Costa Rica had 138 schools, 278 teachers, and 14,478 students. Ten years later, it had 316 schools, 718 teachers, and 21,829 students.[33] The government also sponsored libraries and archives, establishing the Archivo Nacional in 1887 and the Biblioteca Nacional in 1888.[34]

Improved educational opportunities corresponded with a growth of journals and newspapers. A lack of funds, combined with illiteracy, had limited the activities of the press in the early republican era, although the government had passed laws guaranteeing the press's freedom. As literacy grew, so did the press. In 1878, the first daily, *La Gaceta*, started printing, and in 1885 a commercial daily, *El Diario de Costa Rica*, began publishing.[35] From this point, with few exceptions, the government adhered to the earlier commitment of freedom of the press, a fundamental democratic principle.

The new emphasis on civics, civil liberties, and literacy aided the expansion of democracy in the early twentieth century. An increase in political participation accompanied broadened educational opportunities and civil liberties. In the 1897 presidential elections, Costa Ricans cast only 24,065 votes, compared to 71,453 in 1923 (over 71.2 percent of the registered voters in the republic).[36] Much work remained, but the process had gained momentum and would not end.

Costa Rica's democratic development quickened in the first part of the twentieth century. With middle-class support, leaders such as Cleto González and Ricardo Jiménez sponsored innovations such as expanded suffrage.[37] Problems developed with the rise of the short-lived dictatorship of Federico Tinoco, but the country continued moving from a limited to an all-inclusive democracy. Reformers introduced the direct election of the president (1913), a national agency to monitor elections (1925), the secret ballot (1928), and obligatory voting (1936). Voting rates increased, and although the élites still monopolized the most important government positions, Costa Rica possessed a viable democracy by the middle of the century, a point often underscored by observers in the United States and the international community.[38]

The decline of the military aided Costa Rica's democratic evolution. Although no long-standing legacy of a strong military existed, the military had gained some power in the early twentieth century under the leadership of Federico Tinoco and as a result of border disputes with Panama. In 1918, Costa Rica's military had 5,000 soldiers and 700 policemen. By the mid-1940s, its military had shrunk to only 300 soldiers, with a police force of just over 1,100 men.[39] The weakening of the military would remove another repressive political force that undercut democratic development in other Central American republics.

The lack of a military tradition also influenced Costa Rica's literature and other forms of cultural expression. Costa Ricans appeared less aggressive than their neighbors. Their literature encouraged simplicity, shyness, timidity, hesitation, plainness, sympathy, and compassion. Short fiction such as the *Tio Conejo* (Brer Rabbit) stories typically ended happily rather than violently. Even in sport, violence was reduced. In bullfighting, for example, Costa Ricans traditionally spared the animal.[40] This relative absence of militarism and aggressiveness encouraged democratic development and created favorable images of Costa Rica in the United States and Europe.

Like citizens of much of the rest of the world, most Costa Ricans focused on the positive features of their society throughout the early part of the twentieth century. The Great Depression, however, uncovered domestic problems. Especially among the middle and working classes, new leaders arose who wanted an activist government to direct the economy and ensure a minimum standard of living for all citizens. By 1940, they began implementing programs to modernize Costa Rica's social, political, and economic systems. This movement set the stage for dramatic changes that occurred with the rise of reformers in Costa Rican society including Rafael Calderón, Manuel Mora, and José Figueres.

The realities and myths surrounding Costa Rica's historical development created in 1940 a belief among most American observers that in its political, social, and economic institutions, Costa Rica more closely resembled the United States than most countries in Latin America. The two countries shared many common views on capitalism and democracy. Costa Rican élites encouraged political participation and ameliorated discontent with limited social reform. Problems existed, but Costa Rica appeared a model of stability, a point underscored by many U.S. politicians, journalists, and members of the informed public from 1823 forward.

Democratic growth, careful diplomatic choices, and values shared with the United States, along with an absence of internecine fighting, helped the Costa Ricans mold a distinct pattern of relations with the larger nation during the nineteenth and twentieth centuries. San José typically supported Washington on major international issues such as the American Civil War, World War I, diplomatic recognition of the Soviet Union, and World War II. The Costa Ricans frequently clashed with Americans, however, over regional issues, such as the proposed building of a Nicaraguan canal and Washington's heavy-handed interventions in the Caribbean Basin in the first half of the twentieth century. Although perturbed by these displays of Costa Rican independence, the United States rarely viewed them as threatening its vital interests and security, and comparative mutual respect characterized relations between the two countries.

A historian of U.S. foreign relations cannot underestimate the importance of the mutual perceptions among national leaders. The apparent congruence of cultures played a significant role in creating amicable relations. Both Americans and Costa Ricans emphasized the shared values of democracy, capitalism, as well as racial homogeneity. Akira Iriye and Frank Ninkovich have recently advanced understanding of the importance of culture in foreign affairs by stressing transnational intellectual and political contacts.[41] Iriye emphasizes that culture "is the sharing and transmission of memory, ideology, emotions, life-style, scholarly and artistic works, and other symbols."[42] This view exposes a notable part of culture that has relevance to the study of U.S.–Costa Rican relations. Unlike other relationships in the Caribbean Basin, that of the United States and Costa Rica was based on common views that made economic, cultural, and political exchanges easier to accomplish and contributed to cordial relations between the two countries.

The shared symbols and mutual values caused Americans to develop positive perceptions of the Central American nation. From the 1820s forward, American travelers, businessmen, and diplomats viewed Costa Rica as distinct from other Central America countries. John Lloyd Stephens, an American lawyer who visited the region in the 1830s, noted that "the State of Costa Rica enjoyed at that time a degree of prosperity unequaled by any in the disjointed confederacy." "At a safe distance, without wealth enough to excite cupidity, and with a large tract of wilderness to protect it against the march of an invading army," he added, "it had escaped the tumults and wars which desolated and devastated the other states."[43] In addition, he praised Costa Rica's "industriousness," the whiteness of the population, and its record of religious tolerance.[44]

Stephens's portrayal became the standard. Several features of the description remained constant. Race was important because the whiteness of the Costa Ricans, while often exaggerated, provided many Americans with an explanation for the Costa Ricans' exceptionalness. Outside observers also highlighted the lack of distinct social and economic divisions, which contributed to the perception that Costa Rica was a Jeffersonian-style agriculture society characterized by diligent farmers dedicated to egalitarianism and democracy. Finally, the ability of the Costa Ricans to solve problems without combat further confirmed the concept that Costa Rica was a distinct Latin American country.

Throughout the nineteenth century, Americans continued emphasizing the uniqueness of the Costa Ricans. In 1887, the prominent historian Hubert Howe Bancroft underscored the nation's uniqueness, calling the Costa Ricans "a well-formed people . . . generally intelligent, and noted for their absence of hauter in their manner." "They are sedate, industrious, economical, fairly honest, and peaceable," he added, and "indigence is almost unknown." He also emphasized that "all Costa Ricans own property of some kind, and even the humblest of them has the ambition of possessing a piece of land."[45] Finally, he praised Costa Rica's dedication to education, democracy and "the most perfect freedom of religion."[46]

As American economic and cultural influence in Costa Rica and Latin America expanded during the nineteenth century, the Costa Ricans played a more prominent role in highlighting their country's uniqueness to create favorable impressions on foreign investors, immigrants, and diplomats. In 1895, Richard Villafranca declared, "We have, indeed, reached a time when the tide of emigration should go South, to Costa Rica, the tropical land, with a prolonged May day splendor, where neither oppressive heat nor freezing cold prevail, and the flowers are ever in bloom."[47]

Villafranca's countrymen such as Fernando García also pointed out positive features, writing in 1907 that "the country has always supported more school teachers than soldiers. . . . Costa Rica is fortunate in having an industrious and frugal middle class of small farmers who own land, horses, and oxen." García added, "If all the Latin Americans countries were as peaceful and progressive as little Costa Rica they would soon lose their evil fame."[48] Other writers and academicians, including Francisco Montero and Joaquín Bernardo Calvo, promoted their country as the most democratic and egalitarian nation in Central America. Each stressed the whiteness of the population, religious and political freedom, and the republican values of the majority of their countrymen.[49] Costa Rican business and political leaders promoted these images, embellishing them at times to win additional economic and diplomatic concessions from Americans. They often promoted myths such as the whiteness of the population and the notion that the country had more teachers than soldiers in the nineteenth and early twentieth centuries when they were not the case.[50] They understood the need to emphasize Costa Rica's exceptionalness and utilized shared symbols of democracy, capitalism, and race to win support. In the final analysis, the perceptions of Costa Rica among Americans were more important than the reality in influencing actions by the United States.

The basic characteristics of the earliest perceptions did not change dramatically in the twentieth century.[51] Even during disputes such as those of the Tinoco era, images remained remarkably good. In 1918, at the beginning of the conflict, the diplomat and historian Dana Munro emphasized that in Costa Rica there had matured "a nation which is entirely different from any of the other Central American Republics."[52] He underscored the traditional representations, including that regarding race, emphasizing that "the inhabitants of the central plateau are distinctly Spanish in race and civilization."[53] He also noted the number of small farmers, which created an absence of the class distinctions that plagued other countries in the region. "The inhabitants of Costa Rica now enjoy more stable and nearly democratic institutions than any of their Central American neighbors," he added, noting that "the leaders of the opposition carry on their propaganda in San José without hindrance or persecution."[54]

Over the next twenty years, few changes occurred in American views of Costa Rica. On the eve of World War II, historian Hubert Herring wrote that "Costa Rica is unique among the Central American states in the whiteness of the population, the honesty and constitutional orderliness of her political life, the intelligence of their citizenry." "For eighty years, with few interludes," he added, "political life has been tranquil, and Costa Rican elections are exemplary." "The school system is the best in Central America," he concluded, adding that "Costa Rica boasts more schoolteachers than soldiers."[55]

Favorable portrayals of Costa Rica were important because they translated into actions. The positive perceptions led to increased U.S. investment in Costa Rica and cultural exchanges between the two nations. In regional affairs, a belief developed among many U.S. policymakers that the Costa Ricans deserved more respect and independence because they ruled themselves without the contentiousness and instability that characterized other countries. This view also led many Americans to uphold Costa Rica as a model of social and political advancement, especially after the United States encountered problems dealing with the Nicaraguans, Hondurans, and Panamanians.[56]

These positive perceptions provided a solid foundation for the establishment of comparatively cordial relations between Costa Rica and the United States. During the period following Costa Rica's independence in the 1820s, few North Americans knew much about the country.[57] U.S. officials focused more on the larger and more prosperous countries of Latin America and the Central American Federation than on tiny Costa Rica. Changes took place after the federation collapsed in the 1840s and U.S. leaders became interested in constructing a transisthmian canal that included the San Juan River, a passageway shared by Nicaragua and Costa Rica.[58]

Although problems developed over the canal issue, Costa Rica's response helped lay the foundations for future cordial relations.[59] Prominent Costa Ricans recognized the potential of the United States as a regional and world power, especially after it defeated Mexico in 1848. When the dispute arose, San José dispatched its representative to the Court of St. James's, Luis Molina, to Washington as a minister plenipotentiary. Within three months, he negotiated a Treaty of Friendship, Commerce and Navigation that contained a most-favored-nation clause and guaranteed the rights of American citizens in Costa Rica.[60]

The arrival of Charles N. Riotte as U.S. minister to Central America in 1861 further strengthened the foundations for amicable exchanges. The new minister worked closely with the Costa Ricans on such problems as the relocation of freed American slaves in Costa Rica, the use of Central American ports by Confederate ships, and reduction of French influence in the region.[61] He successfully promoted U.S. interests while respecting Costa Rican rights and sensibilities. In return, Costa Rica denied the use of its ports to Confederate privateers and worked to prevent French expansion in the Americas, although they refused to allow freed slaves to settle, fearing the introduction of such a divisive issue. When he left his position in 1868, Riotte had firmly established the groundwork for future U.S.–Costa Rican relations. From this point on, clashes occasionally developed over regional questions, but San José typically supported Washington on important international issues.

For the most part, relations continued along peaceful lines through the remainder of the nineteenth century. The most important nonpolitical event was the arrival of Minor Keith in the 1870s. Brought to Costa Rica by a relative to finish a railroad line from Limón to San José, Keith encountered severe financial and logistical problems. To offset his company's fiscal shortfall, he planted bananas in the coastal areas on lands given him by the government. By the early 1880s, his rapidly expanding United Fruit Company (UFCO) dominated the export of tropical fruit.[62]

Keith became a major political and social figure in Costa Rica. His importation of black workers from the Caribbean islands significantly altered Costa Rica's racial demography.[63] In addition, he assumed more prominence after he negotiated a contract with the Costa Rican government that committed UFCO to finishing the railroad and absorbing the existing debt. In return, he received 800,000 acres of land and a ninety-nine-year lease on the railroad.[64] Additional negotiations placed a banana export tax of one cent per stem, a low rate that remained in effect until the 1930s.[65]

Although coffee remained Costa Rica's most important crop, growing bananas became a profitable enterprise. Over the years, UFCO gained control of more and more of the nation's finances and active capital, although it never controlled the finances and capital of Costa Rica as much as it did those of other countries, such as Honduras and Guatemala. A new influx of American businessmen, missionaries, and adventurers followed. Cultural, political, and economic exchanges flourished, and the United States became the dominant power in Costa Rica.

The Costa Ricans did not resist the incursion. Most people lived in the central highlands, far from the industrial enclaves of the coastal areas. Most laborers were Caribbean immigrants, not a major concern to most Costa Ricans or their government. Furthermore, Costa Rican leaders enjoyed the tax revenues and infrastructure generated by UFCO. As a result, few clashes occurred between American businesses and the Costa Ricans until the 1930s, when the Communists began to organize banana workers.

By the turn of the century, relations between Costa Rica and the United States were good. American businesses received favorable concessions and the stability of the country provided a prime investment environment. U.S. policymakers increasingly viewed Costa Rica's democratic institutions and social system as a model for the region. At the same time, the Costa Ricans tried maintaining their freedom in regional affairs. San José frequently clashed with Washington over U.S. attempts to organize the Central American nations into political and economic alliances because Costa Ricans feared a loss of autonomy to the larger states.[66] While bothersome, the disputes never threatened the overall pattern.

In regional affairs, Costa Rica supported U.S. proposals at the Washington Conference on Central American States of 1907. Some propositions included a ten-year period of peace and amity, compulsory arbitration of disagreements, the removal of dangerous political refugees from bordering countries, and the nonrecognition of governments that gained power by force.[67] Washington and San José also worked together in other areas. Costa Rica backed the United States during World War I and on the nonrecognition of the Soviet Union, refusing to recognize the Soviets formally although it maintained limited contacts in the 1920s through its legation in Paris.[68]

While U.S.–Costa Rican relations were relatively stable throughout the nineteenth and twentieth centuries, they were not without problems that at times threatened the traditional pattern. In the 1850s, William Walker had damaged early relations with his adventurism in Nicaragua and Costa Rica.[69] Tensions were high during Walker's escapades, but the period from

1910 to 1920 most threatened to destroy the normal models.[70] The first major controversy revolved around the signing in 1914 of the Bryan-Chamorro Treaty, in which Nicaragua granted the United States a ninety-nine-year canal concession in return for $3 million.[71] The Costa Ricans protested that Nicaragua had not consulted them as mandated by the Cañas-Jerez Treaty of 1858. They refused a U.S. financial settlement and took their case to the Central American Court, which ruled in their favor. Secretary of State Robert Lansing refused to acknowledge the judgment and the problem persisted into the 1920s.[72]

The most damaging crisis developed from the hotly contested Costa Rican presidential election of 1913. No clear winner emerged from the election, but after some shrewd political maneuvering, Alfredo González became president in May 1914.[73] Problems immediately plagued his administration. He lacked the support of the major parties, and World War I increased his difficulties as Costa Rica's exports and imports dropped, leading to many bankruptcies and foreclosures. In response, the president promoted several controversial programs, such as an unpopular income tax.[74] Discontent grew until January 1917, when the minister of war, Federico Tinoco, overthrew González. A confrontation immediately took place between the United States and the Tinoco government when President Woodrow Wilson refused to recognize the new administration, arguing that Tinoco had seized power unlawfully.[75]

The controversy continued for two years. The United States insisted that it would not recognize Tinoco even if elections took place. U.S. officials tried pressuring him from office by warning American businessmen that Washington would not protect them as it did its citizens in countries with which it had normal relations. Tinoco tried buying recognition by offering the United States leases on Pacific islands to use as naval bases to guard the Panama Canal. In addition, he held elections in April 1917, winning 50,000 out of the 70,000 ballots cast. His attempts to placate the U.S. government partially succeeded, and he received support from some UFCO representatives and American diplomats, such as the ambassador to Costa Rica, Edward Hale. Wilson remained steadfast, however, denying Tinoco formal recognition.[76]

Throughout 1918 and 1919, Washington intensified its attempts to isolate Tinoco and force him from power. More important, the Costa Rican opposition had organized resistance to Tinoco's dictatorship. The pressure proved too much for Tinoco. In the summer of 1919, after a series of clashes with various groups, he resigned and fled to Europe. A crisis of succession followed, but the problems subsided after general elections took place in December 1919 and Julio Acosta took power.[77]

The dispute with Tinoco represented the worst episode to date between the United States and Costa Rica, but Washington at least had refrained from using the sort of military solutions employed in Mexico, Haiti, Cuba, Nicaragua, and the Dominican Republic, permitting the Costa Ricans themselves to solve the problem. American business interests such as UFCO did not regard Tinoco as a direct threat to the United States, especially when compared with the radicalism of the Russian or Mexican revolutions. The absence of heavy-handed interventionism prevented the development of widespread anti-Americanism in Costa Rica and allowed relations to revert to a more normal pattern in the 1920s, a scenario later repeated during the fighting in 1948.

Costa Rica's political system stabilized in the 1920s and provided interesting leaders whose regional policies resembled those that would develop during the early career of José Figueres. There was tension when some Costa Ricans tried asserting independence of action in regional affairs. While most Costa Ricans readily accepted U.S. attempts to act as a mediator and mentor in Central America, others, such as Alejandro Alvarado, the minister of foreign relations (1920–1922), heartily opposed the intrusions. From various governmental positions, Alvarado sharply criticized U.S. policies in Latin America during the 1920s, but at the same time hesitated from aligning himself with perceived threats to U.S. security.[78]

In 1923, for example, Alvarado headed the Costa Rican delegation to the Pan American Conference in Santiago, Chile. With President Acosta's approval, he promoted the creation of a Pan American International Court of Justice, a resolution tabled by U.S. representatives, who feared that the court would side with the Latin Americans. Undeterred, Alvarado pushed for restructuring the Pan American Union (PAU) (a group that, until 1923, had been totally dominated by the United States), challenging its policies on accreditation and election of leaders. Although he lost on the methods of accreditation, he won a victory when the United States agreed to allow the PAU governing board to elect the president and vice-president of the union rather than permitting U.S. representatives to control the positions automatically.[79]

Alvarado challenged the United States in other areas. While serving as a congressional deputy, he led an antiimperialist movement in the Legislative Assembly. Overcoming opposition from conservatives and strongly pro-U.S. groups, he ultimately secured a resolution condemning the U.S. intervention in Nicaragua. In addition, he aided Nicaraguan exiles living in Costa Rica, supported the renegotiation of existing UFCO contracts, and opposed loans from American banks that he believed threatened Costa Rica's economic autonomy.[80]

Alvarado's challenges to U.S. policies appeared muted when compared to those of nationalists in Mexico and Nicaragua, who sought to undermine U.S. hegemony by implementing more radical programs. Alvarado criticized the United States and annoyed Washington, but his actions did not directly threaten American security. U.S. diplomats realized that most Costa Ricans remained strong allies, and although disputes occasionally arose, cordial relations continued through the 1930s. This pattern would reemerge in the 1940s and 1950s when the *figueristas* took control.

Despite the efforts of Alvarado and other Costa Rican nationalists, the United States gained more economic and political influence in Costa Rica after 1918. An important consequence of World War I was the continued expansion of American economic interests in Costa Rica. Trade increased and American businesses assumed more dominant positions in finance and construction. In 1913, 50.4 percent of Costa Rican exports went to the United States, while 41.8 percent went to the United Kingdom and 4.9 went to Germany. In the same year, 50.4 percent of Costa Rica's imports came from the United States, 14.5 percent from the United Kingdom, and 15.1 percent from Germany. By 1920 the percentages had changed dramatically in favor of the United States: of Costa Rica's total exports that year, 71.1 percent went to the United States, 20.8 percent to the United Kingdom, and only 0.2 percent to Germany, while 52.1 percent of its imports came from the United States, 14.2 percent from the United Kingdom, and 13.4 percent from Germany. While the other countries regained parts of the Costa Rican trade during the 1920s, the United States retained its economic dominance.[81]

Cultural exchanges accompanied the expanded commerce. Costa Ricans increasingly visited the United States, and many stayed to study at North American universities. In addition, American culture, most notably movies and literature, became more popular in Costa Rica. The introduction of new American technologies such as aircraft and farm machinery led many Costa Ricans to view the United States not only as the regional leader but also the world leader. (Indeed, viewing the United States as the world leader was an international phenomenon in this era.)

During the 1930s, the Great Depression caused domestic problems for both countries, but their relations remained stable. The United States sought stronger ties with its hemispheric neighbors, a program aided by the pronouncement of the "Good Neighbor" policy and withdrawal from Nicaragua, Cuba, and Haiti. Washington wanted to establish peaceful political and economic contacts to strengthen alliances. For its part, Costa Rica backed the U.S. initiatives that expanded hemispheric cooperation at conferences in Havana (1928), Montevideo (1933), Buenos Aires (1936), and Lima (1938).[82]

In the late 1930s, the United States concentrated on containing fascism in Latin America. Although several prominent leaders such as Costa Rican President León Cortés harbored pro-German sentiments, most Costa Ricans supported the Allies. San José backed U.S. attempts to organize hemispheric defenses and promote regional unity at the 1940 Havana Conference. At the request of the United States, the foreign ministers voted to take over European colonies in danger of being transferred to Germany. They also agreed to act collectively in the event of aggression against a nation in the western hemisphere. At the start of World War II, Costa Rica solidly backed the United States.[83]

By 1940, in the eyes of most Americans and other foreigners, Costa Rica had distinguished itself from its neighbors. Its social, economic, and political systems had evolved differently, laying the foundations for democratic and capitalist development. Costa Ricans shared many values with the United States, preventing problems that might have developed if the cultures had differed more dramatically. In addition, the Costa Ricans retained relative control of most of their own production facilities in the major population centers, limiting European influence and reducing U.S. fears of foreign domination. Costa Rica's domestic stability and the strength of its political institutions denied the United States any excuse to intervene to protect American lives and property. The resultant absence of U.S. intervention reduced anti-Americanism in Costa Rica. Finally, Costa Rica proved a very loyal supporter of U.S. international policy, although problems sometimes arose over domestic and regional issues. The difficulties, however, never endangered the friendly relationship that had developed after Costa Rica secured independence.

Throughout the nineteenth and twentieth centuries the United States enjoyed better relations with Costa Rica than with almost any other nation in Latin America. As World War II approached, there were no indications that the existing pattern of relations would be broken. The newly elected president, Rafael Calderón, and his supporters in the National Republican Party would cement the relationship even further by strongly backing the United States in World War II. Nevertheless, the political alliances formed by Calderón to pass his social programs would ensure domestic enemies such as Cortés and Figueres and guarantee changes that threatened the normal pattern of relations. The Calderón presidency marked a turning point in Costa Rican history. How the Costa Ricans adapted to the alterations definitely influenced the nature of U.S.–Costa Rican relations in the postwar era.

2

LAYING THE FOUNDATIONS OF CHANGE
The United States, President Rafael Angel Calderón, and the Rise of José Figueres, 1940–1944

CHARLES WILSON NOTED in 1941 that "Costa Rica remains a land of order and peace. [It is] also a land of hard work. A majority of its farms and a majority of its homes are owned by their residents. So Costa Rica endures and grows greater; a vivid, personalized world of eternal spring; a land neither of tears nor of loud laughter."[1] Not everyone agreed with this positive assessment. A Chilean journalist, Tancredo Pinochet, commented that, instead of land being equally divided, "what is well distributed in Costa Rica is poverty."[2]

Differences existed between the perceptions and the realities of Costa Rica in 1940. Costa Ricans enjoyed a better standard of living and more political freedoms than their Central American neighbors, but the Great Depression had exposed many problems. Although the administration of León Cortés (1936–1940) had implemented some reforms, its programs lacked the scope and coverage to ease the suffering and economic disparity. By 1940, many Costa Ricans worried that their country's system too closely resembled that of its socially and politically stratified neighbors. A fear of conflict and a genuine concern for the plight of the less fortunate drove members of the élite and the emerging middle class to seek change. Two of the nation's most important political figures responded to the call: Rafael Calderón and José ("Don Pepe") Figueres.

For the next twenty-five years, Calderón played a significant role in Costa Rican politics, both as president and as leader of the opposition in exile. During his presidency, he sponsored reforms for the poor and working classes in Costa Rica to provide them better health care, education, and housing. As was the norm for Costa Rican culture, the policies of the

Calderón administration were hardly radical departures from the past. They revolved around private enterprise and created little additional direct government involvement in the economy, in many ways resembling the changes implemented in the United States in the 1930s. Dictatorships dominated Latin America, but Calderón further strengthened Costa Rica's democratic social and political system by providing more services and distributing wealth more equitably, reducing the potential for revolution and totalitarian rule.

While making numerous changes at home, Calderón followed traditional patterns in international affairs. The United States and Costa Rica maintained a close friendship during World War II. Calderón supported the Allied war effort by ensuring the free flow of raw materials to the United States. He also backed Washington's attempts to strengthen the inter-American system through military cooperation, accommodated the United States on the isolation of domestic and regional Fascist threats, and provided uncompromising support of most U.S. initiatives. The United States rewarded his loyalty with grants for public works programs and with loans. By 1944, the alliance between Washington and San José had reached a high point.

There were few indications in 1944 that the wartime cooperation between Calderón, the National Republicans, and the United States would not continue in the postwar period. Yet the groundwork for future difficulties also arose during his presidency. Calderón and the National Republican party worked closely with the Communist party, contributing to future tensions in U.S.–Costa Rican relations as the wartime alliance between the United States and the Soviet Union disintegrated in the postwar era. In addition, the opposition, primarily José Figueres and the members of the Center for the Study of National Problems, emerged as important political actors in Costa Rica. While they had limited influence during Calderón's presidency, they developed a tightly knit organization that later provided a vehicle for seizing power in 1948.

When Calderón entered office, he had a well-developed political ideology. His background strongly influenced his development. Born in San José into the family of a respected physician and educated in exclusive schools, he displayed early leadership qualities, so much so that his friends toasted him at his graduation as "the future president of the Republic."[3] Afterwards, he studied medicine at the Catholic University of Louvain and the Free University of Belgium. In 1927, he returned to Costa Rica and established a thriving practice.[4]

His educational experience in Europe significantly altered Calderón's political orientation. The ideals of leading Christian socialists, especially Cardinal Mercier, strongly influenced him. Based on Pope Leo XIII's 1891 encyclical *Rerum Novarum,* Christian socialism emphasized the individual citizen's responsibility to alleviate the suffering of the poor and working class. Designed to undermine communism and other atheistic ideologies, it sought state intervention to promote economic programs that guaranteed jobs and better working conditions, although the right to private property underlay most reforms.[5]

After Calderón returned to Costa Rica, he made plans to alter his country's social system along Christian socialist lines. He worked privately and as a legislator to implement changes in public health and other areas. His social activism corresponded with his rise up the political ladder. He built his base of support among the rapidly expanding population that had started flocking to the cities to seek work. By late 1939, he won the presidential nomination of the powerful National Republican party. After a relatively easy contest, he became president in 1940.[6]

In his inaugural address, Calderón outlined a multifaceted program. He promised to restructure the tax system, provide low-cost housing, found a national university, and develop a social security program. In addition, he pledged more rural credit and land reform. Like many of his American contemporaries, he wanted to alter a society that had failed to serve the needs of the majority, but to do so within the democratic-capitalist framework.[7] From their first days in office, Calderón and his associates pushed reformist rather than radical programs, a point underscored by many U.S. diplomats. This fact was important because the perceived convergence of the political cultures of Costa Rica and the United States created common ground on which to build a close relationship during the war, a process accentuated by Calderón's unwavering support of the Allied war effort.

In a flurry of activity following his inauguration, Calderón fulfilled many campaign promises. He helped establish the University of Costa Rica, making higher education more accessible for Costa Ricans from modest backgrounds.[8] He also increased funding for public housing by expanding the existing National Housing Board, broadening housing options for low-income families.[9] Like other social programs implemented by Calderón, this one emphasized private ownership and relatively limited direct government control. Calderón avoided extremes and tried practicing consensus politics within the existing framework of the Costa Rican political system.

The most controversial policy of the first half of Calderón's term was the establishment of Central America's first social security system. Before 1941, the Costa Rican government had gone no further in social planning than limited ventures in workmen's compensation and retirement pensions designed to supplement private ecclesiastical initiatives. Once in power, Calderón actively promoted social security laws in the Legislative Assembly. After successfully outmaneuvering conservatives, who feared expensive health care and retirement initiatives, his supporters in the assembly passed a social security law. Patterned after the Chilean system, the legislation created an insurance institute to guide the program, with funding provided by mandatory contributions from employers and employees. The monies went into a pension program and provided medical care for people whose salary fell below certain levels. Initially the system covered only a small percentage of Costa Ricans, but Calderón planned to expand the program gradually to cover everyone.[10]

Although he succeeded in most areas during his first two years, Calderón faced increasing opposition in the Legislative Assembly from several sectors, primarily dissatisfied conservatives often aligned with the large coffee growers who had dominated Costa Rican politics for many years.[11] The discontent was evident in the midterm congressional elections. The loosely organized opposition leveled accusations of corruption and fraudulent voting practices against the president and the National Republicans. In the election, Calderón's party lost majority control of the assembly. Frustrated and facing a deadlocked legislative body, the president responded by creating a political alliance with the leading reformist group in Costa Rica, the Communists.[12] This move was to have long-term consequences. While U.S. policymakers initially accepted popular-front movements, the alliance laid the groundwork for future disputes in the postwar era, when Washington turned its attentions from defeating the Fascists to containing the Soviets.

The Communist party in Costa Rica had begun in 1909 when a small group of intellectuals had organized the nation's first permanent Marxist party, the *Sociedad de Trabajadores* (Workers' Society). It published a newsletter and founded an institute to promote class consciousness, but the group remained small until the Great Depression. In 1929, a coalition of leftist parties formed the *Confederación de Trabajadores de Costa Rica* (Workers' Confederation of Costa Rica, CTCR). Under the leadership of the young lawyer Manuel Mora, it grew rapidly in the banana enclaves and in some industries.[13]

The CTCR gained members and prominence in 1934 when it successfully led a strike against the United Fruit Company. Laborers left their jobs, demanding better working and living conditions. When company officials failed to break the strike and the Costa Rican government refused to intervene, workers gained a twelve-hour work day, wage increases, and improved living quarters.[14] Mora's success ensured increased membership and had important long-term consequences, establishing the foundations for the expanded unionism and social reform of the 1940s.

Throughout his early political career, Calderón had openly criticized the Communists, especially the atheism and authoritarianism of the Soviet Union. At one point Calderón declared, "Social Christianity, in contrast to Marxism or deification of the State, does not achieve justice arbitrarily, by violence. . . . One may and one must fight against injustice, but not to substitute the dictatorship of the proletariat or whatever other social class."[15] His attitude changed after his opponents mounted resistance to his administration, and he recognized that he needed allies to pass additional parts of his social agenda during the second half of his term. He emphasized that the CTCR differed from its Soviet associates, arguing that the party was first Costa Rican, then Communist. In addition, Calderón believed that the National Republicans would require assistance in guaranteeing that his hand-picked successor, Teodoro Picado, would win the 1944 presidential election. These political exigencies pushed him into an alliance with the CTCR.[16]

The CTCR's power base and social policies provided Calderón with an attractive partner in 1942. In the congressional elections of that year, the CTCR received 16 percent of the vote, giving it the balance of power in the Legislative Assembly between the *calderonistas* and the opposition.[17] While Calderón and Mora differed over religion and the role of the state in the economy, relations changed after 1942 when it appeared that both sides could gain by working together. Mora opened the door further when he refused to participate in a coup against Calderón in early 1942.[18] The president rewarded his loyalty by forging a mutually beneficial association.

Mora worked hard to ease the transition to an alliance between the

National Republicans and the CTCR. Immediately after the thaw in relations with Calderón, he renounced controversial aspects of the Communist doctrine, including class warfare. Instead, he underscored his party's desire to work with the National Republicans to improve Costa Rican society.[19] An unlikely ally, the Archbishop of San José, Victor Sanabria, further legitimized the CTCR. After a series of meetings with Sanabria, Mora agreed to dissolve the CTCR and form a popular-front organization, the *Vanguardia Popular* (Vanguard). He also issued public statements in which he promised that the new party would not adopt policies that contradicted church principles. In return, Sanabria published a decree allowing Catholics to join the new party without any "burden of conscience."[20] Believing that Mora had eliminated the most controversial aspects of his program, Calderón merged his National Republican party with the Vanguard to form the *Bloque Victoria* (Victory Block).

In early 1943, spearheaded by Mora and wasting no time, the alliance introduced its most controversial piece of legislation, the Labor Code. A 628-section statute, it guaranteed labor's right to organize, outlawed arbitrary dismissals, mandated sanitary and safe working conditions, and created labor courts to mediate disputes. It also created a Labor Ministry with power to implement and monitor congressional mandates. The alliance's collective strength pushed the code through the assembly in August despite resistance from conservatives. Delighted with the success, Calderón rewarded the Vanguard's allegiance by placing party members in important positions in the Social Security Institute and the Labor Ministry.[21]

The *Bloque* also promoted other programs, such as land reform. Designed primarily to create a new class of small farmers and reduce crowding in the *meseta central,* the legislation allowed landless peasants to settle on unclaimed lands and secure title after cultivating them for a time. The coalition also expanded housing projects and passed laws limiting foreign ownership of Costa Rican businesses. In health care, the government built new water filter plants, distributed information on nutrition, and gave shoes to children from low-income households to reduce the spread of parasitic disease.[22]

The policies supported by the Communists were hardly radical. They promoted neither seizure of property nor class warfare and focused on gradual, evolutionary reform rather than revolution. This approach reflected the traditional Costa Rican political culture, which emphasized moderation over radicalism. Much as Calderón had argued, the party was a Costa Rican entity that possessed only limited ties to the international Communist movement. While some Communists wanted more extreme policies that corresponded with Soviet desires, the major leaders, including Mora, sought gradual change that accomplished their goals without alienating large segments of the society and outside forces. The middle-of-the-road path ensured success for Mora and his associates. Their cooperation with the National Republicans dramatically strengthened the political position of the Vanguard in Costa Rica, a position that it did not relinquish in the postwar era.

The alliance with the Vanguard guaranteed that upon leaving office in 1944, Calderón left a legacy of political activism that dramatically altered the way Costa Ricans viewed government, a process not easily reversed. Yet prominent sectors of Costa Rican society battled the changes. Disparate groups formed the opposition. The most vocal were wealthy conservative landowners and businessmen who feared that expensive social programs and labor legislation would erode their dominance. In addition, middle-class reformers resented the perceived corruption and nepotism of the Calderón administration. Finally, a small association of young professionals disagreed with Calderón's methods, protesting that he had gone too slowly.[23] The opposition groups, although loosely organized, caused many difficulties for Calderón and his successor, Teodoro Picado.

The strongest opposition came from the conservatives and anti-Calderón moderates who rallied behind León Cortés. The former president had broken with the National Republicans in 1941 and formed the Democratic party. Disappointed with the radicalism of the *calderonistas,* he relied primarily on *personalismo* and a promise to stop the social programs to attract followers.[24] In 1944, he ran a spirited but unsuccessful campaign for president. His followers uncovered many cases of electoral fraud, but the ruling National Republicans ignored the charges. Although disenchanted, Cortés continued battling Picado and the National Republicans, while planning eventually to gain control in future elections.

The most important opposition group that arose during the Calderón administration developed in the late 1930s. Several educators in the law school at the University of Costa Rica led by Carlos Monge, Isaac Felipe Azofeifa, and Brenes Mesen, encouraged their students to organize into small study groups and propose remedies for Costa Rica's problems. Their pupils Rodrigo Facio, Alberto Cañas, Jorge Rossi, Gonzalo Facio, and Daniel Oduber responded to their call, forming the nucleus of the men who dominated Costa Rican politics for the next forty years.[25]

In March 1940, the students joined with a select group of educators, businessmen, and other professionals to form the Center for the Study of National Problems. They established seven research committees and began publishing a monthly journal, *Sucro*. Their short-term goals included fair elections as well as nonpartisan programs designed to uplift their countrymen and battle communism, a perceived threat to their society. Members of the center also formulated long-range plans for creating a political party that promoted government policies to alleviate social, economic, and political inequities in Costa Rica.[26]

Although initially nonpartisan, the center took stronger political stances as its members became increasingly disenchanted with the alliance between the National Republicans and the Communists. Its research reports increasingly denounced Calderón's "unscientific" projects, urging more governmental activism through the creation of autonomous government institutions with mandates to promote economic and social development. Along with underscoring the alliance between Calderón and Picado with the Communists, center members also linked the president and his allies to the notorious dictators of the region, such as Anastasio Somoza García and Rafael Trujillo.[27] The center's membership grew as people searched for a forum to challenge National Republican rule. In 1944, the center supported Cortés's candidacy in order to protest Calderón's poor handling of the government, and later its members joined together to found a political party.

A close associate of the center, José "Don Pepe" Figueres, emerged as the most virulent critic of Calderón and Picado. A coffee-grower of Spanish descent, Figueres had traveled to the United States to study in the 1920s. Originally, he had planned to enroll at the Massachusetts Institute of Technology; instead, he spent most of his time in the Boston Public Library reading on economics, history, and sociology. Charles Fournier, Leo Tolstoy, and Thomas Jefferson strongly influenced his ideology, as did the U.S. political system and its values. He viewed the Soviets and Marxism with much suspicion because he believed that they stifled individual initiative and represented a new form of authoritarianism. When he returned to Costa Rica, he purchased a *finca, La Lucha Sin Fin* (The Struggle without End). Driven by ambition and his newly acquired knowledge, he created a thriving business, producing sisal and other crops. He also implemented social experiments that provided health care, education, and other benefits for his workers. Although he maintained close ties with the members of the Center for the Study of National Problems he had met during his secondary education, he remained preoccupied with his business enterprises and avoided politics until the early 1940s.[28]

When Figueres entered politics, he proved an enigma for domestic and foreign observers. He was aggressive and driven.[29] He had an incredible amount of energy, and his mind worked incessantly on new concepts, some of them characterized by his opponents as hare-brained. More idealistic than pragmatic in his early years, he liked to experiment, although his attention often waned and he moved onto new projects. His critics also stressed that, much like Napoleon Bonaparte or Simón Bolivar, Figueres was short in stature and often overcompensated by constantly challenging others to demonstrate his abilities. They also emphasized that Figueres was quite vain and sometimes overestimated his self-worth and his ability to manipulate others, especially after he became a prominent political figure in the 1950s. While some of these criticisms appeared valid, detractors could not question Figueres's commitment to restructuring Costa Rica to maintain its traditional democratic institutions and, more important, to provide for the majority of the people who had been underrepresented in the past. He also sought to extend this system of government to the other countries of Latin America that languished under the totalitarian regimes, a project that remained important to him until his death in 1990. His assertiveness and genuine concern for his countrymen manifested themselves when he emerged as a vocal critic of the National Republicans in the early 1940s.[30]

Figueres burst onto the political scene with a series of attacks on Calderón's wartime policies. Until 1942, he had avoided politics, focusing instead on his business. In July of that year, however, he purchased radio time to criticize the president for allowing his followers to ransack Italian and German businesses in retaliation for the embarrassing sinking of a UFCO ship by a German submarine in the harbor at Limón. As Figueres vigorously attacked the administration's incompetence, police officers broke in and arrested him. Several days later, the outraged Calderón pressured him into voluntary exile in Mexico.[31] From this point forward, Figueres dedicated himself to overthrowing the National Republicans and establishing a new Costa Rica based on his social democratic theories and those of his friends at the Center for the Study of National Problems. During his exile and after he returned to Costa Rica in 1944, he actively participated in the center and helped form the Social Democratic party (PSD).[32] He would seize the political spotlight and remain in it until his death.

Though loosely organized, these disparate groups—the Democratic party and the center—continued to oppose the National Republicans throughout Calderón's term and during Picado's tenure (1944–1948). Their movement gained momentum in the period immediately preceding the presidential election of 1948, when Calderón tried regaining Costa Rica's highest office. Although unified by their disdain for Calderón and Picado, each group promoted different policies for restructuring Costa Rica. In the end, however, Figueres and his associates emerged as the dominant political force in the aftermath of the civil war of 1948, ushering in an important new political force in Costa Rica.

Figueres and the opposition arose at a time when rapid changes in Costa Rican society closely mirrored developments in the international arena. World War II exacerbated existing economic and social problems in Costa Rica. The response by Calderón and the National Republicans favorably impressed U.S. officials because their political culture resembled that of Roosevelt and the New Deal Democrats. Like their American counterparts, the *calderonistas* were reformers, resolute to utilize the government to sponsor substantial social programs that improved the living and working conditions of a majority of their countrymen while undermining radical alternatives.

The National Republicans also shared Washington's opposition to fascism. As in the past, San José backed Washington on major international questions in time of war. Costa Rica firmly supported the Allies throughout the war, accommodating the United States on issues such as the handling of German and Italian nationals and the question of diplomatic recognition of Argentina. Furthermore, the Costa Rican government provided the United States raw materials and military bases and aided American attempts to isolate potential subversives in Latin America. In return, the United States provided the Calderón administration with military assistance and funded the building of Costa Rica's infrastructure. The wartime alliance strengthened economic and military ties between the two countries but at the same time laid the groundwork for potential difficulties in the postwar period, when the Soviet Union replaced the Nazis as the primary threat to the United States. The National Republicans' cooperation in a popular-front government with the Costa Rican Communists would have long-term effects on the relationship, although it did not affect that relationship during the war.[33]

When Calderón took office in 1940, the United States sought to further strengthen its alliance with its hemispheric neighbors. As a result, U.S. officials actively courted Calderón. Before his inauguration, the president-elect visited the United States, staying four days in Washington, where he met with Secretary of State Cordell Hull and Assistant Secretary of State Adolf A. Berle, Jr. During a reception, Hull publicly praised Calderón for the "constant and unfailing support which your people and your government have given the movement for Pan American unity."[34]

Washington's attempts to impress Calderón succeeded. Once in office, he established close ties with the United States, declaring to the U.S. embassy that "under this administration I hope that you will feel free to express to me frankly any views that you may have as to both foreign and domestic affairs. I want your cooperation and help."[35] He backed up his rhetoric by appointing a pro-American delegate to the Havana Conference in 1940. In addition, he offered the United States bases in Costa Rica from which to protect the Panama Canal.[36]

U.S. diplomats in San José urged Washington's acceptance of Calderón's proposals, especially in light of the impending conflict. U.S. Minister to Costa Rica William Hornibrook stated that "we are on trial at the present moment in Latin America, and unless we are prepared to make good our assurances by a substantial contribution to the defense of this part of the world . . . we may expect as an alternative a successful German 'blitzkrieg' in the not far distant future." He added that "without encouragement from us, they are not going to buy arms and ammunition to defend the Sabana airport . . . even though they know that commercial planes basing on such a field may possibly be used for an attack on the Canal locks." Hornibrook concluded that "aid should be given speedily and without cost to the Costa Rican government."[37]

Throughout the war, the United States sought to help Costa Rica defend itself from both internal and external Axis threats by strengthening its military. In June 1940, Calderón opened talks on the establishment of an American military mission in Costa Rica and the rearmament of the small Costa Rican army. Negotiators immediately encountered several obstacles, especially Costa Rica's unwillingness and inability to finance the military mission and the arms purchases. Calderón feared that the additional expenditures would undercut funding for his social programs, and he also disliked U.S. proposals for enlarging the army and lengthening the terms of enlistment. Concerned, Hornibrook promoted favorable payment terms for the Costa Ricans and by August, the parties had reached a tentative agreement on creating a mission, the first step toward preparing Costa Rica for its role in hemispheric defense.[38]

This military alliance continued throughout the war despite the absence of direct Fascist threats (other than internal subversion by pro-German elements). Although the cooperation tapered off in the postwar period because of Costa Rica's budgetary restraints and its natural inclination toward a weak military, the United States maintained its influence as the country's adviser and arms supplier.[39] This position gave it an important lever to influence Costa Rican politics, especially in the period immediately preceding the revolution in 1948.

In addition to establishing closer military cooperation with the United States, Calderón accommodated Washington even when its actions caused him domestic problems. An example occurred in March 1941 when U.S. and British officials expressed concern that the captains of two Axis merchant vessels in Puntarenas might scuttle their ships in the mouth of the port, thus preventing Allied use of the harbor. When informed about the danger, the Costa Ricans at first reacted cautiously because they still maintained diplomatic relations with Germany and Italy. After a month of discussion with Allied officials, however, Calderón finally agreed to seize the ships. The State Department approved the plan and promised to back all necessary measures.[40]

With this U.S. green light, Calderón ordered his brother Francisco Calderón, the Costa Rican minister of war, to move ahead. Alerted beforehand to Costa Rica's intention, the crews set their vessels afire. In response, the Costa Ricans arrested the sailors and charged them with arson and willful obstruction of navigation.[41] Washington wanted to intern the crews in the United States, but Calderón initially refused on constitutional grounds and for fear of aggravating the Germans and Italians. After some diplomatic haggling, he acquiesced and sent the foreign nationals to the Panama Canal Zone. Although members of his own cabinet protested that the deportations violated Costa Rica's sovereignty, Calderón refused to rescind his decision.[42] The whole episode demonstrated his desire to work with U.S. officials even at a domestic political cost, a policy he continued throughout his presidency. While his motivations were not always clear, he proved a dependable ally when the United States needed him.

Another good example of Calderón's and Costa Rica's willingness to back the Allied cause occurred on 8 December 1941. Indignant about the Japanese sneak attack on Pearl Harbor, the Legislative Assembly, at the president's urging, declared war on Japan several hours before the U.S. Congress approved a similar measure. For many years afterwards, Calderón and Picado proudly boasted that their nation had been the first in the western hemisphere to act, a fact U.S. policymakers acknowledged. Calderón and Picado restated this fact often, usually to demonstrate their pro-American record after the onset of the cold war.[43]

Although Costa Rica's direct contribution to the war effort consisted primarily in the production of raw materials such as coffee, bananas, rubber, and sisal, it assisted the Allies in other areas. Early in the war, American and British agents identified potential Axis threats in the region, especially Japanese, German, and Italian nationals living throughout Latin America. They feared that the Fascists might sabotage the movement of supplies or seek to undermine individual governments' support of the Allies. Washington and London identified problems in most Latin American countries, including Costa Rica, and implemented plans to eliminate the menace.

With some prodding from the United States and Great Britain, the Calderón administration acted quickly. When the war began, Costa Rican authorities arrested all Japanese citizens in their territory, including those who had entered the country at the request of the government to develop a cotton industry. After only limited deliberation, they sent the Japanese to the United States for internment and auctioned off their possessions.[44]

The handling of Germans and Italians proved more difficult. In the late nineteenth and early twentieth centuries, a large number of Germans had moved to Costa Rica. Many became prosperous coffee growers and married into Costa Rica's most prominent families. The new immigrants and the German government sponsored schools to educate Costa Rican élites in the virtues of German culture. By the late 1930s, Nazi Germany took 19 percent of Costa Rica's exports and also sold large quantities of finished goods to Costa Rica. During the Cortés administration, the Germans had gained additional status. Educated in Germany, Cortés openly admired that country, and in 1937 his son traveled to Europe to receive a decoration from the German government. U.S. officials linked members of the

Nazi Party to officials in the Cortés administration, such as Cortés's director of public works, Max Effinger. They emphasized that in Central America, only Guatemala possessed a German population as large and influential as Costa Rica's.[45]

The Allies relied on several methods to destroy Axis influence in Latin America. The State Department implemented a controversial program in January 1942 by issuing a circular, "Proposed Position on Proclaimed List for Other American Republics," the main objective of which was the "elimination of Axis financial and economic influence in the hemisphere."[46] During the war, U.S., British and Latin American officials compiled a registry of Fascists, the proclaimed list, and moved against them, interning many in the United States and allowing local governments to confiscate their property.

After an initial push from the Americans and British, the Calderón administration began working with U.S. authorities to expose Costa Rican Fascists. In 1942, the Legislative Assembly passed Law No. 79 that supplemented existing statutes and permitted the president to revoke the citizenship of native-born Costa Ricans and naturalized citizens who adopted the political doctrines of countries at war with Costa Rica.[47] By the end of the war, the Calderón government had placed more than two hundred persons of German and Italian descent in internment camps in the United States.

Calderón's commitment to the proclaimed lists proved very unpopular among the wealthy and influential coffee oligarchy. The perceived persecution of the hard-working and loyal Germans heightened animosity toward Calderón and the National Republicans. Charges of corruption also surrounded the confiscation of the internees' properties. Many people believed that the *calderonistas* benefited unfairly from the sale of the seized possessions. These accusations further undermined Calderón's power base, causing him to increase his reliance on the Communists and ultimately leading to a confrontation between the National Republicans and the United States in the postwar period.[48]

At the time, however, most U.S. policymakers and the informed public believed Calderón was a reliable ally. Public perceptions were typically positive. *Time* described Calderón as a "handsome polo player, farmer and practicing physician who epitomizes Costa Rican political liberality and the Old World manners of its 90% white population."[49] To demonstrate Costa Rica's strong emphasis on rural democracy, Joseph Thorning highlighted the fact that Calderón drove a jeep instead of a fancy car and depicted him as a person equally at home in the country as in the city.[50] Finally, Irving Child noted, "People in this country [the United States] may be glad to know . . . that the general attitude of Costa Ricans towards the war is faithfully represented by the enthusiastic participation of the Costa Rican government as one of the United Nations."[51] These portrayals were consistent with the traditional ones. Americans looked on the Costa Ricans and their leaders as unique, evidenced by the title of an article in *Harper's*, "Four Strong Men and a President." The authors underscored Costa Rica's democratic tradition and its president over the totalitarianism and dictators of the other countries in the region.[52] For the most part, Americans believed that the Costa Ricans represented democracy. With few exceptions, these perceptions were to remain unchanged into the immediate postwar era.

U.S. diplomats shared the media's positive perceptions of the Calderón administration's support of the war effort. In January 1942, the Latin American Section of the Office of the Coordinator of Information reported that "Costa Rica is cooperating wholeheartedly with the United States in the current war effort."[53] Calderón's approval of U.S. attempts to coerce Argentina, Brazil, and Chile into severing relations with the Axis powers also earned Washington's appreciation. San José backed the United States in the major confrontation between the United States and the reluctant Latin American nations that occurred at the Rio Conference in 1942. The U.S. envoy, Undersecretary of State Sumner Welles, tried forcing all the American republics to break ties with the Fascists and aid the Allies. Costa Rica supported Welles's proposals, even though U.S. officials failed to achieve their goal.[54] Throughout the war, Calderón followed Washington's policy of isolating pro-Fascist nations, especially Argentina. In 1944, he refused to recognize the Argentine government, denouncing as unacceptable its proposals to meet to discuss the impasse.[55]

The United States rewarded Calderón's loyalty by providing loans and sponsoring internal improvements in Costa Rica, part of an overall U.S. policy to help offset some of the dislocations caused by the war. In late 1940, U.S. authorities helped Costa Rican officials secure a $4.6 million low-interest loan from the Export-Import Bank to construct a section of the Pan American Highway from San José to the Panamanian border. Washington also made engineers available for the important project. Although the work slowed toward the end of the war, it infused millions of dollars into the Costa Rican economy and solidified cooperation between Washington and San José.[56]

There were other examples of Washington assisting Costa Rica. During Calderón's second year, the United States rescued Costa Rica from a financial crisis. In January 1942, the government encountered increasingly difficult fiscal burdens as the war reduced its income from import-export taxes at the same time that the government added expenditures for new social programs.[57] Instead of increasing taxes and aggravating conservatives, Calderón sought loans from the United States. When problems developed over the form of payment, Ambassador Robert Scotten urged favorable terms. "President Calderón has as the Department is aware," he stated, "cooperated with us to the fullest extent as regards the international situation and is I believe a sincere friend of the United States."[58] The State Department complied with the request and Costa Rica received a $2 million loan at 4 percent interest.

As large sums of money entered the country, the charges of corruption and misuse of the public trust against Calderón increased. Nepotism was commonplace. The president's family took personal trips at the government's expense and many family members received important positions. Critics also highlighted the president's association with Nicaraguan strongman Anastasio Somoza. Reportedly, the two men shared profits from a lucrative cattle-smuggling enterprise that allowed Calderón to build up *Chomes,* his *finca.* The rumored abuse of power also antagonized some U.S. officials in San José who resented the Calderón administration's misuse of rationed supplies like rubber. Rumors circulated that Calderón's friends had unfairly received the scarce commodities and sold them at inflated prices.[59] Although bothered by the questionable practices, most U.S. diplomats overlooked the president's faults, dismissing them as relatively muted when compared to others in the region and focusing primarily on his loyalty to the United States.

In foreign affairs, the most important long-term consequence of Calderón's first presidency was his collaboration with the Communists. During the war the United States had accepted the efforts of governments to establish closer ties with the Soviet Union and the Communist movements in various countries. With U.S. approval, in 1942, Calderón began efforts to establish diplomatic relations with the U.S.S.R., succeeding by March 1944. The Costa Ricans accepted the Soviet ambassador to Mexico as a negotiator, but he died in a plane accident while traveling to Costa Rica in early 1945. As a result, the relationship never matured.

Despite the failure to establish direct ties between the Soviet Union and Costa Rica, the issue of Communist influence did not disappear during or after the war. Suspicions of the Communists resurfaced as the conflict neared its end, and several embassy officials and others in Washington began monitoring the Vanguard and Calderón's relationship with domestic and international communism.[60] Ambassador Scotten characterized Manuel Mora as an instrument of Soviet dictator Joseph Stalin and stressed his ties to the Costa Rican government. His portrayals aggravated Calderón's supporters in Washington, including Welles. After several exchanges, the situation quieted when the State Department reassigned Scotten to Ecuador.[61]

Scotten's successor, Fay Des Portes, also questioned the Vanguard's intentions, although he never tied it as closely to the international Communist movement and did not emphasize the relationship between Calderón and Mora. He wrote that a "striking similarity exists between the programs" of the Vanguard and the former Communist party. "The statutes of the former Communist Party admitted that Costa Rica was not ready to participate in the Socialist regime and it was not working to impose socialism here," he concluded, "but [it] believed [in] the liberation of [the] country from imperialism, [and] obtaining vast land reform, which would allow each farmer to have his [own] farm."[62] At this point, the U.S.–U.S.S.R. alliance remained intact, preventing confrontations. Costa Rican culture also played a role in moderating fears of Communist influence because of the traditional absence of radicalism in Costa Rican politics, an idea stressed by Calderón and his associates when discussing the issue of communism with U.S. officials. They continued arguing that the Vanguard was uniquely Costa Rican and dedicated primarily to improving Costa Rican society through democratic and evolutionary change and that it was not part of an international conspiracy to replace capitalism with authoritarian communism.

Others outside the State Department harbored suspicions of the Communist role in Costa Rica, especially the Federal Bureau of Investigation. As early as 1941, the FBI had established a base of operations in Costa Rica.[63] In September 1943, it issued a memorandum entitled "Totalitarian Activities in Costa Rica Today," in which it emphasized that "there is no doubt but that the Communists of Costa Rica wield considerable power."[64] The Communist organization contained an executive committee and local cells composed primarily of workers in the government and banana industries. The FBI expressed "doubt as to the genuineness of the dissolution of the Communist Party," pointing out that it continued with the same leaders and propaganda.[65] It concluded that "the Communist Party of Costa Rica (PCCR) governs its acts according to the principles of Marxism, Leninism, and Stalinism."[66] While the study downplayed the Communists as a threat to U.S. security at that moment, it laid the groundwork for a much harder line against the Vanguard in the postwar era, when anti-Communist paranoia swept the United States.

The rise of the Communists alarmed a few U.S. policymakers in Washington and diplomats in San José, but no one advocated working with the opposition because of the focus on hemispheric unity and the absence of overt hostility toward the Soviet Union before 1946. The most powerful member of the opposition was the former president, León Cortés, but most Americans feared his association with the Fascists. Therefore, they began looking elsewhere.

Suspicious U.S. officials also disliked Figueres as an alternative. They possessed only limited information about him. In July 1942, the embassy reported that "Jose Figueres prominent coffee grower, naturalized Costa Rican, Falangist and Pro-Nazi last night made subversive broadcast against government. Immediately arrested. President desires his immediate deportation to the Canal Zone."[67] U.S. diplomats made few other references about Figueres during the war, mainly because he spent most of the time in exile in Mexico, where U.S. officials believed he posed no threat.

Associates of Figueres received more attention from Washington, although only limited contacts occurred. In October 1943 Ambassador Des Portes reported that the Center for the Study of National Problems "represents one of the few organizations with a concrete program for the welfare of the country. The Centro is also endeavoring to introduce a party or institutional approach to politics here, which, as the Department is aware, customarily revolve around individuals." "While the present influence of the Centro is perhaps not great" he added, "it is steadily bringing its viewpoints to the attention of the public here and it may well evolve into an organism of definite political importance in the future."[68] The ambassador correctly appraised the situation. At the time, most U.S. diplomats avoided direct contacts with the Center or other groups in the opposition. This policy changed later when the Cold War heated up and it appeared that Calderón and Picado would sustain the importance of the Communists in Costa Rican politics.

While some U.S. officials monitored the Communist movement in Costa Rica, most ignored it and focused on the war effort. Other events highlighted Washington's lack of concern with Calderón's association with the Communists. During anti-Fascist parades on 4 July 1942, the chief of the U.S. military mission, Colonel R. E. Jones, stood alongside Communist leaders.[69] When Vice-President Henry A. Wallace visited San José in March 1943, Calderón declared a national holiday, and a crowd of approximately 25,000 people greeted the American. At the reception, members of the Vanguard carried pro-Soviet placards and several of its leaders made welcoming speeches, but the embassy voiced no concern about the Communist presence and chose instead to stress the wartime alliance between the two countries.[70]

The most important reason U.S. officials expressed little concern about the Communists in Costa Rica was the existing geopolitical conditions. The Americans devoted their energies to defeating the Nazis, rarely questioning Calderón's loyalty. During his tenure, he readily accepted most U.S. initiatives, especially in relation to the Allied war effort. His actions and statements consistently demonstrated his dedication to the Allies and there was no indication that his pro-American stance or that of the majority of Costa Ricans would change anytime soon.

Although U.S.–Costa Rican relations were relatively harmonious from 1940 to 1944, Calderón's administration laid the foundation for difficulties in the postwar era. One event that foreshadowed the future problems occurred in 1944. In the presidential race, the National Republicans and the Vanguard supported Calderón's hand-picked successor, Picado, against Cortés.[71] During the spirited campaign, the Vanguard organized bands of thugs to intimidate Cortés's groups and ransack the offices of opposition newspapers and radio stations. On election day, government officials reportedly stuffed ballot boxes and destroyed returns from several opposition districts. Not surprisingly, Picado won easily. Disgusted, Cortés protested and dispatched a representative to Mexico to request that Figueres return home and lead a revolt. Figueres returned to San José to a crowd of over 10,000 well-wishers, but the situation grew calm before any clashes broke out. Nevertheless, many members of the opposition remained determined to challenge National Republican rule in the future at the ballot box and with force if necessary. The stage was set for conflict.[72]

While some problems appeared brewing, Calderón left office with a long list of significant accomplishments, including the labor code and the social security program. In international relations, especially with the United States, Calderón distinguished himself. He epitomized the kind of leader the Roosevelt administration wanted in office, a reformer without radicalism. In foreign affairs, he proved a reliable ally, backing the Allies on the issues of Argentina, the internment of German and Italian nationals, and rebuilding the military even when it proved unpopular at home. U.S. officials acknowledged the loyalty, a point Calderón underscored when he tried returning to office in 1948.

Nevertheless, like the domestic potential for conflict, Calderón's policies laid the basis for future disputes with the United States. The alliance with Mora and the Vanguard continued into Picado's term. Although most Americans did not view that alliance negatively during the war, it caused problems afterward. As Soviet-American relations deteriorated, Calderón and Picado failed adequately to discern the shift in U.S. policy until it was too late, while the opposition, led by Figueres and others, used the issue to their advantage. While Calderón's ideology appeared not to change during this time, the onset of the cold war altered American attitudes toward the former president and members of the National Republican party. For U.S. policymakers, the question remained when Calderón sought the presidency in 1948: What was his true position in relation to the United States?

3

THE TIMES ARE A-CHANGING

The Emergence of Problems between the Picado Administration and the United States, 1944–1948

In early 1947, U.S. Ambassador to Costa Rica Hallet Johnson remarked, "Peaceful democratic procedure is the best tradition of Costa Rica. Violence, therefore, is a strange, sinister departure. Not long ago, the municipal water works were blown up; the railroad system dynamited, gun-toting is not infrequent. All these happenings are straws in the wind." "Appreciating the wonderful friendship of the Costa Rican People for the people of the United States," he added, "I am grieved to know that this earthly Paradise in Middle America is confronted with the ugly sight of a serpent of violence, due to the political bickering. We who love Costa Rica are disturbed."[1]

Violence was a common occurrence throughout the Picado administration. The transitional nature of Costa Rican society during the postwar era contributed directly to the upheavals. When Picado took office, he inherited a weak economy and an unstable political situation.[2] Wartime dislocations had reduced imports and exports, limiting the availability of consumer goods and diminishing government revenues in a period characterized by expanded programs and increased expenditures. In addition, the opposition coalesced, seriously threatening National Republican control. Calderón's continued domination of the party exacerbated Picado's political woes and undermined his political authority. Finally, Picado lacked strong ties with prominent public groups, such as the Catholic Church.[3] Without a strong base of support, his programs succeeded only in areas where he received the support of Calderón or Mora. Unable to create a consensus, Picado was susceptible to many challenges that culminated in the civil war of 1948.[4]

In foreign relations, problems deriving from the cold war replaced the security of the wartime alliance with the United States. From 1944 to 1947, the United States remained preoccupied with events in Europe and Asia, leaving the embassy in San José to shape policies toward Costa Rica. Ambassador Johnson and his staff maintained close ties with Picado, ignoring or downplaying his association with the Vanguard. As the cold war escalated, however, some State Department and intelligence officials as well as opposition members led by Otílio Ulate and José Figueres increasingly focused on the Communist presence in Costa Rica. Despite warnings from the FBI and others, Johnson's group molded perceptions in the State Department. For his part, Picado failed to discern the shifts in American attitudes, falling victim to the belief that the Vanguard was uniquely Costa Rican, not a tool of international communism. He steadfastly resisted pressures from the United States, the opposition, and his own advisers to dissolve his alliance with the Communists. Relations began to change in early 1947 when the State Department replaced Johnson with diplomats who did not accept the cooperation between the government and the Communists. By the presidential election of 1948, U.S. feelings toward Picado and his apparent successor, Calderón, had cooled noticeably.

Picado faced the difficult task of succeeding an activist president. A competent and honorable man, Picado lacked the political connections and charisma to control the National Republican party and promote his own agenda. Born into humble origins in San José in 1900, he earned a law degree at an early age but abandoned the legal profession to teach. Soon afterward, he became the director of secondary schools for the province of Alajuela and, in 1932, the minister of public education. In 1938 he entered the Legislative Assembly, and by 1941 his peers had elected him its president. Utilizing his important position, Picado pushed many of Calderón's social and economic reforms although his own politics remained more moderate. Calderón rewarded his loyalty by supporting his successful presidential candidacy in 1944.[5]

In domestic affairs, Picado spent most of his time trying to maintain and extend the programs begun during the Calderón administration. Like his counterpart in the United States, Harry S. Truman, Picado fought those determined to undermine the labor and social advances secured during Calderón's term. On the defensive throughout his term, he passed few new initiatives because he faced fiscal difficulties and a stronger opposition throughout his term. The president worked hard to balance the budget, promoting very unpopular proposals such as an income tax.[6] Throughout his tenure, he held the line but made few dramatic changes.

While there were few major innovations in domestic affairs during Picado's administration, many changes occurred in U.S.–Costa Rican relations. At the start of his term, the wartime alliance appeared likely to continue. U.S. policymakers invited Picado to visit the United States in April 1944. President Roosevelt warmly received Picado in South Carolina, and afterwards Picado traveled to Washington to participate in press conferences, photo opportunities, and dinners with Secretary of State Cordell Hull and Coordinator of Inter-American Affairs Nelson Rockefeller, Jr. Picado made a favorable impression, and at a special session of the Pan American Union, Hull praised his dedication to education and democracy.[7]

Picado also impressed embassy officials in San José. In January 1944, Chargé d'Affaires Edward Trueblood emphasized that although Picado lacked a "pleasant and attractive personality," he presented "the impression of being a hard worker and a responsible man, who will do all he can to administer the nation well."[8] Trueblood also portrayed him as more moderate and less dedicated to dramatic social changes than his predecessor. Finally, he predicted a future break between Picado, Calderón, and Mora since the president had promised to steer an independent course in domestic affairs and to end his party's relationship with the Communists.[9] The political climate of the country would prevent Picado from fulfilling his promise to sever ties with the Vanguard. Nevertheless, most of the embassy officials remained firmly pro-Picado and continued promoting a positive perception of the administration.

The position of Picado among U.S. officials received an additional boost in January 1945 when Hallet Johnson became the U.S. ambassador to Costa Rica. A career diplomat with good political connections in Washington (including his cousin, U.S. Senator Theodore Francis Green), Johnson became a strong proponent of Picado and Mora.[10] From the start, he played down the connections between the Vanguard and the Soviet Union, in part contributing to Picado's inability to recognize the shift in American attitudes toward communism. Johnson also praised Picado's allegiance and willingness to accommodate American interests on major international questions in the Pan American Union and the United Nations. At the same time, the ambassador condemned the opposition's conservatism as a threat to Costa Rican democracy. For over two years, Johnson and his allies in the embassy in San José effectively molded U.S.

policy toward the country and helped sustain cordial relations with Picado.

An examination of Johnson's tenure provides some insights into the mechanics of U.S. foreign relations during the early years of the cold war. Because Washington remained preoccupied with events in Europe and Asia, U.S. diplomats in the embassies in Latin America and lower level officials in Washington maintained prominent roles in determining policy. In Johnson's case, he and his allies set the tone for U.S.–Costa Rican relations from 1945 to 1947. Nevertheless, U.S. policy was not uniform. The infighting between various groups in the State Department, the FBI and Central Intelligence Agency provides an interesting case study in bureaucratic politics.[11] Johnson used his position effectively to shape U.S. policy toward Costa Rica, momentarily outmaneuvering other groups in the State Department and intelligence organizations that tried portraying Picado as a Communist dupe. His ability to mold perceptions began changing as the cold war heated up and U.S. policymakers increasingly focused attention on any perceived Communist threat. This modification led in part to Johnson's removal and replacement by a more hard-line representative who pointed out the dangers of the alliance between the Communists and the Costa Rican government. This conflict within the foreign policy establishment helps underscore the point that U.S. policy cannot be viewed as one-dimensional and coherent but is always in flux.

Upon setting up shop in San José, Johnson began promoting positive images of Picado and Mora in the State Department, highlighting a speech in which Mora denounced class warfare as an outmoded concept.[12] "The former Communist Party which for years based its policy on a bitter condemnation of 'Yankee Imperialism,' " Johnson stated, "is offering collaboration and support to foreign capital."[13] Instead of focusing on the negative aspects of the Vanguard-government cooperation, the ambassador pointed out instead recent opposition attacks on foreign interests, especially the United Fruit Company.[14]

Johnson continued his campaign to distance the Vanguard from charges of communism, affirming "that the members of the Vanguardia Popular can no longer be accurately described as Communists."[15] To substantiate his point, he forwarded a statement made at the founding of the Vanguard in May 1943. "We declare that the Vanguardia Popular is a party authentically Costa Rican [and] that it profoundly respects the religious sentiments of the people; and that its social aim is to prevent misery and ignorance in Costa Rica."[16] Mora tried to assist Johnson's efforts by emphasizing that his group was uniquely Costa Rican and pro-American, writing in the summer of 1945 to President Harry S. Truman, "The Costa Rican people at a meeting held July 4 greet you and express hope for the maintenance of a peace based on the unity of all free peoples."[17]

While downplaying Communist influence in Costa Rica, Johnson and other embassy officials simultaneously stressed the achievements of Picado and his associates. At the end of Picado's first year in office, the embassy reported that his record "in international affairs . . . has been one of close cooperation with the United States and of the maintenance of peaceful and friendly relations with neighboring countries."[18] It added that the president had demonstrated a great "sincerity of purpose" in his social, financial, and electoral reforms and that although an opposition existed, dissension dominated its ranks.[19]

The embassy maintained the upper hand in the battle to determine U.S. policy toward Costa Rica, but not everyone accepted its appraisal. Some officials of the State Department increasingly had monitored the Costa Rican Communists as the war neared its end. In early 1945, reports began circulating that the Soviet Union was using its embassy in Mexico City as a base to initiate subversive actions in the western hemisphere. In January, Soviet Ambassador to Mexico Constantine Oumansky died when his plane crashed en route to Costa Rica. Mexican officials reportedly discovered over $150,000 in $1,000 bills in the plane. U.S. Ambassador to Mexico George Messersmith concluded that "we must take it for about definite proof as we have yet had that Oumansky was using large sums of money for various, what we would call, improper purposes." "The only way in which the money could have been used," he added, "would be to suborn Government officials or labor leaders in Costa Rica or some of these other Central American countries."[20]

The FBI also continued observing the Vanguard and its leaders. The old Communist hunter of the 1920s and 1930s, J. Edgar Hoover, provided the State Department with information on the Vanguard, a group he characterized as the "Communist Party of Costa Rica."[21] In August 1945, the FBI highlighted the party's association with prominent Latin American Communists and its possession of a complex indoctrination program and a large library of books on communism, socialism, and the class struggle.[22] For men such as Hoover, guilt by association and the presence of socialist literature were proofs enough to condemn the Vanguard as a tool of Soviet expansionism. Yet, in 1945, the crusade against communism had not reached epidemic proportions, and most U.S. officials in Washington and San José had not fallen victim to the paranoia that would sweep the United States soon after.

In Costa Rica, the opposition shared Hoover's preoccupation with the National Republican–Vanguard alliance. Political opportunism played an important role in the opposition's effort to make the alliance a major issue in the congressional elections of 1946. Its propaganda influenced some conservative and middle-class Costa Rican voters and effectively raised additional suspicions of Communist influence among some U.S. officials. Over Johnson's protests, some U.S. diplomats responded by moving closer to various opposition leaders. They wanted to play both sides of the fence and maintain connections with the opposition in the event it wrested power from the National Republicans. In addition, some wanted to develop connections with anti-Communists in Costa Rica to act as a counterbalance to the Vanguard.

U.S. officials identified Otílio Ulate as a potential presidential candidate with good credentials. Editor and publisher of the *Diario de Costa Rica,* Ulate had an up-and-down relationship with the United States. In the 1920s, he had worked with Augusto Sandino's Anti-imperialist League, publicly criticizing the U.S. occupation of Nicaragua. At times, he also had denounced the United Fruit Company and other foreign businesses.[23] As he matured, however, his views moderated. During the war, his anti-American rhetoric decreased, and he strongly supported the Allied war effort. Disillusioned with the right-wing tendencies of León Cortés, U.S. officials saw Ulate as a moderate alternative to the former president.

As early as 1945, some in the State Department actively courted Ulate by inviting him to the United States. When he visited in early 1946, Ulate met with President Truman and Undersecretary of State Spruille Braden. After he returned to Costa Rica, he tried capitalizing on his ties with Washington. When the Vanguard accused U.S. officials of favoring Ulate, they denied the charges.[24] Although the relationship cooled after Ulate printed anti-Semitic articles in his paper, he remained a leading choice among U.S. leaders to replace Picado and peacefully reduce Vanguard influence.

While U.S. officials claimed impartiality in Costa Rican affairs, they associated with other opposition leaders such as prominent labor organizer Father Benjamín Núñez. With the support of Archbishop Sanabria, Núñez had founded the Catholic labor union *Rerum Novarum* in 1943 to serve as a Christian alternative to the Vanguard.[25] A consolidated group of fifteen unions, *Rerum Novarum* promoted education for the working class and a regulated form of capitalism that defended labor's rights.[26] More important to U.S. diplomats, it was anti-Communist, a point that Núñez often made. In the May Day celebrations of 1945, Núñez declared: "Our organization . . . is fully disposed to finish with [the] Marxian communism existing in Costa Rica."[27]

In April 1945, Núñez solicited assistance from various domestic and international groups. In a meeting between U.S. Attaché for Civil Affairs Edward D. Cuffe and prominent members of the opposition, Núñez sought money to battle the Communists. All the persons present promised aid, except the embassy representative, although his presence legitimized the proceeding. Núñez also solicited funds from the president of the Central Committee of Democratic Unions for the American Federation of Labor, Matthew Woll, and labor organizer Serafino Romualdi, both of whom received assistance from the State Department and the CIA in the postwar period.[28] The additional funds allowed Núñez to strengthen his organization, providing an alternative to the Communists. The growth of the union was important, as many of its members, including Núñez, participated in large numbers in the rebel army during the fighting in 1948. Although Washington avoided direct subsidies to *Rerum Novarum*, its loose association with the group demonstrated its growing concern with the Communist movement in Costa Rica.

While the United States courted various opposition leaders, it developed relatively few ties with the group that would emerge as the dominant political force in 1948. In March 1945, the members of the center joined with other reformers to form the Social Democratic party (PSD). The new party differed from many predecessors because its members sought to promote political principles rather than a presidential candidate, although personalism never disappeared. The PSD platform called for the establishment of a fourth branch of government (an electoral tribunal to monitor elections), the destruction of communism, and the nationalization of the energy and communication industries. With revolutionary zeal, its most visible member, José Figueres, urged the creation of a Second Republic in the final address of the founding convention. Although he temporarily broke with the party soon after, he returned later and used the PSD as a vehicle for gaining power in 1948.[29]

Because the PSD lacked political power, the embassy maintained only limited contact with the party. Nevertheless, it monitored the party's activities. Johnson correctly characterized the new party as lacking support outside the *meseta central.* "Briefly, it may be said," he recounted, "that the outstanding characteristics of these persons are their youth, opposition to the traditional 'personalism' of Costa Rican politics, and their lack of political experience in government affairs."[30] When the fighting broke out in 1948, however, this group formed the nucleus of the revolutionaries that took to the hills to battle Picado, Calderón, and Mora. Strongly dedicated to establishing a new government, they proved to be a formidable force in 1948.

Whereas in 1954 Washington orchestrated a coup in response to a perceived Communist threat in Guatemala, U.S. representatives never approached the PSD or others to utilize as surrogates to overthrow Picado, Mora, and Calderón. The timing was crucial. Communism was an important issue, but the United States had more pressing problems in Europe and Asia. Furthermore, Costa Rica did not have a long history of radicalism, and this fact prevented U.S. suspicions from developing quickly. Finally, divisions within the State Department canceled each other, preventing hard-liners from pushing a policy that punished the administration for its alliance with the Vanguard. Potential problems still existed because the geopolitical conditions continued to change almost daily in Washington, further destroying the tenuous wartime alliance between the two superpowers.

As relations between the United States and the Soviet Union worsened, political tensions rose dramatically in Costa Rica in 1946. The opposition intensified its attempts to wrest power from Picado and the National Republicans. The unexpected death of León Cortés in March 1946 momentarily disrupted its activities, removing its most likely presidential candidate. After Cortés's death, dramatic changes occurred as Costa Rica's political system began to resemble more closely its quarrelsome neighbors. Radicals increasingly moved outside the normal political channels. In June, a group led by Roberto Brenes and funded by the new leader of the Democratic party, Fernando Castro, attempted to overthrow Picado. Approximately thirty men seized a radio station and broadcast an appeal to the Costa Rican people to revolt against the corrupt National Republican dictatorship. The army responded immediately and arrested the conspirators, crushing the rebellion. In an act of generosity, Picado pardoned the plotters.[31]

The government's quick actions failed to discourage the radicals, who changed their tactic to isolated acts of terrorism. In early November, someone threw a bomb into Mora's home while he and his family slept, causing some minor injuries.[32] Outside observers believed that the lunatic fringe wanted to spark armed confrontations with outraged *vanguardistas* to discredit the government and force its downfall.[33] Demonstrations followed, but no altercations occurred. Problems persisted as some Costa Ricans relied on violence to solve their disputes. The economic dislocations of the postwar period and the frustrations regarding charges of government corruption heightened tensions, resulting in some Costa Ricans rejecting their traditional political heritage and utilizing violence to settle their differences. The terrorism and conflict also caused Americans to focus more attention on events in Costa Rica as Costa Ricans acted abnormally, leading to more speculation on the country's possible direction.

Despite the increased internal disorders, Ambassador Johnson continued backing Picado. In early 1946, he praised the president's support of Washington. "The attitude of the Picado government towards the United States has been from the beginning one of complete cooperation," the ambassador reported.[34] One month later, he added: "I have the honor to report that President Picado and the Minister of Foreign Affairs have many times assured me that the international policy of Costa Rica will be guided by that of the United States."[35] Johnson characterized Foreign Minister Julio Acosta as vehemently anti-Communist and emphasized that although Picado did not share the minister's obsession with communism, he wished to retain a warm and close relationship with Washington.[36]

The Picado administration continued to reinforce Johnson's appraisals with actions. It backed the United States on international issues in the UN and Pan American Union.[37] In October 1946, Acosta instructed his country's UN delegates to follow Washington's lead even if U.S. opinions conflicted with their own.[38] The Costa Ricans also granted the U.S. War Department indefinite control of the radio station at Parrita and the right to land at their airports.[39] Finally, the Picado administration supported U.S. attempts to destroy the remnants of the Nazi presence in Latin America by restricting the immigration of former Nazi party members.[40] These activities fit nicely into the overall pattern of relations as Picado supported U.S.

initiatives on major international questions while remaining reluctant to alter all of his domestic policies to appease the United States.

While Johnson remained intensely loyal to Picado, the views of the embassy regarding the Vanguard fluctuated as the cold war escalated. In March 1946, Johnson described Mora as "an opportunist and an admirer of the Soviets," although he noted his record of cooperating with American businesses.[41] He further speculated that Mora's lieutenants openly sided with the Soviets but that "Mora himself would be governed by the circumstances and it is difficult to predict accurately what his attitude would be."[42] His aides controlled the Vanguard paper, *Trabajo,* that frequently attacked capitalism and Washington's policy toward the Soviet Union.[43] Johnson concluded that a majority of Costa Ricans favored the United States over the Soviet Union, but he found the Vanguard's position indeterminable.

The embassy followed this relatively negative portrayal with more positive descriptions, obscuring the role of the Vanguard. In April, Johnson stated: "The Vanguardia Popular may or may not have some tenuous connection with Moscow, but apart from securing the enactment of the much needed Labor Code, their program has been a mild one."[44] A month later he concluded, "The Vanguardia Popular Party . . . was able to elect only five deputies in February last, and the program of the party is leftist only to the extent of what would be known as liberalism in Anglo-Saxon countries."[45] Other observers, such as Archbishop Sanabria, informed U.S. officials that the Communists posed no danger. He denied that Mora followed Moscow's orders, characterizing him first and foremost as a Costa Rican and not an agent of international communism.[46]

The embassy continued presenting fairly positive portrayals of the Vanguard in October. In a sixty-one-page report entitled "Communism in Costa Rica," it found no direct relationship between the Vanguard and Soviets, although the party's propaganda from the U.S.S.R. arrived in open mail, as did its assistance from organizations such as the Friends of the Soviet Union. The *vanguardistas,* especially the publishers of *Trabajo,* maintained close contact with Mexican and Spanish Communists. Still, U.S. officials emphasized that the Vanguard remained a home-grown socialist organization that charted an independent course.[47]

Although Johnson and his associates supported Picado and tolerated the *vanguardistas,* other State Department and intelligence officials viewed the Costa Rican situation differently. In the postwar era, many in Washington had become increasingly suspicious of Soviet expansionism. The United States adopted a harder line toward the Soviets through 1946 and 1947 as President Truman and his advisers fell under the influence of George Kennan and others who argued that the Soviets were aggressive and intent on world domination. They encouraged the president to develop policies that contained the Soviets, policies first manifested in the Truman Doctrine. The influence of the hard-liners contributed to a new round of anticommunism in the United States, resulting in activities to undermine the Communists in countries where beforehand the United States had tolerated popular-front governments.[48]

Costa Rica was no exception. Throughout the postwar era the FBI had continued monitoring the Vanguard and its leaders. When Mora traveled to Mexico in the summer of 1946 to visit with the suspected Communist organizer Vicente Lombardo Toledano, the FBI trailed him.[49] In July, Hoover's agents outlined Mora's relationship with Rafael Ruano, a Spanish Republican and director of the social security office in Limón who had close ties with prominent Latin American Communists.[50] Finally, the FBI noted that Rodolfo Guzmán, secretary general of the Vanguard, planned to attend the Congress of World Federation of Trade Unions, reportedly a Communist front organization.[51] The FBI was the first to focus attention on the possible threat posed by Costa Rican leftists to the Panama Canal and the Caribbean trade routes. The Central Intelligence Agency and some members of the State Department followed its lead and more carefully watched the Vanguard and its influence in the government, causing Washington to adopt a harder line against the Picado administration.

By October 1946, the State Department had become increasingly critical in its analysis of the Vanguard. The department's Bureau of Intelligence informed senior State Department officials that three groups composed the Vanguard. Hard-line Marxists dominated the party's newspapers and unions while Mora managed a more opportunistic branch interested primarily in improving the lot of Costa Rican labor. The majority, composed of the rank-and-file laborers, knew nothing about communism and had joined only to better their working conditions and wages. The bureau concluded by characterizing the party as Communist and a menace to liberal democratic rule in Costa Rica.[52] Although Johnson successfully parried this attack, a small group in the State Department led by the Central American desk officer, William T. Bennett, Jr., increasingly viewed the Vanguard as a potential threat to U.S. security.[53]

As suspicions of the Vanguard grew in Washington, U.S. military aid decreased, although it is difficult to establish a correlation between the two developments. Military cooperation had continued into 1945, when the two countries signed an agreement maintaining the U.S. military mission in Costa Rica.[54] While continuing to train the Costa Rican army, the United States significantly reduced the flow of arms and ammunition to the country, part of the overall demilitarization in the postwar period. State Department officials opposed additional military assistance because the Picado administration had not serviced its lend-lease debt. They also feared that providing additional military hardware would be construed as interference in Costa Rica's domestic politics. Finally, the Costa Ricans proved reluctant to seek military assistance because of the fear of added expenditures and the desire to maintain a small military establishment.[55] Although U.S. officials eventually allowed Costa Rica to acquire some arms, they reduced the quantities.[56]

Restricting arms shipments had long-term consequences. By 1948, the Costa Rican military was inadequately armed. When the fighting began in March 1948, the government failed to exploit its initial advantage because it lacked equipment. This shortage allowed the rebels to organize an offensive against the government while it tried to replenish its supplies in the United States and Latin America. By limiting arms purchases, U.S. officials effectively undermined Picado's abilities to defeat the opposition, especially when his forces quickly expended their ammunition in the early stages of the fighting in 1948.

The year of 1947 was pivotal. Costa Rica's political scene continued to deteriorate as both sides increasingly relied on violence and many leaders, including Figueres, prepared for a prolonged struggle. During the year, more U.S. officials began focusing on the Communist presence in the country. The process picked up steam when the State Department reassigned Johnson, whose departure removed a powerful ally who had deflected a great deal of criticism (originating in the FBI and among some members of the State Department) of the alliance between Picado and Mora. While some U.S. officials grew more alarmed about the degenerating situation, for the moment they refused to intervene directly in Costa Rican politics because of the continued dedication by some to the principles of the "Good Neighbor" policy and the fact that while the Costa Rican situation was much worse than normal, it was relatively calm when compared to other areas where the United States had interests in the developing world.

The major reason for the increased tensions in early 1947 was the preparation by all sides for the 1948 presidential election. The National Republican candidate, former president Calderón, appeared the front-runner. Although he initially denied his intention to run for the office, his attitude changed in 1946 as he made plans for the contest. In response, the opposition mounted a campaign in the *Diario de Costa Rica* and its other mouthpieces characterizing him as a corrupt Communist stooge and Mora's servant.[57] Understanding the importance of the Communist question in his country and the United States, Calderón vigorously denied the opposition's charges. After leaving office, he had worked in a New York City hospital for several years and had seen firsthand the growing Communist paranoia in the United States. Before returning to Costa Rica in 1946, he visited with Assistant Secretary of State Spruille Braden to stress his dedication to democratic principles and anticommunism.[58] Once he returned home, Calderón continued distancing himself from the Vanguard. In a newspaper interview, he argued that he associated with the Vanguard only because he shared its dedication to improving the welfare of Costa Ricans. He emphasized, however, that he differed dramatically from the Communists on many issues, such as class struggle and religion. "I am not, nor can I be a communist," the former president declared, "but I continue believing that communism is not combated by showing it the big stick or jail."[59]

Johnson supported Calderón's claims, stressing that his association with the Vanguard had been driven by political opportunism, not acceptance of Communist ideology. "There is no evidence that Calderón-Guardia is a member of, or has any sympathy for groups with communist leanings," Johnson observed.[60] Subsequent reports emphasized a "cooling of the former warm relations" between the Vanguard and the National Republicans, and both groups denied any alliance in the approaching February 1948 elections.[61]

While Calderón battled the Communist issue, a more immediate problem for his candidacy developed in February 1947 when the various opposition groups united behind one candidate. Meeting in the national stadium, they chose between Ulate, Figueres, and Fernando Castro in a situation one observer described in these terms: "Castro will lead us to a deal; Figueres to a revolution; Ulate to nowhere."[62] After several ballots, Figueres and his followers backed Ulate, who received the nomination. Unified for the first time, the opposition agreed to participate in the electoral process, but Ulate appointed Figueres "*jefe de acción*" with orders to prepare for potential armed actions against the National Republicans in the event that they tried rigging the election.[63]

Some U.S. diplomats viewed the opposition's choice of candidates skeptically. Although the United States had once courted Ulate, the relationship had cooled after he published several anti-Semitic articles. Immediately after his nomination, State Department officials characterized Ulate as subordinating "everything to his personal ambition," adding that he "has on more than one occasion made it impossible for the Government and the Opposition to arrange political rivalry on a reasonable basis."[64] Most U.S. officials wanted to avoid interfering in the election, believing that the Costa Rican system would rebalance itself. Some thought Calderón would win and follow through on his promise to disassociate himself from the Vanguard.

Ulate's candidacy improved in the eyes of some Americans, however, as the position of Picado and Calderón worsened in early 1947. A major turning point occurred in February when the State Department replaced Johnson with an interim ambassador, Walter Donnelly. Dismayed, Johnson complained to Truman that his embassy was "working as smoothly as a Swiss watch." "Thus, I am desperately puzzled to understand," he asserted, "why I have been dismissed so abruptly after thirty-five years of service, and six years before usual retirement age." He added that his cousin, Senator Green, had informed him weeks earlier that he would retain his position.[65] Unmoved, administration officials justified his reappointment as part of a plan to promote younger diplomats in the service.[66] Johnson's departure was important because Picado, Calderón, and the National Republicans lost a strong supporter. Afterwards, the embassy and State Department became noticeably more hostile toward communism and its perceived allies in the Costa Rican government.

In part, the Vanguard contributed directly to the adoption of a tougher U.S. policy against Picado. U.S. officials increasingly noted the domination of the Vanguard by the more radical, pro-Soviet clique. On 11 April the party organized a march of over two thousand people to celebrate the defeat of nineteenth-century American imperialist William Walker. Some participants carried placards denouncing the Truman Doctrine, one of them reading, "Down with the Truman Plan: we do not wish to be cannon fodder for Yankee imperialism." Vanguard vendors also hawked Mora's 1940 pamphlet, in which Mora attacked State Department interventionism. U.S. officials concluded that the Vanguard now appeared "at least open to Moscow penetration" and held to a "way of thinking far from ours."[67] Although embassy analysts speculated that a break could occur between the National Republicans and the Vanguard, they believed it would "not be due to any deep conviction that we are in the right, but rather to a careful weighing, in the scales of local politics, of political opportuneness."[68]

The Vanguard's reorganization in May 1947 caused additional anxiety among U.S. policymakers. Its new platform emphasized the Marxist-Leninist principles of democratic centralism, anti-imperialism, and a radical socialistic restructuring of the Costa Rica economy.[69] Sufficiently concerned, Bennett requested and received additional information on the Vanguard including a translated copy of a 1946 pamphlet, "Los Principios de Organización del Partido Vanguardia Popular" (Organizational Principles of the Vanguard Popular Party). This booklet called on Vanguard members to organize a well-disciplined party of the masses dedicated to the socialist struggle.[70]

The Vanguard's more radical orientation and Johnson's removal damaged Picado's relationship with the United States. The increased attention devoted to the Vanguard by U.S. diplomats led several of Picado's advisers to intensify their efforts to persuade the president to reorient his relationship with the Communists to ease growing tensions with Washington. Picado did not, however, sufficiently recognize the depth of the problem. He resisted U.S. attempts to interfere in domestic politics and pressure him into dissolving his relationship with Mora and the Vanguard. The president lacked an understanding of the evolving geopolitical situation in which the wartime alliance of the United States and Soviet Union dissolved quickly after 1945. Furthermore, his personality hindered him. Both critics and friends highlighted his uncompromising sense of loyalty. He ignored the pleas of his closest advisers and refused to betray a faithful ally, ultimately undermining his relations with the United States.[71]

While Picado refused to sever relations with the Vanguard, Calderón continued downplaying his relationship with it. In his first meeting with Ambassador Donnelly, he concentrated on the Communist question, reiterating his dedication to democracy and capitalism and recounting his adoption of peaceful methods to battle communism. The former president emphasized that in 1940 the Communists had received 16,000 votes but that when he left office in 1944 they received only 5,000. "Unless we put an end to Communism and other anti-democratic forces in the western hemisphere," Calderón stated, "Communism will be victorious, with a consequent return of the countries of Latin America to a colonial status."[72] Donnelly left the meeting with ambivalent feelings. Calderón appeared willing to dissolve his relationship with the Vanguard for political expediency. Because he had collaborated with the Communists in the past, however, the ambassador refused to accept his statements at face value.[73]

As Calderón lobbied the State Department and campaigned for the presidency, Picado created additional difficulties for himself by refusing to follow the U.S. lead on a regional question. He antagonized the United States by taking Somoza's side during a confrontation with Washington in mid-1947. In May, the Nicaraguan dictator allowed a presidential election in which his hand-picked candidate, Leonardo Argüello, won easily. Problems arose when Argüello asserted his independence by deposing several Somoza henchmen from the government and restricting the activities of the National Guard. The dictator quickly replaced Argüello with his uncle, Victor Román y Reyes.[74] Disgusted, the State Department withdrew the U.S. ambassador and urged other countries to follow its lead.[75]

The Nicaraguan situation trapped Picado between his neighbor and the United States. Calderón and Somoza had maintained very close ties, working closely in economic and political matters (privately and publicly) during the Costa Rican's presidency. Picado had strengthened the relationship during his tenure by sustaining good relations with the Nicaraguan government. He won Somoza's gratitude in 1944 by assisting in crushing an invasion attempt by a small group of Nicaraguan exiles led by General Alfredo Noguera. The Costa Rican army intercepted the force at the border and helped Somoza's National Guard disperse the rebels.[76]

Although Picado wanted to support Somoza and his puppet, he steered a neutral course at first to avoid alienating the United States. In September 1947, a Nicaraguan official, Mariano Argüello, tried persuading him to recognize the Román y Reyes government. The president initially resisted, offering instead several compromises, such as Somoza's departure from Nicaragua, to allow Román y Reyes to rule independently. Ambassador Donnelly questioned the feasibility of Picado's proposals, arguing that Somoza's influence could not be destroyed so easily. Still, he warned Washington that unless it devised a formula to settle the impasse, Managua's pressure would force Picado to recognize Román y Reyes.[77]

For several months, the issue remained unsettled. Despite Somoza's lobbying, Picado parried his overtures. The president continued promoting compromise, but Washington adamantly opposed recognizing Román y Reyes.[78] Somoza increased the pressure by withdrawing the Nicaraguan consul general and ambassador from San José, effectively stranding thirty thousand Nicaraguans in Costa Rica without any diplomatic representation. This act was important because all of these Central American citizens, according to an 1838 law, possessed the right to vote in Costa Rican elections. With the presidential election approaching and no consular officials to verify status, the Nicaraguans could not vote. This maneuver constituted a major threat to Picado and the National Republicans because they relied on the Nicaraguans to vote for their party. Somoza's measures ultimately succeeded and on Christmas Day 1947, Costa Rica recognized Román y Reyes. Dismayed, some U.S. officials worried that Picado and the National Republicans had moved too close to Somoza and could possibly follow his dictatorial example in the upcoming elections.[79]

The events of the summer of 1947 further strained relations between the United States and Picado. A clash known as the "*Huegla de los Brazos Caídos*" (Strike of the Fallen Arms) erupted on 20 July. The police in Cartago fired on a demonstration of Ulate's supporters, killing two people and wounding several others. The government immediately denied any responsibility and blamed local officials instead. An incensed opposition took to the streets of San José and other cities, causing clashes. On 23 July, opposition leaders changed tactics and called for a general nationwide strike. Businesses, transportation facilities, and banks closed down, and when the government tried reopening the financial institutions, patrons responded by making withdrawals. A desperate Picado issued a radio plea for calm and for the people to return to work. Citizens ignored his requests, and the government responded forcefully. Armed supporters of the government entered the streets and plundered businesses while the police watched the destruction, justifying their inactivity on the grounds that the shopkeepers had caused the violence by refusing to feed the starving people.[80]

The chaos concerned U.S. diplomats in Costa Rica, who vigorously protested the destruction of American-owned businesses. Washington criticized the lack of safeguards for American citizens and property and increased pressure on the Picado administration to stop the looting and violence. In response, the president guaranteed protection of American interests, but some embassy staff expressed much skepticism about whether Picado possessed the power to keep his promise. They had watched the disorder and noted the government's inability or unwillingness to maintain order. It appeared to American observers that Mora had more control over the events than either Picado or Calderón.[81]

Compromises by the government in August ultimately eased tensions, but Picado's response to the crisis was important.[82] The "Strike of the Fallen Arms" had alarmed U.S. officials. Afterwards, they further reduced the flow of military supplies, believing that the demonstrations underscored the government's inability to maintain order. To U.S. diplomats the conflict also provided more evidence of the Vanguard's growing prominence in the Picado administration and its potential threat to Costa Rica's democracy. During the most volatile period of the crisis, Mora had imported *vanguardistas* from the coastal areas to help break the strike. Government sources reportedly provided arms to them, and the police and army watched while the Communists wreaked havoc in the cities. These actions did nothing to ease Washington's fears about the Communist presence in Costa Rica.

The situation quieted slightly but only on the surface. Figueres and other members of the opposition continued preparing for an armed struggle against the National Republicans and the Vanguard. Since his return to Costa Rica in 1944, Figueres had stockpiled military equipment and trained his associates at his *finca*. In December 1947, he met under the watchful eye of President Juan José Arévalo in Guatemala with leaders of exile organizations from Nicaragua and the Dominican Republic. They signed the "Caribbean Pact" that created a Supreme Revolutionary Committee to coordinate their activities. The delegates appointed Figueres and his Nicaraguan friend, Rosendo Argüello, Jr., to the committee. The pact authorized the committee to collect supplies, dispense funds, and implement plans to overthrow the region's dictators. Figueres contended that Costa Rica constituted the weakest link in the dictatorial chain, but the group concentrated instead on a more obvious target: Rafael Trujillo in the Dominican Republic. Only after Trujillo defeated an invasion in early 1948 did the committee turn its attentions toward assisting Figueres in Costa Rica.[83]

For several years, U.S. officials had recognized that Figueres posed a threat to Costa Rica's stability. In October 1946, the State Department had noted that Figueres had traveled to Honduras to confer with Arévalo about moving arms and ammunition from Mexico to Costa Rica. Picado responded by characterizing Figueres as "a dangerous man" but complained that he lacked spies to monitor his movements.[84] Several months later, Johnson described Figueres as a "hothead" whose recklessness and hatred of Calderón and Picado could easily cause violence. Trying to pinpoint Figueres's ideology, Johnson emphasized that it combined strains of authoritarianism and socialism, creating a confusing and often indeterminable policy.[85] The State Department followed Figueres's movements throughout 1947, but it worried more about the problems plaguing the government and especially the Vanguard's increasing audacity.[86] Washington apparently never approached Figueres to orchestrate a coup against a suspected Communist sympathizer as it did later in Guatemala because it continued hoping for a peaceful settlement that would reduce tensions and the prominence of the Vanguard in Costa Rica. In addition, the State Department remained dominated by diplomats not willing to return to the heavy-handed interventionism of the 1920s. Still, some State Department and intelligence officials continued watching Communist activities in Costa Rica.

As domestic conditions in Costa Rica deteriorated in late 1947, attitudes among some U.S. diplomats grew more hostile toward the National Republicans and the Vanguard. In October 1947, Donnelly appraised the upcoming and potentially bitter presidential and congressional elections, underscoring that the Vanguard had designated only candidates for the assembly. He described Mora as a popular labor leader with close ties to Carmen Lyra, Costa Rica's top Communist organizer. The party demonstrated no open hostility toward the United States, but Mora was anti-American and opposed U.S. foreign policy and private ownership, favoring instead state-owned enterprises. In the impending elections, the Vanguard supported Calderón, expecting in return key positions in the government. The former president continued downplaying his association with the Vanguard, but "the fact is, however, that he is aligned with them," the ambassador reported, "and in doing so has contributed to their standing and influence in Costa Rica."[87] Donnelly nonetheless concluded that regardless of the outcome, the United States would maintain a favorable position in the country because the majority of Costa Ricans still supported it.[88]

In late 1947, another emerging force in Washington focused on the Communists in Costa Rica. The increased fear of communism and the withdrawal of the FBI from surveillance responsibilities in Latin America had caused the newly formed Central Intelligence Agency to scramble to provide information on Soviet movements in all regions.[89] In November 1947, the CIA issued a document, "Soviet Objectives in Latin America," outlining Latin America's role in the event of hostilities between the United States and the Soviet Union. In a very pessimistic tone, it emphasized that Latin America would provide the Communists only limited supplies and support during warfare. Instead, the Soviets planned espionage and sabotage operations to deny the United States access to the region's strategic materials.[90]

The bulk of the report was a review of Communist plans in the event of a conflict. For the Soviets to achieve their goal of subverting U.S. interests in Latin America, they needed labor unions in areas of strategic value to Washington. The Russians also wanted to create an effective propaganda machine that could secure popular support for the Soviet Union and provide an organizational base for coordinating underground activities. The CIA judged that few Latin American nations outside Argentina, Mexico, Paraguay, Honduras, El Salvador, and the Dominican Republic could prevent the Communists from achieving their goals.[91] It did not ignore Costa Rica. "With the possible exception of Costa Rica," the agency noted, "no Latin American Government is today publicly cooperating with the Communists."[92]

The CIA and certain diplomats monitoring the situation in Costa Rica did not believe the Vanguard posed a clear and present danger. While its small membership held a disproportionate share of power in the country, it possessed limited potential for expansion. Opposition to the group had grown, primarily among the middle and landowning classes. Calderón also appeared willing to distance himself from the organization if he won the impending election. Some Americans correctly had noted Calderón's modifications, but the presence of the Communists in a country so close to the Caribbean trade routes and Panama Canal created an uneasiness among some U.S. policymakers. Nevertheless, the Truman administration had not adopted plans involving direct U.S. intervention to destroy perceived Communist threats. While the Costa Rican situation concerned some in Washington, most policymakers worried more about the volatile situations in Italy, Austria, France, the Philippines, and Japan. The circumstances would change quickly, causing U.S. diplomats to adopt policies that became increasingly hostile toward the Picado government. The intelligence provided by the CIA and certain State Department officials was important because it kept the Communist issue at the forefront of debates over U.S. policy toward Costa Rica.

The increased U.S. suspicion of Communist influence in Costa Rica immediately preceded the most important event of Picado's administration, the presidential election of 1948. When he had entered office in 1944, Picado had enjoyed Washington's support and few American policymakers had questioned his loyalty or that of his country. He had worked closely with U.S. diplomats on a variety of domestic issues, and his programs had not been radical. In international and regional affairs, the president followed the traditional pattern of relations. He consistently supported U.S. efforts to destroy the remnants of fascism and repeatedly backed U.S. initiatives in the United Nations and Pan American Union designed to undermine international communism and uphold America's strategic interests. At the same time, he maintained freedom of action in domestic and regional affairs, primarily in his association with the Vanguard and in his recognition of Román y Reyes, but this independent behavior was not enough to destroy cordial relations immediately.

Although Picado proved uncompromisingly pro-American in most areas, his relations with the United States deteriorated as the cold war took form. From 1944 to early 1948, the evolution of a tougher U.S. policy toward the Soviet Union and communism was gradual and in some cases subtle. There was a divergence of perceptions as Picado failed to discern this shift adequately and resisted pressure to sever ties with the Communists in Costa Rica, believing that they posed no threat to Costa Rican or American security. The opposition, primarily the followers of Figueres and Ulate, proved more capable of understanding the situation in the United States and utilized the Communist issue further to harden American attitudes toward their opponents. Before March 1948, the United States avoided interfering directly in Costa Rica because of the dedication by many State Department officials to the "Good Neighbor" policy, the historic absence of direct intervention in Costa Rican affairs, and their focus on other more dangerous problems elsewhere. Yet, when the opportunity presented itself to remove the Communist threat following the disputed presidential election, U.S. diplomats adopted an antagonistic stance toward the Picado administration and its *vanguardista* allies, threatening the traditional pattern of amicable relations. The question would be whether the Costa Ricans could settle their own problems without direct American military or covert involvement before irreparable harm occurred.

4

THE FIRST LATIN AMERICAN BATTLEGROUND OF THE COLD WAR

The U.S. Response to the Costa Rican Civil War of 1948[1]

On 22 March 1948, the former secretary general of the Social Democratic party, Gonzalo Facio, publicly charged that the Communists in Costa Rica planned to seize control of his country as part of their overall strategy for dominating the Americas. "Few foresaw the Czechoslovak crisis," he added, "but now we have the same thing in our front yard." Facio characterized the situation in his homeland as alarming because it marked the first instance of infiltration "by those serving Soviet interests without the support of the Russian Army."[2]

Heightened tensions between the United States and the Soviet Union significantly influenced U.S. responses to the Costa Rican civil war of 1948. The opposition effectively manipulated the Communist question, making it more important during the fighting that followed the disputed presidential election of 1948. It caused the United States to intervene more directly in Costa Rican affairs, threatening the pattern of traditionally cordial relations between the two countries. While U.S. officials claimed impartiality, their actions belied their rhetoric. As the conflict escalated in March 1948 and the Communists took an important military role in defending the Picado administration, U.S. diplomats adopted measures that undermined the government's position. They prevented Picado's agents from purchasing arms in the United States and Latin America and stymied Somoza's attempt to aid Picado and Calderón, while also turning a blind eye to Guatemalan assistance to the rebels. Furthermore, U.S. Ambassador to Costa Rica Nathaniel Davis and other embassy officers legitimized the rebel movement by openly working with it during cease-fire negotiations, giving the movement the tacit recognition of the most powerful nation in the region. Finally, at a crucial juncture in the peace talks, U.S. officials intimidated Picado into resigning, guaranteeing a rebel victory. The U.S. role in the revolution was important, helping remove a perceived Communist threat by aiding Figueres's triumph, which ensured a major change in Costa Rican leadership and returned relations between the two countries to more normal patterns in the post–civil war era.

While significant, the U.S. role was secondary to that of the Costa Ricans. In contrast with its policy in Guatemala, the United States did not orchestrate in Costa Rica the overthrow of a government it perceived to be collaborating with the Communists. Instead, the Costa Ricans themselves settled the problem before the United States concluded that it needed to intervene militarily or covertly to remove the National Republican–Vanguard coalition. As in the past, the Costa Ricans adapted to changing geopolitical conditions, preventing direct conflict between their country and the United States. They were aided by the fact that Costa Rica's internal struggle took place in the early years of the cold war, before direct U.S. interventionism returned in full force as a policy alternative, as later evidenced in Guatemala (1954), Cuba (1961), the Dominican Republic (1965), and Chile (1973). In the end, relations returned to more normal forms, although Figueres and his associates hardly proved subservient to the United States.

The crisis that provoked the conflict was the presidential election of 1948. In the months preceding the balloting, the two major candidates, Ulate and Calderón, mobilized their forces by staging rallies, making speeches, and denouncing their rivals in partisan newspapers. Although most Costa Ricans and U.S. diplomats predicted that Calderón, with Vanguard assistance, would win, Ulate campaigned hard. His associates tried discrediting the coalition of Calderón, Picado, and Mora by focusing on National Republican electoral fraud such as the purchasing of *cédulas* (voter registration records) and the processing of its members' voter registrations at higher rates than the opposition.[3] The *ulatistas* also criticized the government's purchase of twenty-five submachine guns from the United States, arguing that Calderón and Picado intended to use the weapons to invalidate any returns that went against them.[4] The charges of corruption and the arms sale further undermined the National Republicans' base of support, confirming fears that they planned to maintain their rule at any cost.

Even more damaging to Calderón was his alleged alliance with the

Communists, a point often raised by the opposition. During the latter stages of the campaign, the *Diario de Costa Rica* published stories recounting a meeting in which Calderón had reportedly showed Vanguard leaders a map of Europe and Costa Rica dominated by communism. The newspaper also carried a photograph of the former president shaking hands with the Mexican labor leader and purported Communist agent Vicente Lombardo Toledano.[5] Calderón denied cooperating with the Communists, but the propaganda played well in conservative sectors of Costa Rican society and in the anti-Communist middle class.

The opposition campaign linking Calderón to communism further heightened U.S. suspicions. In late January, the Central American desk officer, William T. Bennett, Jr., emphasized that the editorials in *Trabajo* had moved from muffled criticisms of the United States to "undisguised approval and support of Soviet policy and vigorous attack on nations engaged in defending themselves from the communist threat."[6] The 10 January edition, he added "contained for the first time an unequivocal admission that the individuals responsible for *Trabajo* are communists."[7] Earlier in the month, the embassy had emphasized that the Vanguard would hold the "balance of power" in the new congress that convened in May, affording it an excellent bargaining position from which to secure concessions from the new president.[8] Bennett failed to establish adequately any direct relationship between the Vanguard and the Soviet Union, but these reports increased fears in the State Department of expanded Communist influence in Costa Rica—but not enough to provoke a direct response at the time.

As the 8 February election approached, the candidates issued last-minute appeals to the voters.[9] Calderón denounced his opponent's reported ties to the Communists, while Ulate chastised the former president for running up a massive debt during his term. The speeches and publications inflamed emotions, provoking disturbances and occasional brawls, many in front of the National Registry. Such violence foreshadowed the future confrontation. "If Calderón wins I will respect his victory," Ulate announced, "[but] if I should win I doubt if he will have the same respect for me."[10] Many Costa Ricans shared his pessimism. On the eve of the election, San José store owners boarded up their windows and the police stepped up its patrols.[11]

Despite such fears, few clashes took place on election day. Early returns showed Ulate maintaining a small lead, and as the polls closed the unofficial results had him winning by a substantial margin.[12] Calderón immediately denounced the outcome, charging the opposition with vote fixing and warning that Picado would call a special legislative session to annul the election.[13] Ulate challenged their accusations, stressing that any attempt to invalidate the election was an attack on the Costa Rican constitution. His supporters announced their determination to fight for their rights but simultaneously encouraged everyone to remain calm while the electoral tribunal tabulated the votes.[14]

An air of uncertainty dominated the country during the deliberations of the electoral tribunal, a three-man committee created in 1944 to monitor the election and validate the returns. Difficulties immediately developed when a fire destroyed a large number of ballots before they could be counted.[15] Logistical problems also slowed the review. While the tribunal worked, Picado pleaded for patience.[16] Life gradually returned to normal, but tensions persisted. No major confrontations occurred as everyone seemed intent on letting the tribunal make its ruling before acting.[17]

U.S. officials also maintained a wait-and-see policy. The new ambassador, Nathaniel P. Davis, had arrived in early 1948 and was still adjusting to the position. A veteran diplomat, he had developed a reputation as an authority on communism during his service in the Philippines, leaving Costa Rica in 1949 to serve in a similar position in Hungary. As he organized his post, reports began circulating in San José that both candidates had prepared plans to respond if the tribunal ruled against them. On 12 February, Davis reported that Calderón had marshalled his congressional allies for an extraordinary session of the assembly to annul the election.[18] A week later, Davis entertained prominent *calderonistas* and *ulatistas,* who hinted that a compromise candidate might be selected.[19] On the eve of the tribunal's decision, Davis met separately with Ulate, Picado, and Calderón to ascertain the truth surrounding the rumors, but they provided no definitive answers. Afterwards, he criticized Picado for failing to bring the two groups together. Instead, the president remained pessimistic and unwilling to promote a peaceful resolution.[20] Although concerned, U.S. officials stressed that they favored neither side and actively encouraged a settlement, a policy that changed only after the fighting began and the Communists started taking a prominent position in the defense of the government.

After some intense deliberation, the tribunal declared Ulate the winner on 28 February. In response, Calderón's followers protested in the streets and Picado called a special session of the Legislative Assembly to decide whether to accept the tribunal's decision.[21] On 1 March, the Legislative Assembly convened to resolve the issue. In an unruly and undisciplined session, the National Republican–Vanguard coalition annulled the election by a vote of twenty-six to nineteen.[22] Calderón's legislative allies announced that when the assembly reconvened in May they would nominate Calderón as first-designate. From that position, he would rule until the next scheduled election in 1952.[23] For the first time since 1917, the country did not have a peaceful transition of power. The annulment sparked a violent clash as Costa Ricans fought to return their country to democratic traditions, leading the United States to interfere more directly in Costa Rican politics.

Immediately, some isolated skirmishes broke out as the government tried to arrest opposition leaders.[24] U.S. officials in Costa Rica, primarily Ambassador Davis, could not escape involvement as the feuding parties immediately sought his intervention in the conflict. First, Davis helped secure medical assistance for people wounded following a shoot-out between opposition members and police intent on seizing Ulate.[25] He then worked with Archbishop Sanabria to guarantee Ulate's safe passage to a government jail after Picado had threatened to bombard the president-elect's sanctuary, a friend's home in San José.[26] Ulate remained in government custody for only one day before a judge ordered him released and cleared him of all charges in the death of the two policemen.[27]

The situation in the first two weeks of March calmed momentarily as Ulate, Calderón, and Picado began negotiations to settle the impasse. From this point forward, the ambassador was quite visible as a mediator. While Davis and other U.S. diplomats in San José and Washington claimed impartiality, they clearly favored a peaceful solution that achieved several goals, primarily peace and the reduction of Communist influence in the country. They wanted neither Calderón or Ulate to be president, fearing that having either one in office would cause additional instability. Furthermore, a third party also appeared less likely than Calderón to allow the Communists a prominent status in his administration. As the U.S. representative, Davis held a historically important position in Costa Rica, providing him with an opportunity to affect the outcome. While hesitant at first, he began exerting himself over the next few weeks to secure the desired outcome.

As the negotiations progressed, both sides tried drawing the United

States into the conflict. In Costa Rica, a well-known lawyer and Picado's former minister of labor, Miguel Brenes, visited Davis to gauge U.S. responses to the invalidation of the election. Brenes queried the ambassador about possible solutions. "Neither Ulate nor Calderon," he emphasized, "could take the presidency and maintain order."[28] Davis urged the disputants to stop political activities and meet under the guidance of a neutral intermediary.[29]

The progovernment forces also worked in Washington. In a meeting with State Department officials, the Costa Rican ambassador to the United States, Francisco Gutiérrez, tried to justify the annulment of the election. More concerned with the role of the Communists in Costa Rica, U.S. diplomats questioned him about the strength and orientation of the Vanguard. On the defensive, he denied any ties between Mora and Moscow, stressing that, in the event of hostilities between the United States and the Soviet Union, the Vanguard would side with Washington. "Ambassador Gutiérrez gave the impression that he was trying to indicate that Mora and the Vanguardia party were not Communists," a U.S. official noted, "while he perhaps in fact questioned Mora's real position himself."[30] The Communist issue remained an important factor in influencing U.S. responses to the conflict, increasing in significance after the fighting started the following week.

Although both sides continued negotiating, members of the opposition, in a move comparatively unusual for Costa Ricans, planned a military solution to the political deadlock.[31] The central figure of the movement was Figueres, who had fled to his farm outside San José when the government arrested Ulate. Joined by allies, he armed them with equipment he had stockpiled since his return from exile in 1944. While Calderón and Ulate debated in San José, Figueres trained his followers and waited for the right moment to strike.[32] Unlike the participants in many movements in Central America, the insurgents were driven by a passion for democracy and change, not personal greed or power. It proved a very potent force.

Figueres relied on the easily defended terrain around his farm while he secured additional supplies and reinforcements from Guatemala. He planned to build a citizen army patterned after the minutemen of the American Revolution. While he organized, Figueres also wanted to initiate an urban guerrilla campaign to disrupt the government's defenses and undermine morale. Finally, he wanted to establish a network in the

United States and Latin America to denounce the alliance between Picado, Calderón, and the Communists, hoping to secure sympathy for his cause.

When the mediation efforts failed, Figueres launched the War of National Liberation on 11 March, declaring that he began with "seven shotguns, some festival rockets borrowed from the Church in San Isidro del General, and the people."[33] A group led by Figueres's chief lieutenants, Alberto Martén and Father Benjamín Núñez, seized the San Isidro airport and three DC-3 airplanes. They immediately sent the aircraft to Guatemala, where President Arévalo fulfilled his commitments under the Caribbean Pact, releasing over six hundred rifles, several machine guns, ammunition, and supplies to the rebels. In addition, seven exiled Nicaraguan, Honduran, and Dominican military officers boarded the planes for the return flight.[34] As the fighting escalated, Figueres was joined by additional mercenaries and idealists, a group labeled the Caribbean Legion by journalists. The military experience of its members proved invaluable, helping turn the tide in favor of the rebels. The CIA later characterized the Caribbean Legion as "a deciding factor in the 1948 Costa Rican civil war."[35] Arévalo's aid was also important. His chief military officer, Col. Francisco Araña, supervised the airlift that continued throughout the forty days of fighting. During that time, the rebels flew nineteen missions to Guatemala to secure supplies and men.[36]

Before Figueres could fully coordinate his plans, the government forced him to retreat from his farm to defensive positions overlooking the Inter-American Highway at El Empalme. Picado's inexperienced officers halted and failed to press home their original advantage. Their lack of practical experience limited their effectiveness. Furthermore, some believed that the rapidly growing militia, composed primarily of *calderonistas* and *vanguardistas*, posed as great a threat as the rebels. They moved slowly, fearing that by overextending themselves, they might ensure a Communist takeover. Meanwhile, Figueres waited for his civilian army to materialize. Within several weeks, over seven hundred men joined him. At the same time labor leader Luis Alberto Monge organized attacks on bridges, communication facilities, and power stations around San José.[37]

The fighting pushed U.S. diplomats to adapt to the rapidly changing conditions, moving away from supporting a compromise candidate and toward choosing a side in the conflict. The most important component that shaped the U.S. response was the Communist question. Increasingly, the reports from the embassy and the desk offices in Washington became negative, focusing on the failure of the Picado government to maintain order and the possibility that the Vanguard could utilize the chaos to their advantage. Davis, often working within broad parameters established by U.S. officials above him, helped move the United States toward a policy that aided the insurgents. The escalation in the conflict mirrored the increasing fear among U.S. officials of a perceived Communist threat and became a major factor in the U.S. response to the Costa Rican civil war.

For the first week, U.S. officials carefully monitored the fighting and put most of their energies into protesting government abuses against American citizens. On 14 March, *Chicago Tribune* reporter Jules Dubois complained that the police had detained him until he promised not to send reports home. That same day, Davis traveled to the airport to inspect three unmarked planes. As he approached them, several policemen fired on him, barely missing the mark.[38] The ambassador lodged complaints about these incidents and others that involved beatings of Americans and illegal seizures of property by progovernment forces.[39] Picado's inability to restrain his troops angered some U.S. diplomats in San José and Washington and increased suspicions that his administration had lost control and that the Communists might fill the void.[40]

Picado's position worsened after 20 March when the rebels repelled an attack by his best-trained group, the Mobile Unit. In San Isidro, the insurgents also defeated a militia composed primarily of three hundred Communist banana laborers led by the influential Vanguard organizer Carlos Luis Fallas. These setbacks weakened morale and caused additional dissension within the government coalition, especially the *vanguardistas,* who bitterly complained that Picado had withheld ammunition to prevent their victory in San Isidro.[41]

The victories inspired new confidence among the rebels who began claiming that victory was near. Many including Davis expressed skepticism and continued urging compromise.[42] By 24 March, however, Davis's position hardened. As conditions worsened in San José, the Communists took additional defensive positions, ignoring government orders and obeying their party commanders. "Definite impression [that the] government lacks strong control leadership while Communists [are] too well organized [and] disciplined," Davis reported to Washington, "but unlikely [to] use this advantage to stage outright coup unless present situation degenerates to chaos."[43] The problem was that no U.S. officials could accurately predict the future.

The increased presence of the Vanguard after the outbreak of the conflict corresponded with heightened Communist paranoia in the United States at approximately the same time. New problems had arisen in Europe and Asia to cause U.S. policymakers additional concern about Communist aggression. According to John Hickerson of the State Department, the fall of Eduard Benes in Czechoslovakia in February 1948 had "scared the living bejesus out of everybody," confirming fears of Soviet expansion in Europe, Asia, and Latin America.[44] On 11 March, President Truman declared: "We don't want a Communist government in China, or anywhere if we can help it."[45] The intensified anticommunism in Washington translated into actions by some U.S. officials that clearly favored the rebels.

The *figueristas* understood the importance of the Communist question and manipulated it to their advantage. Many had studied and visited the United States during the period immediately preceding the fighting and had seen the increased Communist paranoia. Rebel propaganda played upon growing U.S. fears of an alliance between Picado, Calderón, and Mora. The rebels' supporters in the United States made numerous attempts to sway American opinion. The most important group was the Costa Rican League against Communist Domination. Organized by Dr. Carlos Gutiérrez and Gonzalo Facio, the league staged protests, published editorials condemning the Vanguard, and presented leaflets and handouts to State Department and Organization of American States officials outlining Communist aggression in their homeland.[46] The league's activities caused prominent U.S. congressmen, diplomats, and individual Americans to focus on the Communists in Costa Rica.

On 11 March, the day the revolution began, Senator H. Alexander Smith of New Jersey arranged for Facio and Gutiérrez to meet with Norman Armour and Bennett. The Costa Ricans emphasized the deteriorating conditions in their country, according to U.S. officials "ascribing most of the blame for the present crisis on the influence and maneuvers of the communist Vanguardia Popular party."[47] Gutiérrez requested that the State Department demand the return of lend-lease equipment, but Armour insisted that the United States would remain neutral.[48] While the U.S. diplomats claimed impartiality, Facio observed that the U.S. officials, primarily Bennett, possessed detailed information about the position of the Communists in the government and armed forces.[49]

The league utilized other methods to highlight the alliance between Picado, Calderón, and the Communists. It organized protests outside the offices of the Soviet delegation to the United Nations to denounce Communist aggression in Costa Rica.[50] Prominent Latin Americans including Víctor Raúl Haya de la Torre, the Peruvian Aprista leader and close associate of Monge, agreed to help the rebels. In a lecture at Columbia University in late March, Haya de la Torre characterized Figueres as a "liberal and democrat" struggling to prevent a second Czechoslovakia.[51]

The rebels won some adherents who in turn pressed the State Department to do something in Costa Rica. On 16 March, Senator Homer E. Capehart of Indiana complained that the newspapers in his district had focused on increased Communist activities in Costa Rica.[52] Others urged Washington to help restore Costa Rica's democratic institutions. Elton Hocking, chairman of the Department of Modern Languages at Purdue University, declared, "I understand that the democratic winners in a recent election in Costa Rica have been cheated out of their positions by reactionary elements there."[53] An American businessman in San José, Archie Davis, described Costa Rica as ruled by a "Communist-dominated regime" that censored the press and detained people without provocation.[54]

The American press also stressed the Communist presence in Costa Rica. On 15 March, the Associated Press characterized Picado as a figurehead in a country dominated by Mora, adding that the Communists controlled the army barracks and openly displayed the hammer and sickle flag.[55] A week later, the *New York Times* noted that the government forces had divided into two factions. The regular army remained loyal to Picado and its commander, Rene Picado, the president's brother. The majority of the troops owed their allegiance to Mora and Calderón, however, and reportedly received their orders from José Tavio, a Cuban colonel with Communist ties.[56]

The rebel propaganda and increased reports of Communist domination of the Picado government swayed the opinions of some in Washington. In the third week of March, Bennett distributed a memorandum to State Department officials documenting the infiltration of the Picado regime by the Communists. The Vanguard consisted of only seven thousand militant members, he warned, less than 1 percent of the population, but it controlled more than 15 percent of Costa Rica's congressional representation. This position provided it the balance of power in the Legislative Assembly because the two other major parties were evenly split. Bennett also pointed out that Picado and Calderón maintained intimate ties with Mora, who had stiffened Calderón's will to resist and repeatedly sabotaged negotiations. The Communist strength could not be underestimated, he emphasized. More than 70 percent of the police and army were party members, and they owed their allegiance primarily to Communist commanders. The *vanguardistas* also dominated important offices throughout the government bureaucracy, most notably in the social security administration. Bennett reported that their "greatest achievement has been the replacement of members of the Costa Rican middle class in Government positions by Vanguardia members." He concluded that the uncertainty and insecurity resembled that of eastern Europe, underscoring Haya de la Torre's description of Costa Rica as "the Czechoslovakia of the Western Hemisphere."[57]

The allegations of Communist influence in Costa Rica affected U.S. responses to the conflict. Claims of impartiality by U.S. officials failed to square with such actions as preventing government purchases of equipment and ammunition in the United States and Latin America. During the early stages of the fighting, the inexperienced government forces carelessly wasted their munitions. When Picado's representatives tried to buy small arms and other materials in the United States, Washington denied export licenses. Throughout the civil war, U.S. diplomats successfully pressured Mexican, Honduran, and Salvadoran officials not to sell military equipment to the Costa Rican government.[58] Although Picado argued that the United States would better serve its interests by providing military aid, Washington reiterated its neutrality.[59]

More important, the United States restricted Somoza's assistance to his friends, Picado and Calderón, denying them the aid that could have tipped the outcome in favor of the government coalition. Motivated partly by fears of an expanded conflict among the Central American states, U.S. officials worked hard to prevent Somoza's interference. They succeeded, but only after dangling the possible recognition of the Román y Reyes government as a reward.

When the fighting began, reports circulated that Somoza had sent arms, munitions, and national guard "volunteers" to assist Picado.[60] Washington responded quickly, ordering Chargé d'Affaires Maurice Bernbaum to remind Somoza that existing treaties prohibited him from interfering in his neighbors' affairs.[61] He denied that he planned to intervene in Costa Rica, but rumors continued circulating that more Nicaraguans had flown to San José, reportedly with instructions to prepare to destroy not only the rebels but also the Communists.

Despite his denials, Somoza aided Picado. "I know of my own knowledge that at least four Nicaraguan planes have been here at one time or another," Davis reported on 20 March.[62] The dictator heightened U.S. fears when he massed his troops on the Costa Rican border. The chief of the State Department's Division on Panama and Central American Affairs, Robert Newbegin, ordered Bernbaum to protest and to emphasize the bad timing, especially on the eve of the Bogotá Conference, where delegates would discuss policies on recognition, an issue critical to Somoza. Newbegin requested that the chargé write the message slowly, knowing that the Nicaraguans had tapped the embassy phones, so that they could "get the full import" of the conversation.[63] Later that day, Bernbaum met with Somoza, who threatened to send a thousand troops to San José to destroy the Vanguard.[64] Bernbaum stressed that any invasion, no matter how justified, violated existing treaties.[65] Somoza initially remained undeterred, but in the evening he canceled the invasion.[66]

The State Department also sought the support of other Latin American nations in securing Somoza's compliance. On 22 March, Secretary of State George C. Marshall asked the other American republics to condemn Nicaragua's interference in the internal affairs of another sovereign state. He received statements of condemnation from Argentina, Brazil, Venezuela, and Panama.[67] The pressure succeeded temporarily in restraining Somoza. Although some national guard volunteers lingered in San José, the Nicaraguan threat subsided momentarily at a time when Picado desperately needed assistance. Somoza remained, however, a possibly potent and disruptive force.

While U.S. officials attempted to stop aid to government forces, they made only half-hearted efforts to prevent the rebels from receiving Guatemalan assistance. From an early stage, Picado made Arévalo's interference an issue. During a meeting of the foreign ministers in San José on 18 March, Picado's officials denounced the Guatemalans for aiding Figueres against the "legally constituted and recognized government of Costa Rica" and urged the diplomats to protest Arévalo's actions.[68] Davis acknowledged Guatemalan aid to the rebels, stating that Arévalo's activities were "already known—to this Embassy at least."[69] U.S. officials knew that the rebels relied on Guatemalan assistance. Military attaché Col. J. R. Hughes visited Figueres's camp several days before the fighting started, consulting with the *figueristas* about their proposed operations and making several recommendations to improve their capabilities. While few additional contacts occurred between Hughes and the rebels, the initial appearance of the U.S. representative heartened the rebels.[70]

Other Costa Rican and Nicaraguan officials encouraged the United States to take forceful actions to prevent Guatemalan interference. In Washington, Ambassador Gutiérrez condemned Guatemala in a meeting with the director of the Office of American Republic Affairs, Paul Daniels. He produced boxes reportedly captured from Figueres's forces bearing the legend "República de Guatemala, Secretaria de Defensa."[71] The ambassador asked that the United States provide his government arms and munitions to offset Figueres's acquisitions, but Daniels denied the request.[72] Somoza joined the chorus, declaring that "Señor Arévalo's history of piracy and his disregard of his duties as President of an American country is now quite long."[73] He linked Guatemala's intervention to a complex conspiracy fomented by Arévalo and Figueres to overthrow the governments of Honduras, El Salvador, and Nicaragua, destroying Washington's anti-Communist allies and throwing the region into turmoil.[74]

Reacting to the accusations of Somoza and the Costa Ricans, the State Department requested that U.S. Ambassador to Guatemala Edwin Kyle meet Arévalo and express Washington's concern about his activities in Costa Rica. He confessed that he sympathized with Figueres but denied any involvement.[75] Guatemalan Ambassador to the United States Ismael González supported his president's claims, asking U.S. officials to trace the serial numbers of the captured arms rather than rely for evidence on easily duplicated legends on boxes.[76] Although far from convinced by Guatemalan denials, U.S. diplomats issued only muted protests and never threatened sanctions, a pattern that would be repeated throughout the civil war. When combined with more successful attempts to block Somoza's interference, U.S. actions gave the rebels an important advantage.

Without substantial outside assistance, Picado's position deteriorated. On 30 March, his forces again failed to dislodge the rebels at El Empalme. The small size of the army and lack of practical experience, when combined with internal divisions and a shortage of armaments, prevented the government's forces from succeeding. The failure caused indecision and inaction that aided the rebels. New recruits joined Figueres, and he continued to stockpile Guatemalan weapons. His audacity increased, and on 31 March his makeshift air force bombed the presidential palace.[77] Figueres remained cautious, however, waiting for a more opportune moment to mount a large-scale offensive.

While Figueres planned his final attack in the first week of April, concerned U.S. officials became increasingly pessimistic about the situation in the country. They continued stressing Picado's inability to maintain order and Calderón's ineffectual attempts to mobilize the troops. While the two leaders floundered, the embassy reported that the *vanguardistas* had organized new battalions for the defense of San José. The Communists openly criticized Picado's officers and the policy of distributing arms and munitions. They announced their intention to take power, if necessary, to protect themselves against the reactionaries in Figueres's army.[78]

The instability caused numerous problems for Davis as he attempted to protect American lives and property. On 5 April, he warned that the "internal situation shows signs [of] further deterioration," adding that looting and robbery were commonplace.[79] The embassy's fear of further erosion of the government's position appeared to be justified, leading to new fears that Mora and the *vanguardistas* might use the chaos to seize power and establish a Communist dominated regime. At the least, it appeared the fighting would take a bloody turn, possibly expanding to the other nations of the region. In response, Davis and others moved much closer to openly supporting the efforts of the rebels to win power.

As the perceptions of the Picado administration worsened among U.S. diplomats, so did public portrayals in the United States and Latin America. The American-owned newspaper *The Panama American* described Picado as sleeping "inside a circle of Commy guards armed with machine guns," and urged the United States "to prevent the establishment of a Communist base, virtually on the banks of the Panama Canal."[80] *Time* characterized Picado as dispirited and unwilling to give interviews because "it makes him feel bad to put so many friends in jail."[81] "Manuel Mora and his Communistic Popular Vanguardia allied to the government were reported in virtual control of the city," *Newsweek* added.[82] In addition, students at the National University in Mexico City protested the rumored shipment of Mexican arms to Picado, denouncing any formal or informal aid to a "communist backed" regime.[83]

At the same time, the rebels intensified their efforts to influence American opinion. Davis transmitted to Washington a copy of a leaflet circulating in San José that chastised the State Department for failing to disarm the government forces and their Communist allies.[84] On 8 April, the league produced a bulletin with the headline "Neither Liberal nor Conservatives: Only Patriots and Traitors!" criticizing Picado and Calderón for undermining the constitution and reporting the defeat of the "Communist bigwig" Fallas by the Army of National Liberation. The editors of the bulletin encouraged the United States to provide assistance to the rebels to prevent the spread of communism to Costa Rica, although they rejected direct American military intervention.[85]

The rebel propaganda and increased Communist activity in Costa Rica coincided with mounting anti-Communist paranoia in Washington in late March and early April. The National Security Council (NSC) prepared several papers outlining the Communist menace. In "The Position of the United States with Respect to Soviet-Directed World Communism" the NSC emphasized that "the ultimate objective of Soviet-directed world communism is the domination of the world." "To this end," the report added, "Soviet-directed world communism employs against its victims in opportunistic coordination the complementary instruments of Soviet aggressive pressure from without and militant subversion from within."[86] A week earlier, the NSC had produced another study reviewing Communist activities in Latin America and stressing that "international communism . . . is a direct and major threat to the national security of the United States, and to that of all the other American Republics."[87] It warned of Communist strength in Costa Rica and supported the adoption of measures to undermine Vanguard influence.[88] While the authors avoided calling for direct intervention in Costa Rica, the memoranda underscored a growing concern among U.S. officials about the Communist presence in Latin America that threatened at least to disturb the inter-American system in a period when the United States wanted to focus on other areas.[89]

Events in Bogotá during an inter-American conference further exacerbated fears of expanded Communist activities in Latin America at an important juncture of the Costa Rican civil war. On 9 April, an assassin killed Colombia's powerful Liberal leader Jorge Eliecer Gaitán. Angry crowds thronged the streets, blaming the murder on Colombian president Mariano Ospina-Pérez. Mobs attacked government buildings and ransacked the conference meeting area. U.S. officials, including Secretary of State Marshall, fled to the suburbs and formulated evacuation procedures. They never implemented the plan because Colombian troops regained control after several days, but only after three hundred people had died.[90]

The rioting in Bogotá strengthened U.S. fears of Communist subversion in the region. Marshall charged international communism with creating the disorders during the conference to embarrass the United States in the crucial period preceding the Italian elections. He emphasized that the Colombian Communist party chief, Montaña Cuellar, had called on rioters to burn the presidential palace. Marshall and others such as Rep. Mike Mansfield who had stopped in Costa Rica on the way to Bogotá connected Communist actions in Colombia with increased Communist activities in Costa Rica. Some U.S. officials feared that the Vanguard might repeat its Colombian compatriots' performance and possibly even try to take power.[91]

The heightened fears coincided with the development of new worries for U.S. diplomats after Figueres launched his long-awaited offensive on 10 April. In a multi-pronged attack, his troops captured the important Atlantic harbor of Limón. Simultaneously, Figueres and three hundred men marched over narrow oxcart trails and passed through enemy lines unobserved. On 12 April, they surprised government forces in Cartago and after intense fighting emerged victorious. The following day, the final major battle of the civil war took place when the rebel army defeated a government relief column from San José. The insurgents now controlled the country's best port and its second most important city, located less than twenty miles from the capital.[92]

Figueres's victories demoralized Picado, forcing him to request Davis's assistance in settling the conflict. "The government would accept anything I could arrange with Figueres," the ambassador recounted.[93] Several army officers visited him and warned that chaos would reign if the parties did not reach a settlement immediately. Davis agreed, fearing that the militiamen might follow the example of the terrorists in Bogotá.[94] From this point Davis, with the implicit approval of the State Department, worked to ensure a rebel victory and destroy the influence of the Vanguard and its allies. While the process had been evolutionary, the goal to defeat a perceived Communist threat now surged to the forefront of U.S. policy toward Costa Rica.

On 12 April, Picado requested that the foreign diplomats create a com-

Figueres and his lieutenants parade triumphantly through San José after their victory in 1948. (Photograph courtesy Archivo Nacional de Costa Rica)

mittee to negotiate with Figueres. They chose Davis (over the protests of several diplomats who feared the exertion of undue U.S. influence), the papal nuncio, Luigi Centoz, and the ambassadors of Mexico, Panama, and Chile. The committee immediately set about its task and arranged a cease-fire so that the group could cross the front lines and travel to the rebel command post.[95]

The committee's first meeting with the rebels took place on 13 April at Figueres's headquarters in Cartago. When queried about his demands, Figueres responded that he placed little faith in a political transaction. Davis quickly reminded him that the United States considered the Picado administration the constitutional government of Costa Rica, emphasizing that any group that seized power by force faced a problem of recognition. Figueres proved more compliant, proposing the resignation of Picado and his vice-presidents and their replacement by him and his chief lieutenants until 8 May, when Ulate would take control. The committee returned to San José and met with Picado, who issued a counterproposal that was simply restatement of an old compromise. Stressing the futility of presenting the offer, the committee pushed Picado to reconsider. He finally capitulated to all the rebels' demands, with the exception of Figueres's appointment, and agreed to work out the details with a rebel representative.[96]

The next day, Davis and the committee traveled to the front lines and picked up Figueres's emissary, Padre Núñez. Briefly delayed by gunfire from government positions, the group returned to San José. After much discussion, Picado and Núñez reached a compromise that named Santos León Herrera interim president until early May. For his part, Núñez promised to protect the vanquished individuals under the constitution and to maintain existing social legislation.[97]

While the parties negotiated the final details of the settlement, Davis worked to head off possible threats to the negotiations. He had received a disturbing report that a Spanish soldier of fortune, Julio López, had buried bombs throughout the capital and had threatened to detonate the explosives, vowing never to allow another capitulation such as he had experienced in Spain in the 1930s. Fearing that such a maniacal act might destabilize the entire situation, Davis sought Picado's assistance. The president and the ambassador pleaded with López to reconsider. After a heated debate, the Spaniard agreed to stop his activities, thus ending a potential danger to the peace talks.[98]

The most immediate threat to the negotiations was Somoza. After the crisis in March, he had provided limited, covert assistance to government troops. As conditions deteriorated in Costa Rica, his interest in the outcome increased because several prominent Nicaraguan exiles served in Figueres's army. Somoza believed that once Picado surrendered, the rebels would turn their attention toward him. Instead of waiting, he acted.

When the rebels initiated their final offensive, Picado and Calderón sought Nicaraguan aid. On 16 April, Francisco Calderón, at the request of his brother and the president, traveled to Managua to encourage Somoza to defend himself against the Caribbean Legion by occupying strategic areas in northern Costa Rica.[99] Somoza acted almost immediately on Calderón's advice. He requested assurances that Costa Rica could prevent revolutionary activities near his border. The government refused and granted Nicaragua the right to fortify the border.[100] Believing that Picado approved, Somoza ordered his troops to occupy strategic positions in northern Costa Rica, emphasizing the defensive nature of the invasion and his intention not to advance any further.[101]

The Nicaraguan intervention alarmed U.S. officials, who believed it would strengthen Picado's resolve to resist, thereby undermining the negotiations and allowing the Communists more time to plan their activities. They also feared an extended conflict because Arévalo had reportedly promised to declare war on Somoza if the dictator's troops attacked Figueres.[102] On 17 April, Davis encouraged the State Department to denounce Somoza's action and secure, if possible, a condemnation from the delegates at the Bogotá Conference.[103]

U.S. and foreign diplomats in Costa Rica quickly addressed the crisis. On 18 April, Davis and the committee questioned Picado on his role in Somoza's invasion. The president first characterized the Nicaraguan troops as customs patrols, but when pressed angrily left the room. Soon after, he returned with a typewritten statement denying any involvement in the Nicaraguan intervention. He instructed Costa Rican diplomats in Managua to demand that Somoza recall his national guard, effectively undercutting the dictator's rationale for interfering.[104]

The State Department adopted other measures to guarantee Nicaragua's withdrawal from Costa Rica. On 19 April, the U.S. embassy in Managua condemned the Nicaraguan government and demanded that it immediately withdraw its troops from Costa Rica.[105] That same day, Marshall sponsored a formal denunciation of Nicaragua by the representatives at the Bogotá Conference.[106] A member of the U.S. delegation concluded that it "may have been exactly the action required to persuade Somoza to withdraw his troops from Costa Rica."[107]

The State Department's pressure succeeded, and on 20 April Somoza's troops retreated from Costa Rica, removing Picado and Calderón's last hope for victory.[108] The United States rewarded his obedience by accelerating the process of normalizing relations. While the move away from using nonrecognition as a weapon had begun in the postwar period, the timing of the normalization of relations corresponded too closely with Somoza's compliance to be viewed as coincidental. By 6 May, Washington decided to reappoint an ambassador to Managua and returned the embassy to full diplomatic status.[109]

With the threat of Nicaraguan intervention reduced, the disputants and mediators renewed their efforts to reach a final settlement. Davis recounted, "the Nuncio and I started out on, our tenth and I hope final trip through no-man's land."[110] Although he and the committee had accomplished a great deal, several divisive issues remained, including the position of the Communists. While the government had disintegrated and its leaders fled, the *vanguardistas* had continued preparing defenses in San José. Mora traveled through the capital, urging the people to "seal their social gains with blood." "I will not compromise," he declared, "or throw away anything for which I have fought for 25 years."[111]

Padre Núñez successfully defused the potentially volatile issue by negotiating with Mora. On 19 April, they reached a compromise, the "Pact of Ochomogo," in which Núñez guaranteed to consult the Vanguard about the composition of the new provisional government. He also agreed to protect social legislation including the labor code and social security. Finally, he pledged to respect the property and lives of the Vanguard members. In return, Mora promised not to oppose the final transfer of power from Picado to Herrera and vowed that his troops would surrender their arms. Although Figueres later disavowed the pact, it ended Communist opposition.[112]

The capitulation of the Communists removed the final domestic threat to peace. On 19 April, the major parties gathered at the Mexican embassy to sign an agreement that replaced Picado temporarily with an interim president until the rebel forces could take power. Picado remembered that by this day the withdrawal of Nicaraguan assistance and a report of possible U.S. intervention had destroyed his will to resist. During the latter stages of the fighting, he reportedly had received information that U.S. troops were mobilizing in the Canal Zone to invade Costa Rica and eradicate the Communists. The president chose to surrender, rather than subject his country to foreign occupation.[113] With a compliant president and Calderón noticeably absent, the warring factions signed the final settlement, the "Pact of the Mexican Embassy," naming Herrera interim president and initiating the transfer of power. Champagne and "mutual admiration speeches" followed, after which the conferees dispersed to implement the terms of the surrender.[114]

Davis's activities during the civil war were critical. He maintained a very visible position throughout the struggle, and as the conflict escalated and the Communists increased their strength, he used his office to help ensure a rebel victory. His work with the rebels during the negotiations conferred tacit recognition on the movement by the strongest power in the hemisphere, a significant action in Latin American affairs. At important junctures, Davis intimidated Picado with explicit and implicit threats, and he worked tirelessly to stop outside assistance to the government. In the end, Davis helped prevent a possible Communist takeover, an action lauded by the State Department.

With a final agreement reached, the parties began implementing its provisions. Government forces disarmed the militiamen, offering them money for arms and providing free transportation to their homes.[115] The interim regime also released political prisoners and established control of the military installations and government buildings. The departure of Picado and Calderón to Nicaragua and Mora to Mexico also eased tensions. By 24 April, the Army of National Liberation victoriously entered the capital and conducted a triumphal march through its streets.[116]

The fate of Ulate's presidency remained a divisive issue. Many *figueristas* complained that he had forfeited the presidency when he had failed to fight. They advised Figueres to seize control, but he hesitated to establish a dangerous precedent. After several days of discussion, Figueres and Ulate compromised, creating a junta under Figueres's leadership to rule for eighteen months. In that period, a constituent assembly would convene to draft a new constitution and validate Ulate's election. The junta would step down after the allotted time and permit Ulate to serve his full four-year term.[117] This plan went into effect on 8 May when Herrera resigned and Figueres took power.

The junta received immediate international acceptance when Washington recognized it. U.S. officials characterized Figueres as a crusader who had issued promises to create a society that better served the needs of the majority. A U.S. diplomat in San José emphasized that "the forthcoming interim period may well prove to be one of the most critical in the life of Costa Rica."[118] He properly predicted the importance of the transition. The civil war had altered the political system of Costa Rica, effectively shifting the leadership from the National Republicans and Vanguard to the *figueristas* and *ulatistas*. Ulate personified the status quo, while Figueres promoted his own ideology based on a progressive, anti-Communist liberalism. In both cases, the two parties represented groups that the United States believed were unquestionably pro-American, allowing a return to the traditional pattern of relations.

The most important result of the conflict on U.S.–Costa Rican relations was the removal of the Communists from any positions of power. Clearly the United States had overestimated the threat of the Communists. No hard evidence linked Mora and most of his allies to the Soviets. As Picado and Calderón characterized it, the Vanguard was a domestic movement dedicated primarily to improving the well-being of Costa Rican workers. In 1948, the Communist question had jumped to the forefront in guiding U.S. policy, and U.S. officials increasingly failed to distinguish between a domestic movement and the international Communist movement, lumping all parties into the perceived Soviet plan for world domination. Washington would repeat this misunderstanding on numerous occasions.

Despite failing to establish a security threat, the United States implemented an interventionist policy that favored the rebels as the fighting progressed. U.S. officials became hostile toward the Picado-Calderón-Mora coalition, although the U.S. response to the coalition was less organized and more reactive than the ones employed against the governments of Guatemala and Iran in the 1950s. The United States assisted the Costa Rican rebels by obstructing the government's access to military materials. More important, the State Department restricted Somoza's ability to aid Picado while knowingly allowing the Guatemalans to send large quantities of assistance to the rebels. Finally, the activities of Davis and other embassy officials clearly favored Figueres. Picado had declared, "I can assure you that inseparable forces are absolutely determined to have us lose this contest," a direct reference to Figueres, Guatemala, and the United States.[119] His defeat removed a perceived threat to the security of the United States and a potentially divisive issue in U.S.–Costa Rican relations and allowed affairs to return to more normal patterns in the aftermath of the civil war of 1948.

While the United States played an important role in the fighting, the most notable factor in deciding the conflict and reestablishing cordial relations was the Costa Ricans. The country's historic aversion to the extremes represented by the more radical elements of the Vanguard and the opposition's dedication to democratic principles proved vital. Costa Ricans themselves settled the perceived problem of Communist influence and government corruption before U.S. policymakers intervened militarily to combat a perceived threat. They used force of arms as well as diplomatic maneuvers to sway the opinions within the State Department and U.S. government. The *figueristas* and their allies understood the significance of the Communist question and played an important role in the overreaction of some U.S. policymakers to the perceived Communist menace in Costa Rica. Nevertheless, the United States did not simply wave a wand and make the Vanguard disappear or promote an insurgency as it had in Guatemala in 1954. For the most part, Costa Ricans determined the result, although Guatemalan arms and the U.S. diplomatic maneuverings made the task much easier.

With the victory of the *figueristas* and the end of the perceived political threats, tensions in Costa Rica did not disappear. They carried over into the diplomatic arena, where U.S. diplomats continued to express caution about the situation in Costa Rica. While most U.S. officials greeted the defeat of the National Republican–Vanguard coalition favorably, many possessed little information about Figueres and his allies. His course of action remained an unknown. The period of the junta would provide another round of tests for U.S. officials, although the new tests differed significantly from those of the preceding three years. Nevertheless, Figueres would fit well into the traditional pattern of relations. While returning the country to more normal political and social relations, his nationalist domestic and foreign policies would at times displease the United States. Yet, much as he demonstrated during the civil war, he understood the United States and played a game of give-and-take that allowed him to walk the fine line between nationalism and anti-Americanism.

5

THE FIRST TIME AROUND
The Costa Rican Junta and the United States, 1948–1949

AFTER TWO YEARS of constant tension, Costa Rica returned to more normal patterns of domestic affairs, permitting the State Department to recommend that "we need badly to have this pleasant assignment . . . reserved for our use in taking care of deserving Chiefs of Mission who have done their stint in hardship posts."[1] By November 1949, the situation had improved so much that Acting Secretary of State James E. Webb could declare, "we view with profound satisfaction Costa Rica's success in solving serious political and constitutional questions in a democratic manner fully consistent with the country's long traditions of liberty and devotion to the principles of representative government."[2]

The eighteen-month rule of the revolutionary junta significantly altered Costa Rica's society, ushering in a new era of intensified government activism. From the Ulate-Figueres pact, the junta received power to rule without legislative oversight, although the judicial system remained intact and performed as a check to the junta's authority. Utilizing the broad powers granted them by the pact, the *figueristas* built upon the many changes of the preceding eight years in education, health care, and public services. They expanded the role of government, creating agencies to stimulate economic growth and guarantee more equitable distribution of resources and wealth for all Costa Ricans. Within only a short period, the junta dramatically helped modify the way Costa Ricans viewed the government and its responsibilities, a task that Figueres and his associates continued after leaving office in 1949.

In foreign affairs, tensions between the United States and Costa Rica caused by the perceived Communist threat dissipated, and relations returned to more normal patterns. San José supported Washington's international objectives, but resisted U.S. attempts to reduce its independence in domestic and regional affairs. Tensions arose over the junta's nationalism and assistance to Caribbean exiles, but the *figueristas'* anticommunism and dedication to democratic principles counteracted negative perceptions and helped ensure economic, military, and diplomatic assistance from Washington. By November 1949, when the junta relinquished power, relations remained comparatively good, although some U.S. officials looked forward to the more moderate Ulate taking control.

Eleven men composed the junta. They were relatively young, ranging in age from thirty to forty-five, and came from a variety of professions, including business, law, and education. They respected American institutions and attempted to understand the United States, especially Figueres, who had spent a great deal of time there. Furthermore, Figueres's wife Henrietta was an American citizen, giving him another important link to the United States. The minister of economy, Alberto Martén, the minister of justice, Gonzalo Facio, and the minister of labor and social welfare, Padre Benjamín Núñez, had attended school in the United States. In addition, the junta's primary advisers and diplomats, Francisco José Orlich, Mario Esquivel, Alberto Cañas, Daniel Oduber, and Fernando Fournier, had lived in North America for extended periods.[3] Several of the men retained close relations with American businessmen and academicians, traveling to the United States often and viewing firsthand the changing attitudes toward communism and nationalism in the postwar era. Unlike many Latin American nationalists, they prided themselves in having closer ties with Americans than with Europeans or other Latin Americans. As their predecessors, they utilized images and symbols such as republicanism and anticommunism to their advantage, winning overwhelming American support. The *figueristas'* experience with and knowledge of the United States was vital, providing them with a better comprehension of the domestic constraints and international commitments Washington faced. This understanding allowed them to make more informed decisions on economic, political, and international questions at a time when many Americans identified most forms of nationalism as Communist-inspired. It improved their ability to walk the precarious tightrope between nationalism and anti-Americanism.[4]

The dominant figure in the junta was Figueres. While there were other strong members, Figueres gave the group much of its idealism and energy. Since his arrival on the national scene in 1942 and subsequent exile for criticizing the Calderón government, he had developed ambitious plans to recreate Costa Rica. In his book *Ideario costarricense* (1943) he had outlined such goals as the abolition of corruption in public administration, the establishment of a professional civil service, and the development of a foreign policy that aided democratic movements against the dictators of Latin America. He also sought a more activist government that would control the economy by utilizing autonomous planning agencies to ensure more equitable distribution of wealth. Figueres also wanted more educational opportunities, better health care, and increased chances for social advancement for previously underrepresented groups such as blacks and women.[5] Although his ideas changed somewhat over time, these principles guided him for the next forty years.

As scheduled, the junta took power on 8 May. It immediately suspended the constitution of 1871 and began enacting a number of laws that many Costa Ricans and Americans viewed with caution.[6] The civil war had disrupted government operations, and the junta needed money to reestablish basic social services and to fund public works projects. To raise the needed revenues, it issued Decree No. 70 instituting a 10 percent tax on domestic and private capital valued at more than 50,000 colones. The act also created an Office of Direct Taxation to oversee the payments, aggravating wealthy Costa Ricans and foreign businessmen and further eroding the junta's political base.[7]

Simultaneously, the junta issued Decree No. 71 nationalizing the banking system. Until 1948, private individuals associated primarily with the coffee elites had monopolized the public banks. The *figueristas* wanted to diversify the economy and provide more opportunities for industry and small businessmen. When the banking industry refused to cooperate, the junta seized the public banks.[8] Although it encountered problems implementing government control, the expropriation represented the first serious attempt to restructure the Costa Rican economy along the lines envisioned by the *figueristas*.

These policies alarmed some U.S. diplomats and businessmen. The decrees nationalizing the banking industry and implementing the 10 percent tax caught U.S. officials off guard, but the anger vented by conservative and some moderate Costa Ricans failed to carry over into the international arena. The junta accommodated American interests by making clear that the bank seizures applied only to public institutions, although several of Figueres's advisers wanted to seize all banks. In addition, it informed the U.S. embassy that the tax applied only to foreign companies with no existing contract, a loophole that excluded some major American businesses such as United Fruit.[9] Figueres and his associates made a conscious effort not to provoke the United States or the majority of their countrymen. They were realistic, understanding that they possessed a precarious hold on power. Recognizing that some moderate moves forward were better than no advances at all, they proceeded cautiously.

The junta offset much of the criticism of its economic nationalism by stamping out the remnants of communism in Costa Rica. On 30 May 1948, after rumors spread of an impending coup, the government detained two hundred suspected Communists and seized a large cache of arms and ammunition.[10] In mid-June, following reports of a *calderonista* and *vanguardista* plot against the junta, the police arrested the remaining Vanguard leaders.[11] A month later, the junta issued Decree No. 105, which prohibited any Communist organization from operating in Costa Rica on the grounds that communism threatened democracy.[12]

Even though the *figueristas* had removed the *vanguardistas* from positions of power after the civil war, the Communist question remained very important to Washington. Most U.S. officials happily accepted the total elimination of the Vanguard. "To all intents and purposes Vanguardia Popular and its parallel labor organization, the CTCR, have ceased to exist," a memorandum noted in mid-May.[13] The State Department also declared that Mora, Calderón, and Picado "will not soon forget the smarting blow which Figueres has given them," although it warned that they "may attempt a 'comeback.' "[14] Most U.S. officials applauded the destruction of the Vanguard, although a few expressed concern that the party would disappear underground and become a dangerous clandestine group.[15]

During a period of increased anticommunism in the United States, the *figueristas* had moved decisively against a perceived Communist threat. Unlike Somoza and others who used the issue for personal gain, Figueres and his associates genuinely shared Washington's concern about communism, believing that it eroded the social and political fabric of Costa Rican society. They made a conscious effort to emphasize their record against the Communists, portraying themselves as alternatives to the authoritarians on whom Washington increasingly relied to maintain order in Latin America. During the civil war and afterward, they continued to attack the

Communists at home and internationally. Anticommunism would remain an important cause of the many junta members throughout their public careers.

The destruction of the Communists removed a divisive issue that had threatened to disrupt the traditional pattern of U.S.–Costa Rican relations. The outlawing of the Vanguard firmly established Figueres as an anti-Communist in most quarters in the United States. The action was important because Figueres's attacks on the wealthy and seizure of the banks resembled actions taken by nationalists in other countries that the United States identified as Communist. His stance on communism, however, helped maintain comparatively good relations with the United States even when his policies sometimes conflicted with Washington's goals for the Caribbean Basin. It also guaranteed U.S. assistance when the junta faced an attack from Nicaragua by its enemies.

The junta would need outside assistance to battle foreign threats during its tenure. Problems with Nicaragua had arisen for the junta soon after it took office. The conflict fit the long term pattern of relations between the two countries. Monge later recounted, "In Costa Rica, there are only three seasons: the wet season, the dry season and the season when there are problems with Nicaragua."[16] Calderón and Picado had fled to Nicaragua in the days immediately following the civil war and began planning to retake power. They believed that the junta's economic policies provided them a weapon to drive a wedge between the junta and Ulate, Costa Rican conservatives, and the United States. Calderón traveled to the United States after the civil war to lobby U.S. officials to support him against the radical Figueres. First, he denied any ties with Mora and the Communists, pointing out that Mora and Figueres had signed a pact during the fighting. He also warned that Figueres, Arévalo, and Rómulo Betancourt, the Venezuelan leader, would disrupt peace in the region by assisting the Caribbean Legion in operations against Somoza and Trujillo.[17] Picado also attacked the junta. He visited the U.S. embassy in Managua to request that Washington pressure the junta into ceasing persecution of his allies, warning that the animosities created by such arbitrary acts would lead to a counterrevolution.[18]

Despite Calderón and Picado's attempts to discredit it, the junta favorably impressed most U.S. diplomats, and early relations were particularly good. Washington immediately recognized the junta as the constitutional government of Costa Rica.[19] "The new government may be characterized as a group of young civilians," a State Department official noted, "imbued with undoubtable high ideals for reform of the political and economic life." The inexperience and youth of the new government had caused problems, an analyst stressed, but "if the Junta manages to get through its initial period of organization and depuration without hurting too many people, it may well become the forerunner of a new era for the country."[20]

A leading proponent of the junta was Ambassador Davis, who developed a close and lasting friendship with Figueres. In early June 1948, he praised the junta's dedication to democratic principles and the absence of corruption in its rule. He emphasized that its popular support had been obtained without inciting class hostilities. "The plain fact," Davis reported, "is that the Junta is motivated by a desire to give the country a clean and honest government."[21] The ambassador remained a strong supporter of the *figueristas* throughout his tenure. He helped ease some possibly tense situations when the junta's policies clashed with those of the United States, and even after leaving the post continued lobbying for Figueres.

The portrayals of the junta remained fairly positive for most of its early existence. After observing a summer of changes and realignments in Costa Rican society, the U.S. embassy in San José issued a document entitled "The First Hundred Days of the Junta." The memorandum outlined the successes and failures of the junta, noting the serious economic and political circumstances it had inherited. The junta had based its actions on a desire "to reorganize public services, place the country on a sound basis and eradicate the system of misgovernment."[22] While recognizing some defects of the new leaders, the embassy backed their activities, emphasizing that their policies resembled New Deal and Fair Deal programs more than communism. To many U.S. officials, Figueres and his associates were model leaders for Latin America. They promoted social changes that improved the living conditions of the less fortunate without arousing class warfare, undermining the conditions on which the Communists flourished. Furthermore, the *figueristas* were pro-American and anti-Communist. In many ways, their programs paralleled those of President Truman and anti-Communist liberals in the United States in the late 1940s.

While a flurry of activity characterized the first one hundred days of the junta, a period of political and economic consolidation followed. The junta passed decrees raising taxes on imports, stressing that the country needed to reduce its trade imbalance.[23] It also opened negotiations with United Fruit on a new contract to increase revenues, a process that ultimately provided the Costa Ricans with an additional $1.5 million a year in income.[24] The junta also received loans from the Export-Import Bank and the International Monetary Fund to build public works and purchase machinery and materials for small businesses. By September 1948, the economic situation had stabilized so much that the junta could refuse a $5 million loan from the National City Bank of New York.[25]

The junta faced other more pressing domestic problems. Tensions had arisen between Figueres and Ulate when the president-elect had criticized the nationalization of the banking industry, implementation of the 10 percent tax, and the initiation of operations by the Caribbean Legion against Somoza. The president-elect argued that each country should solve its own problems and that Figueres should concentrate on healing the wounds of the civil war rather than opening new ones, ideas echoed by U.S. diplomats.[26] Utilizing his paper, *Diario de Costa Rica,* Ulate charged that the junta had returned to the old days of corrupt, partisan politics. The *figueristas* retaliated, calling Ulate a coward who had avoided fighting in the civil war. By September, several embassy officials warned that the situation presented "dangerous possibilities."[27]

Of all the policies Ulate challenged, Figueres's aid to the Caribbean Legion most aggravated U.S. officials. They believed his alliance with the group and his support of its activities undermined U.S. efforts to maintain the status quo in the region. The attacks on Washington's dictatorial allies threatened to divert American attention and energy away from more important matters in Asia and Europe. Although Figueres understood that U.S. officials opposed his adventurism, he resisted their pressures to abandon his friends and continued assisting their attempts to establish democracies in the Caribbean Basin, justifying his work as moral and necessary. The choice caused tensions in the relationship, but Figueres adamantly refused to abandon his friends and continually criticized the U.S. policy of supporting dictatorships in the Caribbean Basin.

Following the civil war, Figueres had fulfilled his obligations under the Caribbean Pact by providing assistance to other exiles. The legion had received an important position in the victory parade in San José, and the junta housed its troops in the artillery barracks and its leaders in nice homes around the capital. The adventurers organized the Army of National Liberation of Nicaragua under the command of Figueres and his friend, Rosendo Argüello, Jr. Using money and arms provided by Arévalo, the rebels prepared for military operations against Somoza.[28]

Throughout the summer of 1948, the United States and Ulate pleaded with Figueres to stop plotting against the totalitarian regimes. His refusal angered not only Nicaragua but also the Dominican Republic. After taking power, the junta had broken diplomatic relations with the government of Rafael Trujillo, stressing that Costa Rica would not associate with non-democratic nations.[29] Trujillo counterattacked and blamed Costa Rica's hostility on Betancourt, Arévalo, and the Communists who wanted to overthrow pro-U.S. regimes in the region and create chaos from which the Soviets would benefit.[30]

Somoza and his diplomats also criticized Figueres in newspapers and in private meetings with various foreign diplomats. In a meeting at the State Department between Robert Newbegin and Ambassador Guillermo Sevilla, the Nicaraguan criticized the junta and Arévalo, emphasizing that his country might implement measures to protect itself against Costa Rica and Guatemala. Newbegin cautioned Sevilla that "it was thoroughly undesirable that action taken by one country outside its own frontiers should be disguised as defense measures."[31] He urged "the greatest caution and patience" and promised that Washington would encourage the Costa Ricans to live up to their treaty obligations and maintain a policy of nonintervention.[32]

Throughout the summer, relations between Nicaragua and Costa Rica remained strained despite attempts by the United States to ease tensions. No direct confrontations occurred because the legion remained inactive. Corruption and a lack of security plagued the organization, allowing Somoza's spies to infiltrate it. In July, the movement suffered a serious setback when Nicaraguan officials captured an important leader of the exiles, Edelberto Torres. Somoza produced a letter that reportedly contained plans by the Caribbean Legion for attacks against Nicaragua, Honduras, and El Salvador. The disclosure and growing disillusionment with the legion among Costa Rican leaders caused some of the Nicaraguan exiles to move their operations to Guatemala.[33]

During the early fall, U.S. officials continued to encourage the parties to cease their intrigues. While Figueres ignored their appeals, personalities and events eroded the alliance. In mid-August, Figueres clashed with the supreme commander of the Caribbean exiles, General Juan Rodríguez. The Dominican wanted the Costa Ricans to return the arms loaned to them during the revolution, but Figueres declined and instead offered $340,000. The general refused the money, and Arévalo's attempts to mediate the dispute failed. Figueres returned home with the check, vowing to keep the military hardware.[34]

The rebel alliance continued disintegrating slowly as the feud between Figueres and Rodríguez persisted. In October, Rodríguez left San José and moved his headquarters to Guatemala to concentrate on deposing Trujillo. A large number of exiles followed him, many disgusted with Argüello's ineptitude, inactivity, and lack of discipline. Even Figueres tired of defending his friend's incompetence and alcoholism. By the end of September, Costa Rican diplomats promised Washington that no legion activities would originate in their country and assured U.S. officials that the exiles would leave the country within two weeks.[35] Still, on 20 September, Figueres and other junta officials attended a speech by Vicente Saenz at the National Theater. The speaker condemned the dictatorships in Nicaragua, Honduras, and the Dominican Republic, adding that as long as totalitarians ruled they threatened Costa Rica. Saenz encouraged the subjugated people in those countries to utilize armed resistance and civil disobedience to overthrow the governments. He also asked Costa Rica to sever relations with Nicaragua and any country refusing to support democratic ideals.[36]

While the movement against Somoza floundered, his plot to depose the junta flourished. Since June, rumors had circulated that Somoza had armed and trained a force of Costa Rican exiles to attack Costa Rica and install Calderón as president.[37] Somoza initially had denied the reports but vowed to protect himself against Nicaraguan exiles in San José, warning that any movement by them would ensure that his "Guardia would be in San Jose in three days."[38] Recognizing the potential problems, the Costa Ricans complained to U.S. officials about Somoza's alliance with Calderón.[39] U.S. diplomats responded that they had taken "legitimate steps" to encourage peace in the region, but their desire to avoid interference in the domestic affairs of sovereign states limited their effectiveness.[40]

The actions of Figueres, Arévalo, and the democratic left and the counterattacks by the dictators concerned U.S. policymakers who wanted stability in the region. Some believed that Figueres's adventurism threatened Washington's strongest anti-Communist allies, such as Somoza and Trujillo.[41] They feared the Communists might exploit any change in government, allowing them to gain positions of prominence. The issue caused some friction between Figueres and U.S. officials, but relations never deteriorated to the point that Washington would desert the Costa Ricans.

Many agreed that democracy was the best form of rule, but unlike Figueres they hesitated upsetting the balance of power in the region during a period in which they believed they needed to focus on the unsettling events developing in Asia and Europe.

Again and again, U.S. officials cautioned Figueres about his assistance to the democratic left movement. Despite the problems caused by his aid to his friends, Figueres retained a strong following among some State Department officials who respected his anticommunism and idealism. Ambassador Davis and embassy officials proved very loyal to Figueres. Bennett and others in Washington also supported the junta. Bennett criticized an article in the Caracas *El Nacional* that denounced the junta, calling the editor a Communist and adding that "in view of Manuel Mora's close association with Calderon Guardia, it is not surprising that a communist-line newspaper would take up Calderon's cause."[42] The loyalty of these U.S. officials was important because a storm appeared brewing on Costa Rica's northern border. Without the support of the United States, the junta faced a difficult task of fighting Costa Rican rebels and the Nicaraguan national guard.

The junta's position in the early winter had deteriorated under constant attack by the *ulatistas* and conservatives. The tax issue, nationalization of the banking industry, and the assistance to the legion had continued to cause problems. The domestic dissension heartened Calderón, Picado, and Somoza, who intensified their efforts to overthrow Figueres. They hoped to take advantage of the dissension, sweeping in and occupying the country before the *figueristas* could marshal their forces.

The *calderonistas* received additional good news in late November when Figueres announced that his country would reduce the size of its defense forces. He first reported the Caribbean Legion would soon leave the country. At the formal announcement, he praised the legion's service to Costa Rica and its sacrifice in disbanding to ease tensions in the region.[43] Although Davis expressed some doubts about whether Figueres intended to force out the legion totally, the pronouncement gave the appearance that a large part of Figueres's army would depart, dramatically reducing the nation's defensive capabilities. Two days later, Figueres abolished the Costa Rican army in a ceremony at the Bella Vista barracks. After outlining his beliefs on why Costa Rica needed no military, he took a sledgehammer and symbolically struck the building, announcing that it would be turned into a national museum.[44] The army was not immediately dis-

Figueres symbolically strikes the military barracks at Bella Vista with a sledgehammer to celebrate the abolishing of the army in December 1948. (Photograph courtesy of the Archivo Nacional de Costa Rica)

solved, but after December 1948 it remained only a skeleton force and not much of a deterrent to Somoza's national guard or even Calderón's group.

The timing of Figueres's actions perplexed many State Department officials. Reports continued circulating that the exiles planned an attack on Costa Rica. Calderón's military commander, Julio López, had reportedly purchased seven thousand rifles in Mexico and troop movements had taken place on the Costa Rican–Nicaraguan border.[45] While concerned, Costa Rican officials seemed more interested in the upcoming elections for representatives to the Constituent Assembly than the external threat.

U.S. officials responded to the reports of rebel and national guard activities by questioning the Nicaraguans. In a meeting with U.S. Ambassador to Nicaragua George Shaw on 3 December, Somoza and Ambassador Sevilla disputed the existence of any Costa Rican exile army in their territory. Somoza acknowledged the presence of a group of Costa Ricans in Rivas, but insisted that they possessed no military equipment.[46] Despite the denials, two days later the U.S. embassy in Managua intercepted several messages from the *calderonistas* indicating that operations had been initiated, although the messages provided no exact details.[47]

The State Department continued receiving unsubstantiated reports that the rebels had invaded Costa Rica.[48] Finally, on 10 December, Calderón verified the rumors and issued a decree promising to restore democracy to his country. "With absolute faith in the triumph of our cause," he stated, "I call upon my fellow citizens to follow me." "My aim is to restore the state of things destroyed by a group of insensate men led by Jose Figueres," he added.[49] Calderón dedicated himself to the movement, declaring that "it is preferable to die on your feet than live on your knees."[50]

The junta reacted quickly to the *calderonista* attack. On 11 December, Figueres requested State Department assistance in purchasing arms. Fears of an expanded conflict caused U.S. officials to reject the Costa Rican request for direct grants of military equipment, but U.S. officials agreed to grant export licenses for commercial sales. Davis promised to inquire about the possible purchase of two thousand rifles, several machine guns, and ammunition through private sources.[51] These arms procurements were important because the junta desperately needed to equip its volunteer army (composed primarily of veterans of the civil war) and the six hundred members of the legion who still remained in Costa Rica.[52]

The conflict between Nicaragua and Costa Rica placed the United States in the precarious situation of wanting to avoid offending Somoza while protecting a model democracy. To do so, they encouraged negotiations rather than confrontation and pressured Somoza to withdraw his support. The United States also tried to remove the major points of contention by pushing both sides to prevent revolutionary activities on their soil. Washington did not act unilaterally. It brought the Organization of American States and individual countries to support the effort to maintain the peace in Central America.

A major problem of the confrontation between Costa Ricans was the role of Somoza. When confronted by Ambassador Shaw, the Nicaraguan dictator denied any collaboration with the Costa Rican rebels, emphasizing that the insurgents had crossed the boundaries because "when Figueres announced he had disbanded his army we decreased our border forces."[53] Shaw pressed him, pointing out that he knew that the rebels had moved across the border unmolested. The dictator changed tactics, admitting that he had allowed the rebels unrestricted passage to force Figueres to settle the problem of the foreign exiles. Shaw emphasized that Somoza "expressed no regret . . . and stated also that if this brought about an armed attack on Nicaragua that he would welcome it indicating that he felt able to cope with this situation by force of arms."[54]

U.S. officials encountered many difficulties in dealing with Somoza because they no longer possessed any weapons, such as the question of diplomatic recognition used during the civil war, to ensure his compliance. On the other side, Ambassador Davis counseled Figueres to be patient, pointing out that the Costa Ricans held the sympathy of most nations and that rash actions could damage their position. He also encouraged the junta to accept a cease-fire until a final agreement could be reached.[55]

Figueres listened to U.S. proposals, but his natural tendency was to confront the problem. He and his advisers remained defiant. "Self-preservation is one of the principles of Christianity," Núñez declared. "With divine guidance, we shall turn back the invaders of our soil—but we also need machine guns."[56] Figueres added, "A people is much harder to conquer than an army. . . . We're not a bit worried."[57] Despite the rhetoric and the impulse to fight, the *figueristas* recognized that they needed outside assistance to defeat Calderón and Somoza. When the fighting started, they went to the Organization of American States (OAS) and denounced the Nicaraguans for violating the nonintervention clause of the Rio Treaty. On 12 December, the OAS convened in special session, but it adjourned without making a decision.[58]

While the OAS recessed, the Costa Ricans organized their defenses. Their efforts proved unnecessary when the rebel movement floundered in northern Costa Rica. When no mass uprising occurred, Ulate temporarily set aside his differences with the junta and joined it to demonstrate unity. The junta moved against internal threats by arresting many of the *calderonistas*. Even the Communists refused to assist Calderón because of his association with Somoza. After a few days, it appeared that Calderón could secure victory only through the intervention of Somoza's national guard.[59]

By 14 December, the possibility of direct intervention by the Nicaraguans appeared unlikely. Some observers concluded that Somoza had reconsidered his role in the invasion, and they reported that Nicaraguan border patrols had detained reinforcements trying to join the rebels. Shaw stated that "this is first definite indication that Somoza is realizing his mistake and unfavorable position and is now looking for an escape."[60] The ambassador warned, however, that Somoza still wanted to destroy the legion. He urged U.S. officials to push the Costa Ricans into making concessions, stressing that "it would be typical of him [Somoza] to cause us extreme trouble and embarrassment even if it cost him his official position."[61]

The international community joined the United States in pressuring Somoza to withdraw his support from the *calderonistas*. On 14 December, the OAS invoked Article 6 of the Rio Treaty prohibiting attacks on member nations by other countries.[62] It created a commission composed of representatives from Mexico, Brazil, Colombia, and the United States to investigate the conflict. The following day, the U.S. Air Force flew the group to Central America to make an on-the-spot report.[63] In response, Ambassador Esquivel stated: "It is finally going to be decided if these treaties [particularly the Inter-American Treaty of Reciprocal Assistance] are platonic romance or if they are capable and effective for maintaining the peace which we all so earnestly crave."[64]

The actions of some U.S. representatives, especially those in Costa Rica, did not always correspond with their rhetoric of neutrality. Washington assisted the junta by making U.S. facilities in Costa Rica available to Figueres's forces. Costa Rican officials requested that the Public Road Administration allow them to use its camp at Macana to house 500 troops. Davis responded that the camp was small and lacked adequate water supplies. Instead, he recommended the installation at Guancímal, approximately thirty miles away and fully stocked. He dispatched Col. J. R. Hughes to inform the junta that under existing contracts the Costa Ricans possessed the right to "house highway workers" at the facilities. He added, "And for goodness sakes, don't ask any official questions."[65]

Some skirmishes developed between the rebels and government troops in northern Costa Rica, but no major confrontations occurred. The *calderonistas* proved reluctant to leave the protection of Somoza's national guard, while Figueres avoided committing his troops close to the Nicaraguan border. Most people focused on the activities of the investigative commission that arrived in San José on 17 December. The junta staged an impressive welcoming event in an effort to play upon perceptions of Costa Rica as a model democracy. A large crowd led by Figueres, Ulate, and other junta members greeted the commission at the airport. A procession followed up the Avenida Central where thousands of Costa Ricans threw flowers and confetti on the motorcade. After dinner and some discussions at the Hotel Costa Rica, Figueres led a large group in the singing of the Costa Rican national anthem. The scene impressed members of the commission, especially the Americans. Bennett affirmed in glowing terms that "this unusual reception, which had nothing of the regimentation or forced participation in its spontaneous enthusiasm, was eloquent testimony to the prestige enjoyed by the Organization of American States among the general public."[66] Throughout the commission's stay, the Costa Ricans continued working to sway its opinions, believing that its findings would vindicate them of any wrongdoing and prove them an innocent victim of totalitarian aggression.[67]

While the commission continued collecting information in San José and later Managua, Costa Rica and Nicaragua issued charges and countercharges. In an interview with the International News Service, Somoza emphasized that if his national guard had been involved it would have already occupied San José. The Costa Rican press responded quickly. The *Diario de Costa Rica* called the statement "vulgar and stupid," adding that the Nicaraguan government was the "body of Somoza and the head of Román y Reyes."[68] Ulate also characterized the invaders as "bobos" who possessed so little intellectual ability that "five dollars and a good push in the back would send them to fight any place."[69]

After a week of traveling in the region, the investigative commission returned to Washington on 24 December.[70] It immediately reported to a special session of the OAS that the Costa Rican exiles had instituted the invasion from Nicaraguan soil although no direct evidence of Somoza's participation existed. The commission stressed, however, that the Nicaraguans had made no attempt to prevent this operation. It also laid partial blame on the Costa Ricans for harboring the Caribbean Legion in San José. After reviewing the commission's findings, the OAS Council rebuked both countries for allowing dissident groups to operate in their territories, and it advised everyone to cease hostilities and submit their differences to arbitration. Following another commission recommendation, the OAS created an Inter-American Committee of Military Experts to monitor the Costa Rican–Nicaraguan border until the tensions subsided.[71]

The commission's report elicited a mixed response. Most U.S. officials supported the findings that pressed both sides to cease the intrigues. Somoza accepted its findings, boasting that the OAS had found Costa Rica guilty of giving shelter to exiles who threatened Nicaragua. He also praised the stationing of the military observers to monitor border activities.[72] Figueres, on the other hand, compared the OAS resolution to *"cantinflas,"* a Mexican clown who talked a lot and said nothing. He wanted a harsher condemnation of Somoza, but Davis counseled caution and suggested that the junta affirm that it would no longer support revolutionary operations against Nicaragua.[73]

For the next month and a half, fighting occasionally flared, although the two countries spent most of their time sparring in the newspapers. Somoza paraded several captured Costa Ricans in front of the press, where they confessed recently seeing legion members stationed in the Bella Vista.[74] The Costa Ricans counterattacked, questioning Nicaraguan Ambassador Sevilla's claims that his country had not supported the December invasion. Ambassador Esquivel went so far as to call Sevilla a liar who employed the "Machiavellian strategy that an untruth, constantly repeated, eventually becomes accepted as truth."[75] He also condemned the Nicaraguans for training and arming the rebels, pointing out that no responsible officer had received any form of punishment.[76] Despite the denunciations, negotiations continued. Finally, the two countries signed a pact of amity that called for arbitration in the event of a new conflict, and each agreed to strengthen its border patrols to prevent any reoccurrences of the past three months.[77]

U.S. officials and other foreign observers praised the OAS's quick response to the crisis. "It is too early to estimate the results of this action," the CIA reported, "[but] the procedure used is of considerable significance and provides a precedent as well as a formula for future use in more serious situations."[78] A member of the OAS investigating committee, Juan Petersen, concluded that "the Nica-Tica affair is far more important than an unsuccessful invasion of one small country," adding that "thanks to the speed with which the gentlemen guiding the destinies of the Organization of American States acted . . . the Rio pact has become a living instrument."[79] Nicaraguan and Costa Rican journalists correctly expressed the pessimistic view that the negotiations had created only a temporary peace, but for the moment tensions subsided.[80]

The United States won a significant victory with the OAS report. It rebuked Figueres and Somoza equally. Some U.S. diplomats had feared antagonizing Somoza as the cold war intensified. For his part, the Nicaraguan dictator secured his goal of focusing on Figueres and Arévalo's meddling in the affairs of some of Washington's staunchest allies in the region. The United States missed an opportunity to strengthen the democratic-left movement because it feared the group threatened the security of the Caribbean Basin at a time when U.S. diplomats wanted to concentrate on Asia and Europe. The stance the United States chose limited the ability of Figueres and others to promote the cause of democracy effectively in Latin America. While the conflict forced Figueres to change his methods, he did not desert his friends completely and continued assisting the democratic struggle despite repeated U.S. warnings that such actions violated existing treaty obligations and threatened to undermine relations between the two countries.

The clash between Nicaragua and Costa Rica had caused some U.S. officials to question their support of the junta because of its uninterrupted attempts to disrupt peace in the region by aiding the Nicaraguan exiles. The Americans continued to want to secure stability in the region so that Washington could focus on more important areas. The United States tried to contain democratic groups opposed to the authoritarians, fearing their nationalism and the instability that might be caused by overthrowing the dictators. The intensification of the cold war made the tyrants more attractive. U.S. officials increasingly moved away from early postwar opposition to pro-American totalitarians and into the camp that accepted their arbitrary rule in return for their opposition to communism. This change in policy ensured additional difficulties for Figueres and others in the democratic movement.

Despite the tensions caused by the junta's assistance to the democratic left, most Americans remained pro-Figueres. In mid-March 1949, Ambassador Davis outlined the successes and failures of the junta on the eve of its first anniversary, highlighting "substantial progress" in domestic programs and "great progress in the elimination of graft." He also noted problems such as "a growing restiveness in the traditional political parties over their exclusion from office; loss of popular confidence in the capacity of the government while granting its good intentions."[81] The Costa Ricans won high marks for their continued anticommunism and support of the United States in the United Nations, but earned low marks for their continued assistance to the Caribbean Legion.

For the moment, OAS mediation and domestic political problems diverted the *figueristas* from foreign intrigues. Immediately preceding Calderón's invasion, the Costa Ricans had held elections for the Constituent Assembly. Figueres and his associates had foolishly maintained neutrality during the campaign, allowing Ulate's party to win thirty-three of the forty-five positions while the *figueristas* took only four seats.[82] The *ulatistas* now controlled the drafting of a constitution and the validation of the election of Ulate. A constant struggle in the Constituent Assembly between the *figueristas* and the *ulatistas* characterized the next eleven months, diverting Figueres's attention from the Caribbean Legion and helping reduce conflicts among the Central American states.

The Constituent Assembly opened on 16 January 1949, and the junta immediately encountered problems. Figueres asked the assembly to validate the junta's policies, a request it denied. He also sought an extension on the junta's rule for six months, threatening to resign and put his economic and political policies to a popular referendum if the body refused. After a standoff, Ulate urged his followers to grant the appeal. This action reduced tensions temporarily, but the potential for conflict remained.[83]

The most immediate threat to the junta developed from conservatives opposed to the junta's economic policies. On 2 April, the minister of public safety, Col. Edgar Cardona, Claudio Cortés, and a small group of conspirators seized Bella Vista. They requested a meeting with Ulate and offered to install him immediately in the presidency. He refused, declaring his allegiance to the junta. Without Ulate's support, the movement collapsed. Figueres issued a statement emphasizing that he would accept only unconditional surrender. When the rebels ignored his ultimatum, Figueres's troops attacked the barracks and forced them to capitulate.[84] U.S. officials had reported that trouble had been brewing for some time but that no American intervention was necessary. The junta's quick reaction to the seizure of Bella Vista prevented any U.S. responses other than the evacuation of the U.S. Embassy located near the Bella Vista barracks. Afterwards, U.S. diplomats concluded that the defeat of the Calderón invasion and Cardona's insurrection would "clear the air" and "should ensure stability of the Figueres regime for some time to come."[85]

Following Cardona's failed coup, the *figueristas* again concentrated on the Constituent Assembly. They suffered a series of setbacks when the assembly rejected the *figueristas'* draft of the constitution and tried to ban Catholic priests from holding office, a direct attack on Padre Núñez.[86] After much debate, the Constituent Assembly adopted a new constitution in 1949. Using the constitution of 1871 as their guide, the assemblymen severely weakened the executive branch.[87] Despite their limited numbers, the *figueristas* secured several major victories. The constitution upheld the social guarantees and labor code and promoted the concept of "public regulation of private property and enterprise," a direct reference to the state's responsibility for stimulating production and promoting equitable distribution of wealth. The document mandated the creation of autonomous government agencies to guide and regulate the economy and social service programs. Well-trained and nonpartisan professionals outside the control of the executive branch were to direct the institutions.[88] In addition, the *figueristas* successfully secured the creation of a fourth branch of government, the Supreme Electoral Tribunal, to direct and validate elections. Finally, they accomplished their goal of extending suffrage to women and ending discrimination against the blacks from the Limón area.[89]

The battle in the Constituent Assembly had important long-term consequences for the *figueristas*. The defeats caused by the failure to push their own candidates convinced them that they needed to organize their forces and expand their base of support to win elections. Upon leaving office, they dedicated themselves to the project. During the four years of Ulate's presidency, Figueres and his associates built a strong political party and emerged stronger in domestic and international affairs when they returned to power.

Although the constitutional debates diverted Figueres's attention from international events, the question of the Caribbean Legion remained volatile. After it moved its headquarters to Guatemala, the legion focused on overthrowing Trujillo rather than Somoza. The move did not convince U.S. officials that the Costa Ricans had ceased assisting the movement. In early June, Bennett reminded Ambassador Esquivel that the State Department opposed adventurism, warning that such activities could invite Dominican and Nicaraguan countermeasures. The ambassador agreed to pass the message along to San José.[90]

Figueres ignored the warnings and continued sending aid to the exiles, although he reduced the amounts sent and adopted more covert methods of transferring it. The assistance centered on providing the legion with support for its plans to overthrow Trujillo in the early summer. Problems developed when the dictator's spies alerted him to the impending attack. Utilizing his radio station, "La Voz Dominican," Trujillo attacked the Caribbean Legion as Communists under the command of the degenerate Arévalo and supplied by the Marxist Figueres.[91]

By mid-June, the revolutionaries were ready to launch operations. Their initial plans called for 1,200 troops to land from planes and ships at strategic locations in the Dominican Republic. On 19 June, they moved, but their plans immediately fell apart when six of the seven planes failed to reach their destination. Trujillo's troops quickly crushed the uprising. After executing several conspirators, including an American pilot, Trujillo tortured the others and forced them to confess the role of Guatemala, Cuba, and Costa Rica in the invasion. Horacio Ornes, a hero of the Costa Rican civil war, accused the three countries of having a "marked Communist tendency."[92]

The failed coup attempt caused tempers to flare throughout the summer and early fall. The Nicaraguans, Dominicans, and Venezuelans complained that Cuba, Guatemala, and Costa Rica had violated the nonintervention clauses of existing treaties and urged the United States to punish the conspirators. Venezuela's foreign minister, Luis E. Gómez, warned that the leaders of his country might respond militarily against the offending parties, especially those aiding Betancourt.[93]

The United States recognized the seriousness of the situation. The CIA stressed that the revolutionaries were "committed to their undertaking [overthrowing the dictators]," but added that "it is obvious that the U.S. security interest in Hemisphere solidarity is not served by constant strife in the Caribbean, even though there is no question that all the countries involved will support the U.S. in a U.S.–U.S.S.R. conflict."[94] As in the past, the United States tried defusing the conflict by pressuring the conspirators to stop interfering in the affairs of other nations.

The Costa Ricans responded that they had reduced their role in the democratic-left movement. Ambassador Esquivel and Daniel Oduber, former secretary general of the junta, met with U.S. representatives to underscore their support for Washington's objectives. Oduber assured the U.S. officials that the Costa Ricans would assist their efforts to create peace and stability in the Caribbean Basin. He promised that revolutionary activities had diminished in Costa Rica, emphasizing that the legion had evolved into a tightly organized leftist movement controlled by Arévalo.[95]

The junta claimed it had not been involved in the plot, but Figueres's continued association with prominent members of the democratic left such as Juan Bosch undermined its argument. At the end of July, Bosch departed Costa Rica after a lengthy visit with Figueres. In an impromptu speech before boarding the plane, he denounced Somoza's record of tyranny, murder, and deceit.[96] Other reports circulated that Figueres had hidden large quantities of arms at his *finca,* where he continued preparing for an attack on Nicaragua. U.S. officials told Figueres to be cautious, pointing out that any activities would cause the dictators to attack his country again.[97]

In mid-August, the United States moved to ease tensions by promoting OAS mediation. At a special session of the OAS, delegates from the Dominican Republic presented a fourteen-page report criticizing Costa Rica, Cuba, and Guatemala for their "imperialistic interventionism." The Cuban delegates responded by blaming the problems on the dictators who ensured political and economic stagnation, arguing that only democracy—as represented by the exiles—could guarantee stability.[98] Unconvinced by the Cuban line of reasoning, Washington maintained that revolutions, even democratic ones, threatened the region and that only gradual changes would accomplish the desired goals. It stressed that "democratic principles were certain to suffer if there continued to be illegal international activities in the Caribbean, with the apparent effort to justify such illegal activities in the name of 'democracy.' "[99]

The problems of instability in the Caribbean Basin remained a priority for U.S. policymakers, a point highlighted in a September 1949 speech by the new secretary of state, Dean Acheson.[100] The difficulties with Costa Rica declined, however, as the *figueristas* neared the end of their term. Although Dominican and Nicaraguan officials continued charging the junta with interference, U.S. diplomats believed that when Ulate took power such activities would decrease.[101] Since the border dispute of December, the issue had been important to the United States but not to the same extent as before the fighting. In the aftermath, Figueres adopted a more covert policy typically directed against Trujillo rather than Somoza. This response limited the potential for direct conflict between the neighbors and placed the responsibility for the problems more on the Cubans and Guatemalans. Still, tensions persisted throughout Ulate's presidency, as Figueres privately continued to aid the attempts of exiles to establish democracies in the region. Costa Rican interventionism resurfaced as a divisive issue after Figueres took power again in 1953.

During the last two months of its rule the junta's problems with Ulate increased, draining most of its energies. At one point, Figueres threatened to resign, form a new party, and run for the vice-presidency. He eventually backed down and retained his position.[102] A more serious controversy developed in late October when the assembly tried classifying all government employees as interim. The junta promised to quit in protest. Ulate had his supporters tone down the legislation, and he guaranteed not to use any powers granted him against pro-Figueres civil servants. Pacified for the moment, the junta stayed in power until the assigned time.[103]

After months of controversy, Ulate's inauguration took place as scheduled on 8 November 1949. A large number of foreign dignitaries attended the ceremony at the national stadium, where Figueres relinquished power despite the protests of his followers, who characterized Ulate as undeserving. "After almost two years of civil war and de facto government," *Newsweek* noted, "Costa Rica had returned to its traditional path of constitutional democracy."[104]

The United States greeted favorably the peaceful transfer of power. Acheson emphasized that it was "important that this government display tangible evidence of its satisfaction over the return of Costa Rica to constitutional government." He had encouraged the appointment of special emissaries to Ulate's inauguration that included the new U.S. ambassador to Costa Rica, Joseph Flack.[105] Acting Secretary of State James E. Webb stated that "we are happy along with many other friends of Costa Rica" that the nation once again had joined the ranks of true democracies.[106] To many Americans, Costa Rica remained an example of democratic rule in a region characterized by the seizure of power with broken promises of turning over command.

The junta had helped return U.S.–Costa Rican relations to its normal pattern. The junta implemented policies that it believed best served its country's needs, even though its programs (primarily the nationalization of the banking industry) sometimes conflicted with U.S. economic views. Junta members understood the growing correlation in the United States between nationalism and anti-Americanism, an understanding provided in part by some Americans, including Davis and others in the State Department, who admired Figueres and his associates and shared many of their beliefs regarding democracy and capitalism. In the end, the Costa Ricans successfully distanced themselves from charges of anti-Americanism by removing the Communist threat and by reducing their radicalism of the policies, although the moderation typically occurred not only because of U.S. pressure but also because of the internal dynamics of Costa Rican politics.

In regional affairs, the *figueristas* also tried to steer an independent course, primarily in their support of the exile movement against neighboring dictators. These actions conflicted with the U.S. efforts to maintain stability in the Caribbean Basin. The United States and its dictatorial allies successfully thwarted the attempts of Figueres and his allies to overthrow the authoritarians, forcing them to change tactics. This pattern followed the established rule of relations as Figueres supported major international issues while struggling to maintain independence of action in domestic and regional affairs. While Figueres's actions were more extreme than those of most of his predecessors, they never directly threatened U.S. security, a point highlighted in 1949 by U.S. diplomats who emphasized that the democratic-left contained little Communist influence.

In the end, Figueres returned his country to more normal forms of political and social relations, an accomplishment that won admiration among U.S. officials who had seen too many times in Latin America the refusal to relinquish power. While Ulate ruled, Figueres gained even more prominence in domestic and regional affairs, implementing many of the lessons learned during the reign of the junta. He returned to power in 1953 with more radical policies that tested the United States in a period characterized by heightened problems with a correlation between communism and nationalism. Nevertheless, the country would receive a brief respite from the upheavals of the preceding decade during the four years of Ulate's presidency.

6

THE CALM BEFORE THE STORM
The Presidency of Otílio Ulate and the Rise of the Partido Liberación Nacional, 1949–1953

In March 1952, Harry Murkland declared that "Costa Rica, after a brief interruption, is back again on its normal road of political peace and economic prosperity. It is showing again the economic steadiness, political good sense and national resiliency which singles it out from its Central American fellows."[1] "It is not that Costa Rica has achieved perfect success," he suggested, "but that it is advancing steadily toward it."[2]

Peace returned to Costa Rica under Otílio Ulate. When he took office in November 1949, the country still faced many problems caused by the civil war and the clash with Nicaragua. The economy and political system remained unsettled after years of rapid change under Calderón, Picado, and the junta. With dogged determination, Ulate addressed the problems. Contrary to widespread expectations, he did not dismantle social programs, but he did slow their growth and promoted fiscal conservatism and the gradual evolution of existing institutions. In many ways his domestic activities paralleled those of U.S. President Dwight D. Eisenhower, who entered office as Ulate left office in 1953.

In international affairs, Ulate promoted few initiatives. He remained very pro-U.S., supporting Washington's policies in the United Nations and in the Korean conflict. In regional affairs, he prevented the democratic-left revolutionaries from using Costa Rica as a base of operations, a policy U.S. officials greatly appreciated. Yet he was not totally subservient, refusing to follow totally U.S. mandates regarding the Costa Rican Communists by allowing them some leeway during his term. Nevertheless, when Ulate left office in 1953, U.S. diplomats praised his policies and contrasted his tenure to the preceding five years, during which Costa Rica had drained off

U.S. time and energy. The Ulate presidency helped reaffirm Costa Rica as a stable ally and strongly reestablished the traditional pattern of U.S.–Costa Rican relations.

Ulate's presidency also corresponded with the growing popularity of Figueres and his allies. While out of office, the *figueristas* created a political party, the *Partido Liberación Nacional* (National Liberation party or PLN), and outlined a plan for taking Costa Rica into the twenty-first century. Their central purpose was to win the presidential and congressional elections in 1953, and they organized on the local and national levels to achieve that goal. The *figueristas'* ideology and programs won them a strong following in Costa Rica and in the international community, primarily the United States. The evolution of the party and its leaders was important, setting the stage for domestic and international tensions in the period after Ulate.

For the four years under Ulate, stability returned to the country. The new president was strongly influenced by his humble origins. He had started as a newsboy in Alajuela, working his way into the editorship and ownership of the *Diario de Costa Rica.* He had only limited political experience before entering the national limelight in the presidential election of 1948. As much as anyone in the nation's politics at the time, he represented the ideals of late-nineteenth-century Costa Rica. When he entered office, he made clear his belief that the country needed no additional transformation of its economic, political, and social systems. More than anything, he wanted to improve the efficiency of existing programs rather than create new ones.[3]

Throughout his tenure, Ulate sought to return the country to more normal patterns of relations characterized by political participation and respect for civil liberties. He resumed the presidential custom of a morning walk to the central post office to sit and chat with the people. As he sat one day on a bench, several drunk *calderonistas* shouted support for their exiled leader. Instead of allowing the police to arrest the men, he encouraged them to "viva whom they wish."[4] During this new era of tolerance, Ulate encouraged exiles to return home. He sought to heal the political and social divisions of the civil war, reducing potential conflicts.

In economic affairs, the regime concentrated on cutting the national debt by slashing unnecessary public expenditures and promoting administrative efficiency. To balance international payments, the Ulate government supported the Law for the Control of International Transactions, a

Costa Rican law that created rules for international exchanges and levied import taxes on a wide variety of luxury items. It also reduced borrowing from international lending agencies, successfully trimming the foreign debt by 20 percent.[5]

While Ulate promoted fiscal austerity, he also expanded public works such as roads, dams, and a new international airport with the funds provided by the new UFCO contract and the junta's 10 percent tax. He supported agriculture, backing programs that encouraged agricultural self-sufficiency and prevented the loss of hard-earned currency on expensive imports. His administration sponsored irrigation projects, provided credit and technical assistance to farmers, and guaranteed prices for such crops such as beans, corn, and rice. The plans succeeded, and by 1953 Costa Rica began exporting some basic foodstuffs.[6]

Ulate also bolstered education and health care. During his four years in office, the government built 317 new schools and augmented the University of Costa Rica, adding schools of agronomy and nursing. It also helped pass in 1950 the General Law of Medical-Social Assistance, which guaranteed medical care to all Costa Ricans, regardless of ability to pay. Working with officials of the United Nations and the United States, the administration made health care more readily available, especially in the areas of preventive medicine and public sanitation.[7]

When Ulate left office in 1953, he had accomplished no major innovations. He had addressed numerous existing problems, such as the foreign debt and the trade imbalance, and continued some of the more popular social programs of the *calderonistas* and *figueristas.* After ten years of rapid change and numerous dislocations caused by World War II and the civil war, most Costa Ricans wanted a leader like Ulate. He brought a sense of stability and well-being back to society. Still, the legacy of change of the 1940s was a constant feature of the activists that succeeded Ulate. In 1953, Figueres and his newly organized National Liberation party stepped to the forefront and again took the lead in trying to restructure Costa Rican society.

While concentrating primarily on internal problems, Ulate did not ignore foreign affairs. His administration shared Washington's aversion to communism and followed the U.S. lead in the international arena, especially the cold war. In regional affairs, Ulate also worked with Washington on such problems as the rise of Communists in Guatemala and interventionism in the Caribbean Basin. Despite some disagreements with Ulate, the United States ensured that he received financial and technical assistance. When he left office, he had a strong following among certain U.S. diplomats, who expressed appreciation for his reliance on democratic methods that promoted the well-being of his people and his unobtrusive international policies that allowed U.S. officials to turn their attention elsewhere.

The most important issue in U.S.–Costa Rican relations during Ulate's presidency was communism. The junta had destroyed most Communist influence in Costa Rica, leading the CIA to conclude that "Communist capabilities for causing political instability in Argentina, Brazil, Colombia, Costa Rica . . . are at present limited largely to causing annoyance."[8] Ulate and his advisers shared Washington's fear of the Communist ideology, although they lacked the *figueristas'* zeal for battling communism. Ulate had denounced the Communists before and during the civil war, backing the outlawing of the Vanguard as a "just and prudent" decision, although his views toward the group moderated over time. Furthermore, he consistently supported U.S. efforts to defeat perceived Communist threats in Asia and Europe.[9] Near the end of his administration, he declared: "Individuality, in the field of inter-human relationships, is what gives form and substance to the dignity of man." "Collectivism, or the exaggeration of the importance given to society as a being or abstraction," he added, "spells the negation of personality and the suppression of its attributes."[10] As in the past, the Costa Ricans supported the United States on the major international issues, standing behind it in the postwar struggle to contain communism.

Although he strongly opposed international communism, at times Ulate's policy toward the Costa Rican Communists vacillated. After taking office, he increasingly resisted U.S. pressures to deny the former *vanguardistas* all rights and privileges. Much like Calderón and Picado, he began differentiating between international communism and native movements such as the Vanguard, arguing that the latter was not under Soviet control and existed primarily to improve the plight of the working class. He believed that everyone possessed the fundamental right to participate in a democratic society, even those that disagreed with him. In response, he encouraged exiles such as Mora and the *vanguardistas* to return home to facilitate the healing process. Many complied, causing uneasiness among some Costa Ricans and U.S. officials who wanted to prevent all operations by perceived Communist organizations.[11] Again, the Costa Ricans tried to maintain independence of action in domestic affairs, although the activities of the Costa Rican Communists and their allies caused Ulate to take a much harder line than he wanted.

Quick actions by Ulate against perceived Communist threats assuaged fears of renewed Communist influence in the government of Costa Rica. In August 1950, Ulate's forces suppressed a plot by *vanguardistas* and followers of Calderón. Reportedly, the Vanguard had infiltrated labor unions and planned a general strike against United Fruit to cause widespread disturbances, possibly bringing about the downfall of the administration. As soon as it uncovered the intrigue, the government arrested 150 *vanguardistas* and *calderonistas,* including Mora and Javier Cortés, the son of former president León Cortés.[12]

In April 1951, the government crushed another plot by the Communists and *calderonistas.* Bombing attacks on the homes of Foreign Minister Mario Echandi and members of the compensation board heightened fears of another invasion by Calderón and Picado from Nicaragua.[13] The police arrested fifty people, including Calderón's brother and uncle, and seized a large quantity of arms purportedly transported from Mexico. The government also secured the Mexican government's promise to prevent any further shipments.[14] The scheme unraveled, but the exiles and their domestic allies remained a threat to the country's stability, although their potential to take power appeared limited.

Although he sometimes allowed the Communists more leeway than U.S. officials wanted, Ulate suppressed direct challenges. His administration seized mail entering the country from Soviet bloc countries, but at the same time allowed Mora to operate openly, rationalizing that this action permitted the government to monitor his movements more effectively than if he moved underground. By 1953, in a move to satisfy his desire to sustain full civil liberties and embarrass the incoming *figueristas,* Ulate tried to help Mora secure permission to organize a labor federation.[15] The attempt failed when Ulate backed away from the effort after the Eisenhower administration expressed its displeasure and many in Costa Rica condemned the measure.[16] While Ulate had resisted persecuting Mora and his associates, he did not want to take the issue too far and risk totally alienating many Costa Ricans and Americans.

At the same time, following the traditional pattern of relations between the two countries, Ulate wholeheartedly backed Washington's international policies. In June 1950, when North Korea attacked South Korea,

Costa Rica denounced the invasion and the rumored Soviet role in the conflict. On 27 June, Foreign Minister Echandi publicly charged that the attack on South Korea was a Communist plot against an independent nation.[17] A day later, Ulate expressed to Truman his nation's support for U.S. and U.N. attempts to protect South Korea.[18]

Throughout the war, Costa Rica supported the United States. President Ulate offered military bases to protect the Canal Zone and promised to send volunteers to Korea if the United States provided military training. San José also stood behind Washington in the United Nations, urging forceful actions to meet North Korean and Chinese aggression.[19] While Costa Rica provided little direct aid, it strengthened its reputation as strongly pro-U.S. and anti-Communist and helped smooth over some of the differences that arose over Communist activities at home.

San José also followed the U.S. lead on the question of Nationalist China. It refused to recognize the Communists on the mainland, choosing instead to maintain economic and political ties with the Nationalists.[20] In the United Nations, Costa Rica consistently voted to sustain the Nationalists as China's representatives. In early 1951, the Ulate administration received a Nationalist envoy, Cheng Cheng-Ya, as minister plenipotentiary.[21] From this point until the late 1970s, Costa Rica proved a dependable ally of Chiang Kai-shek and the Nationalists, many times drawing parallels between the two country's struggles against communism.

The Costa Ricans also supported U.S. policies toward the Soviet Union in the United Nations and Organization of American States, following the historic trend of Costa Rican opposition to the Russians. In 1952, the Costa Rican delegation to the United Nations declared that its "Government and people will resolutely support any measure which reinforces democratic achievements and strengthens absolute respect for human rights."[22] These actions included criticizing the closed society of the U.S.S.R. for preventing the free expression of ideas and prohibiting foreign diplomats from traveling freely.[23] At the urging of the United States, the Costa Ricans also upheld a boycott of the Communist states on arms, chemicals used to manufacture petroleum, and any materials that could be used to produce atomic weapons.[24]

In regional affairs, Ulate won the approval of U.S. officials for assisting their efforts to stabilize Central America and the Caribbean Basin. He had opposed the junta's assistance to the Caribbean exiles, arguing that it endangered the well-being of Costa Rica by causing unneeded tensions with

Nicaragua and the Dominican Republic. While a firm believer in democracy, Ulate was a pragmatic leader who sought primarily to protect Costa Rican interests. Even though the activities of the legion in Costa Rica had declined dramatically after its defeat at Luperon and Figueres's departure from office, Ulate's government wanted to reduce tensions further. It intensified efforts to curtail the activities of foreign adventurers living in Costa Rica. In 1950, it stopped Honduran exiles from using a radio station to denounce their nation's rulers for massacring their people. Although the Costa Rican supreme court overruled the administration's edict, the act demonstrated Ulate's determination to end meddling in other nation's affairs.[25] Despite Ulate's efforts, Figueres and others continued working with the revolutionaries. Somoza responded by plotting with Calderón and Picado, but no clashes occurred until Figueres again assumed office in 1953.

Ulate worked with U.S. officials on other important regional issues. Throughout his term, he and his associates cooperated with the United States against the rise of communism in Guatemala. In a meeting in the summer of 1950, Assistant Secretary of State Edward Miller emphasized that Cuba, Costa Rica, and Mexico had tried impressing upon Guatemalan diplomats the seriousness of the Communist question.[26] Washington often used Costa Rica as a model in economic affairs, advising Guatemala to follow San José's 1949 example when renegotiating a contract with United Fruit. UFCO officials went so far as to leave a draft copy of the Costa Rican agreement with President Arévalo.[27]

Relations between Costa Rica and Guatemala deteriorated throughout 1951 and 1952. Costa Rican officials increasingly criticized the Guatemalan Communists and their emerging alliance with the new president, Jacobo Arbenz. The radicalism of the expropriation of property especially concerned Ulate.[28] The president initially resisted Washington's attempts to further isolate the Guatemalans by avoiding public condemnations of them and refusing to join alliances that excluded Guatemala, but tensions increased. In 1953, San José declared the Guatemalan ambassador persona non grata for reportedly plotting with Costa Rican leftists against the government. These problems persisted until the end of Ulate's presidency, and he turned them over to his successor.

Ulate's policies evoked strong support from the United States. From his inauguration forward, the State Department underscored that the country had stabilized and returned to "a truly democratic and constitutional form of government."[29] It praised the Ulate administration's "genuine and sincere" opposition to the Communists and its support of U.S. policies toward international communism. The CIA described Ulate as "flamboyant and susceptible to flattery. He is an excellent editor and writer, an amusing and charming and, if need be, forceful speaker. Except for heavy drinking, Ulate leads an exemplary life in Costa Rica." "As a bachelor, he is fond of making trips abroad, especially to Panama," it added, "where his heavy drinking and 'night-clubbing' are the source of much amusement and gossip among upper-class circles."[30] Despite this interesting characterization of the president, U.S. officials pointed out that Costa Rica provided a model for Latin America and that the country's "democratic characteristics have made possible a truly genuine friendship with United States." "It is our policy to cultivate this friendship," they added, "as means of strengthening that country and the example it provides of what may be achieved through the democratic system."[31] To demonstrate its approval, the State Department sent Assistant Secretary of State Miller to San José in August 1951 to award Ulate the Congressional Medal of Merit for his commendable service for the cause of freedom and democracy in Latin America.[32]

At the outset of Ulate's rule, U.S. objectives centered around maintaining Costa Rica's traditional democracy and its allegiance to Washington in extracontinental affairs. U.S. officials recognized the country's lack of capacity to combat future domestic and external Communist threats. The government had abolished the army, maintaining a small national guard to deal with internal and external threats. To strengthen the force, the two countries settled Costa Rica's lend-lease debt, freeing San José to secure additional U.S. assistance. Costa Rica also agreed to support inter-American military collaboration and extended the contract on the U.S. military mission for an additional four years.[33]

U.S. policymakers also sought to help strengthen Costa Rica's economy, which had been damaged by World War II and the civil war.[34] As was the norm in the postwar era, Washington funded programs and provided loans through various organizations. In Costa Rica, the United States helped expand public works and create jobs. In 1951 the U.S. Congress appropriated an additional $4 million for the continued survey and construction of the Inter-American Highway.[35] In return, Costa Rica provided approximately $1 million for the project.[36] Increased work on the highway provided much-needed jobs and an infusion of capital into the country. It also improved the infrastructure and opened up new areas for economic development and the resettlement of a burgeoning population.

The Ulate administration also received funds from the Point 4 program. In September 1950, Congress appropriated over $34 million for technical assistance to developing nations, dividing the money among several U.S. and U.N. agencies to develop specific projects. U.S. officials wanted to improve conditions in Latin America by increasing agricultural output, promoting industrialization, and launching health and sanitation projects. From the improved conditions, U.S. officials hoped to secure more markets while simultaneously undermining the poverty on which communism thrived.[37]

Costa Rica was one of the first countries to sign a Point 4 agreement. In September, Ambassador Joseph Flack informed Ulate that the United States would contribute $125,000 to help sustain the *Servicio Técnico Inter-Americano de Cooperación Agrícola,* an agricultural assistance program. The pact made more money available for salaries for the members of the Food Supply Field Staff and extended cooperation on existing ventures through June 1955. The two countries also promised to work to increase Costa Rica's rubber production and on other agricultural extension projects.[38]

Throughout the Ulate administration, the United States provided additional Point 4 funds. Washington allocated more money to pay for food programs and expand existing technical assistance projects.[39] In May 1951, the parties established a cooperative health program. Working through the Costa Rican Ministry of Public Health and the Institute of Inter-American Affairs, the United States gave financial and technical aid to improve sanitation and health through studies and surveys, new joint projects, and increased training of workers and experts.[40]

On other questions, the two countries cooperated. The United States established the Civil Aviation Mission to develop Costa Rica's domestic airlines and create policies that corresponded with international procedures for the country's fledgling airline industry.[41] The two nations also sponsored an exchange of scholars as called for by new regional treaties on cultural relations.[42] In 1952, as the administration neared the end of its term, Washington and San José opened talks through the International Bank for Reconstruction and Development to construct hydroelectric plants on the Reventazón and Grande rivers, projects ultimately completed.[43]

When Ulate left office in the summer 1953, many U.S. officials praised his tenure. He had followed Washington's initiatives in international affairs, supporting the United States in Korea and against the Soviets in the United Nations and the Organization of American States. In addition, he had minded his own business and had not disrupted regional stability by sponsoring revolutionary activities against Somoza and Trujillo. In domestic affairs, Ulate had steadied the economy by streamlining the government and paying off debts. U.S. officials enjoyed the brief respite from the turmoil that had plagued Costa Rica before Ulate's presidency and that appeared again on the horizon as Figueres became the front-runner for the presidency.

The return of Figueres to the political limelight during Ulate's term significantly influenced future U.S.–Costa Rican relations, bringing a nationalist leader to the forefront in a period when Washington often identified nationalism with communism. After leaving office in 1949, Figueres and his associates began preparing to take political control in the 1953 elections. Disappointed by their inability to alter Costa Rica dramatically along the lines envisioned during the administration of the junta, they learned from their mistakes and carefully planned to take power and implement their programs. During Ulate's term, they prepared coherent and effective policies to win the congressional and presidential election in 1953, developing a strong following among Costa Ricans and influential groups in the United States.

The first project the *figueristas* tackled was the creation of a political party. In Costa Rica and other Central American countries, parties had typically been ad hoc groups established to support the aspirations of an individual.[44] The original Social Democratic party closely resembled the old pattern. Determined to offset these tendencies, Figueres and his associates built a strong organization with a coherent ideology. Influenced by party systems in the United States, Europe, and other Latin American nations, the *figueristas* developed a platform to attract wide support.

After much planning and debate the *figueristas* founded the *Partido Liberación Nacional* (PLN) in 1951. They issued a "*Carta Fundamental*" outlining their beliefs and plans for the future, a document strongly influenced by Figueres. The proclamation emphasized the importance of the individual, arguing that a person held certain "inalienable rights." It promised government intervention to meet the basic social and economic needs of all Costa Ricans and to allow the individual to earn a living and maintain the dignity associated with life and liberty.[45]

In the economic sector, the *figueristas* stressed a qualified belief in private property, declaring, "We recognize private property and proclaim its social function, the exercise of which ought to be inspired for the well-being of all. We consider it necessary to establish property as a generalized social fact and to avoid its swollen concentration."[46] "To the extent that it [property] advances the acknowledgment of the social character of the economic function," they added, "the profit incentive should be complemented and ennobled by the spirit of service."[47]

Keynesian and New Deal economics strongly influenced Figueres and his advisers. To ensure more equality of economic opportunity, the PLN promoted a mixed economy in which the government provided general direction to private enterprise. The state would serve as the country's conscience, seeing to it that business promoted the public welfare. Figueres believed that healthy government intervention would protect democracy by guaranteeing that the system represented everyone rather than a select few.[48] The PLN advocated several policies to assure a more equitable distribution of wealth and economic development. The constitution of 1949 provided for the creation of autonomous governmental agencies, free of executive and legislative influence, to promote economic development and administer social programs. The party also wanted high tariffs to increase industrialization and government ownership of public utilities to reduce consumer costs and allow profits to remain in the country.[49]

The *figueristas* made economic independence from outside interests a priority, believing that Costa Rica suffered from "selling cheap and buying dear."[50] Figueres wanted foreign investment, but he opposed outsiders taking advantage of Costa Rican laborers by paying low wages. Convinced that subsistence pay erected barriers to hemispheric unity because of the great disparity between rich and poor nations, he called for higher wages for Latin American workers so that they could purchase U.S. products. This would reduce exchange problems and, more important, eliminate the need for humiliating loans and expensive U.S. government grants.[51] At times, Figueres angered some Americans, especially businessmen and conservatives, who feared that his ideas were anticapitalist. In the period immediately preceding the 1953 election, he caused further alarm when he declared that "we do not want a new wave of colonialism, such as foreign ownership has sometimes implied in the past."[52] "We resent the pretence of speculators who assert that their motive in investing money abroad is to foster the development of our countries," he said. He concluded, "We distrust people who assure us that they are willing to 'run a risk,' for we have discovered that what they really want is to 'make a killing.' "[53]

While some of his rhetoric worried some American business leaders and diplomats, Figueres appeased most fears with his strident anticommunism. He frequently reminded Americans of his role in destroying the Communist menace in his country, and he continued to attack the Communists after he left office. In 1950, he affirmed, "Communism has no political appeal to individualistic, liberty-loving Latin Americans. Its only appeal is economic. Its strategy is to inflame the many poor to class warfare against the few rich. Its opportunity and our responsibility hinge on the same fact: We do have too many poor. The problem can't be solved by a worker's war to destroy wealth; it can be solved by intelligent employers and responsible workers united to utilize the 20th-century techniques that can provide abundance for all."[54]

Figueres firmly believed that democracy and regulated capitalism were the best hope for Latin American development, stressing that communism would destroy that way of life and wreck the region's potential. He wanted Washington to emphasize not only military cooperation but also an economic and spiritual union to defeat the foreign threat.[55] All these concepts related closely to his belief that fairer economic exchanges would ensure greater prosperity and undermine the Communists' base of support.

Although Figueres supported the U.S. crusade against communism, he continued criticizing Washington's assistance to Latin American dictatorships. "Militarism and graft are perfectly acceptable to U.S. in our relations with you," Figueres stated, "as long as your men in power pay lip-service to our side in the world struggle, and see to it that foreign investments are properly respected."[56] "The Soviets stand behind Communism; the rightist totalitarians stand behind militarism," he added; "why should not the democracies stand behind the principles of honest administration and representative government?"[57] Figueres angered some U.S. officials with these statements and his continued participation in the democratic left, activities that threatened peace in the region. U.S. officials monitored his movements and pressured Ulate to stop Figueres's plotting with his friends against Somoza and Trujillo. Their efforts were only partly successful. Figueres persisted in supporting his friends, emphasizing that his actions were pro-American because they would ultimately create democratic stability in Latin America.[58]

Figueres made conscious efforts to win American support for his domestic and international policies, especially among liberal democratic groups. His studies in the United States and frequent visits there had provided him with insight into the country. After an interview with Don Pepe, political scientist Charles Anderson wrote, "Figueres believes that he understands the nature of contemporary United States' society better than many of the citizens of that nation. He is persuaded that much of the friction between Latin America and the United States is due to the failure of Latin American leaders to understand the civilization of their North American neighbors."[59] Figueres utilized this knowledge to advantage and created strong ties with important Americans.[60]

The ideology of Figueres and his allies won them much support in the United States, especially with "vital center" liberals in groups such as Americans for Democratic Action (ADA).[61] The platform of the PLN, especially its social welfare programs and anti-communism, strongly resembled the postwar liberalism of the ADA. Many informed Americans were familiar with the views of Figueres and the PLN because Figueres published many works in the United States, provided numerous interviews, and traveled frequently to the United States to lecture at universities and to assist at other functions.[62] Within the ADA, Figueres developed close associations with historian Arthur M. Schlesinger, Jr., and others who upheld the Costa Rican leader as a democratic model for Latin America.[63]

Figueres also associated with other anti-Communist American liberals. In 1950, Frances Grant, a long-time advocate for the International League for the Rights of Man and Venezuelan leader Rómulo Betancourt helped form the Inter-American Association for Democracy and Freedom (IADF). Prominent Americans from a variety of associations including the ADA and AFL joined the IADF. These included Schlesinger and Robert LaFollette of the ADA; labor activists such as Serafino Romualdi, Robert Alexander, and Ernest Schwartz; and Walter White of the National Association for the Advancement of Colored People. Sol Levitas of *The New Leader,* congressmen including Clifford Chase and Chet Holifield, and celebrities such as Pearl Buck and Eleanor Roosevelt also joined the group. Grant played the most important role as the group's secretary general, coordinating activities from her office in New York. She provided Latin American democratic liberals several forums in which to transmit their message, publishing their writings in the official publication, *Hemipherica,* organizing meetings, and sponsoring lectures.[64] As much as any other group in the United States, the IADF proved a powerful ally of the Latin American democratic liberals.

Sufficiently impressed by Figueres's ideology and dedication to democratic principles, the IADF invited him to speak at its inaugural meeting in Havana. Afterwards, it sponsored a series of lectures by Figueres in the United States in 1951. On 13 April 1951, it hosted a speech in New York City, advertising a presentation by the "former President of Costa Rica who saved his country from 'capture' by totalitarian forces."[65] Soon afterward it awarded Figueres the first citation for "Service to Inter-American Democracy."[66] Grant especially maintained close contact with Figueres and the PLN during the 1950s and would coordinate lobbying for Figueres among the liberals in the trying times of the first two years of his elected term.[67]

Figueres and his associates also had ties with the American Federation of Labor (AFL), especially the AFL coordinator for Latin America, Serafino Romualdi.[68] A Costa Rican and PLN member, Luis Alberto Monge, served as secretary general for the *Organización Regional Interamericana de Trabajadores,* a leading anti-Communist labor movement aligned with AFL.[69] During the junta and the first Figueres presidency, labor received strong support from administration officials, especially Padre Núñez and Monge. A leading adviser on Latin America to the AFL, Robert J. Alexander, reported in a memorandum to the AFL (a copy of which the State Department secured without his knowledge) that the labor "situation in Costa Rica is about hopeful as anywhere in Latin America." After visiting with Figueres, he characterized the new president as a "dreamer" who possessed a strong personal following. He believed Figueres was fundamentally pro-American, although he predicted a strong clash between the Figueres administration and the United Fruit Company.[70] Like other American groups, the AFL held the PLN up as an example for Latin America and for potential cooperation between labor and government.

The most important connection Figueres made with an American during Ulate's term occurred in early 1953. In March, Adolf A. Berle, Jr., traveled at the State Department's request to investigate charges by the U.S. embassy in Managua that Figueres was a Communist. After visiting with Figueres in San José and stopping in Nicaragua, Berle called the charges false. He criticized the U.S. officials in Nicaragua for having no contact with Central Americans other than Somoza's representatives, stressing that they even lacked the ability to speak Spanish. He reported to the Jackson Committee, a special executive group headed by William Jackson to investigate Communist aggression, that Figueres was an "anti-Communist liberal Democrat about comparable with Senator [Herbert H.] Lehman of New York."[71] He praised Figueres as a symbol of the younger intellectuals dedicated to democracy in Latin America. "Of the men who have or are likely to get popular support in Central America," Berle stated, "Figueres is easily the most dynamic, and I think the fairest-minded."[72] In conclusion, Berle denounced Somoza's authoritarianism, emphasizing that Figueres would provide more stability because of his respect for civil liberties and the support of the masses.[73]

Berle had traveled to the region not only to investigate Figueres but also to build support for U.S. efforts to isolate Guatemala. While in Costa Rica, he talked with Figueres about the perceived Communist infiltration of the Arbenz administration. When questioned on the issue, Don Pepe responded that he understood that no Soviet-backed government could be tolerated in Central America, and he recounted his role in expelling the Communists from Costa Rica. At the same time, he advised Washington to refrain from military actions through surrogates such as Somoza. Instead, he advocated pressuring Arbenz to remove the Communists from the government. If that failed, he backed sponsoring democratic groups in Guatemala against the Communists, creating a repeat of the victory in his country in 1948. He wanted changes and understood the importance of the Communist question, but he continued to oppose heavy-handed interventions by reactionaries.[74]

From this point forward, Berle proved a strong backer of Figueres in the State Department. He developed a close friendship with the Figueres family, sending his son to summer in Costa Rica. The connection was important because, although Berle was a loyal Democrat, he remained an adviser to the Eisenhower administration on Latin America. Berle also had close ties with the foreign policy establishment in Washington and New York. He participated in the Foreign Policy Council and numerous study groups that included politicians, journalists, and academicians such as Dean Rusk, Henry Kissinger, Arthur Schlesinger, Jr., Adlai Stevenson, and Chester Bowles. The relationship with Berle provided Figueres with a strong ally when he took office in 1953. Berle helped to assuage fears of Communist influence in Costa Rica and played a major role in helping the Costa Ricans secure U.S. aid in 1955 when the Nicaraguans assisted Calderón's attempt to overthrow Figueres.

Others in Washington continued to support Figueres and the PLN. In the State Department, career diplomats such as William T. Bennett, Robert Woodward, and Norman Armour, and retired diplomats such as Nathaniel Davis who had developed close ties with Figueres during the civil war and the junta era provided the Costa Ricans an important lobby in the State Department to deflect criticisms that developed during the early stages of the Figueres presidency. In addition, the *figueristas* maintained a strong following in the U.S. Congress. Prominent senators such as Paul Douglas, J. William Fulbright, and Wayne Morse, and other congressmen associated with the ADA and IADF also backed Figueres, believing that he served as a model for democratic leadership in Latin America. These connections furnished Figueres and his associates with strong allies at the height of McCarthyism and in a period characterized by an American tendency to equate nationalism with communism. When Somoza, Trujillo, and their cronies tried swaying conservatives in the United States, these Figueres allies acted as a counterbalance.

The convergence of political cultures between the PLN and important groups and individuals in the United States aided the *figueristas'* attempts to promote controversial nationalistic policies while maintaining American support when they took office in 1953. A Figueres biographer, Harold Bonilla, concluded: "José Figueres has made a great impression on international public opinion. In the United States he is considered representative of the best in Latin America and it would be a loss of time to try to convince anyone of the contrary." "To those Americans who believe in José Figueres," Bonilla added, "and they are legions, he is the Blessed Trinity: God the Father, God the Son and the Holy Spirit, all Three in One."[75] These private and public interests maintained contact with the State Department, other government officials, and the media during the Eisenhower administration and lobbied for the Figueres administration during its tenure. Much of the groundwork for the cooperation derived from a conscious attempt by Figueres and his advisers to garner U.S. support during the Ulate administration by actively working with the ADA, AFL, and IADF to promote their agenda.

While prominent Americans promoted Figueres as a model for Latin American leaders, others viewed him as a possible threat to American business and strategic interests. From 1951 forward, some officials in the embassy expressed concern about a possible PLN victory in 1953. First Secretary Alex Cohen called a March 1951 Figueres speech an example of his "well intentioned but highly confused mental process." He characterized Don Pepe's statements as "unintelligible jumble which constitutes the stock in trade of Mr. Figueres and his immediate coterie."[76] Others in the embassy emphasized that the "political struggle in Costa Rica today could be interpreted as one between radical theories of Figueres and his group and Costa Rica conservatism as championed by Ulate."[77] In early 1952, diplomats in the embassy went so far as to predict that Ulate's party would easily defeat the *figueristas* in the upcoming elections.[78]

Attacks on Figueres by his domestic enemies led some diplomats to scrutinize him more closely. The opposition originally backed the candidacy of Mario Echandi, although Ulate remained relatively uninvolved in the process. Vice President Rafael Oreamuno reported to the embassy that Figueres was a "mad man who by himself or through connections with Juan Bosch, Prio Socarrias, Arevelo and Arbenz, would be sure to get Costa Rica into trouble if he ever came to power."[79] Echandi even tried portraying Figueres as a Communist, underscoring his connections with revolutionaries in the democratic left who at one time had adopted communism as their ideology.[80]

While the *ulatistas* and others opposed to Figueres could not sway public opinion in Costa Rica, they did plant seeds of doubt among some U.S. officials. By mid-1952, the embassy recognized the inevitability of a Figueres victory, but embassy officials continued warning that he posed a potential problem. In August 1952 Chargé Philip Williams characterized Figueres as a political opportunist bent on disturbing the peace in the Caribbean Basin by attacking neighboring dictators. He denounced several of Figueres's advisers, especially Rómulo Betancourt, who had become Figueres's close friend after the IADF meeting in Havana, because of their association with the Costa Rican Communist party in the 1930s.[81] Although Betancourt had broken with the party in the late 1930s, Williams believed that he remained a Communist. While he refused to call Figueres a Communist, Williams warned that Figueres's programs might wreck the country.[82] In response, the CIA investigated the charges. Its agents reportedly tapped Figueres's phones in early 1953, but they apparently collected no definite information linking Figueres to the Communists although some CIA representatives remained suspicious of the Costa Rican.[83]

The most damaging blow to Figueres's reputation was the publication of a booklet entitled "Who and How We Were Betrayed" by his former associate Rosendo Argüello, Jr. The Nicaraguan reproduced a letter from

Figueres to his friend Edelberto Torres that called the United States and the State Department fools and promised economic reforms for Costa Rica more radical than the Communists. Figueres immediately denounced the letter as a forgery. While the embassy split on the validity of the charges, Williams wrote that "the Department should not completely disregard this evidence of possible anti-American feelings in Figueres, nor the possibility that he might be closer to communism than is generally believed."[84]

United Fruit officials also expressed concern that a victorious Figueres would challenge existing contracts. They warned of the anti-foreignism in his rhetoric and writing. In a public interview in early 1952, Figueres had stated that long-term contracts could be broken if doing so served the needs of the country. He emphasized that such a concept applied to United Fruit.[85] Second Secretary of the Embassy John B. Crume defended Figueres, pointing out that he had pledged not to nationalize industries without just compensation. He highlighted the junta's record and its commonsense approach to the banking system as evidence of Figueres's record.[86]

As the election approached in 1953, Washington prepared for a Figueres victory. He remained something of an enigma to many U.S. diplomats. For the most part, U.S. officials remained comparatively uninformed about his intentions, a fact compounded by the conflicting reports originating in Costa Rica and the region. With the exception of the year and a half that Figueres had served as president of the junta, he had not held public office, ensuring that U.S. officials had little on which to base their decisions. Few doubted his anti-Communist credentials, although the Argüello letter created some doubts about his sincerity. This uncertainty developed at a time when the U.S. policy was moving toward a much harder line against many nationalist movements. U.S. diplomats increasingly sought stability in Latin America, evidenced by the move closer toward the dictators of the region. U.S. policymakers faced the unknown with some trepidation.

Williams and several other embassy officials would have preferred that Ulate retain the presidency, but the Costa Rican constitution prohibited consecutive terms. To many U.S. diplomats, Ulate had represented a model Latin American leader during the postwar era. He had provided democratic stability, supported U.S. initiatives in international relations, and, more important, concentrated on domestic problems rather than upsetting the existing balance of power in the region. With Ulate, Washington achieved the best of all worlds: accommodation with only minor acts of independence.

Figueres would be more of a challenge for Washington. From past experience and continued surveillance of him, U.S. officials recognized that he would step in and immediately change the internal and international setting with his activist policies. Figueres's accession followed closely on the heels of the inauguration of a more conservative U.S. president, Dwight D. Eisenhower, and his advisers, such as Secretary of State John Foster Dulles. As demonstrated in Iran and Guatemala, the administration tolerated few nationalist challenges to U.S. hegemony. Figueres and his associates would face the difficult task of walking a precarious tightrope between nationalism and anti-Americanism.

7

RESISTANCE AND ACCOMMODATION

The United States and the Nationalism of José Figueres, 1953–1957

In August 1953, the Guatemalan Communist paper *Octubre* characterized the new president of Costa Rica, José "Don Pepe" Figueres, as an "unconditional servant of American imperialism" and the latest "United Fruit Company President."[1] Two years later, a conservative American columnist, Robert Johnson, denounced Figueres in very different terms. "Pinkos sound the same in any language," he stated; referring to the Costa Rican ship of state, he wrote, "Communism thrives on the Figueres!"[2]

Both these portrayals highlight the difficulty the United States encountered when confronting Third World nationalism in the post–World War II era. With leaders such as Figueres, Washington pursued often contradictory policies. In some cases (Guatemala, Iran, Vietnam, the Dominican Republic), it identified economic and political nationalism with anti-Americanism and communism and allied itself with reactionary forces to stem the revolutionary tide. In Costa Rica during his first elected term, Figueres implemented nationalistic programs, but the United States supported him, thus demonstrating some flexibility toward nationalistic governments during the cold war.

The *figueristas* were a major reason for the different American response. They promoted social programs that expanded the role of government in the economy, but they avoided large-scale seizures of private enterprise. While some conservative opponents in the United States and the Caribbean Basin characterized Figueres and his associates as Communists, the *figuerista* programs in fact differed little from those implemented in the United States during the progressive and New Deal eras, a point underscored by supporters of the PLN.

In international affairs, Figueres and his advisers better gauged American attitudes toward their activities than many nationalists, allowing them to navigate more skillfully the troubled waters between nationalism and anti-Americanism. They challenged the United States over United Fruit contracts and U.S. aid to the regional dictators, but Figueres's anti-communism and moderate plan of economic nationalism undermined his opponents' attempts to diminish Washington's support for him. While the Costa Rican leader's actions aggravated U.S. officials, they never really threatened the legacy of amicable relations between Washington and San José.

To secure the chance to promote their agenda, Figueres and the PLN had worked hard during the period leading to the 1953 elections. They had organized at the local and national level, winning broad support for their program and their heroism during the revolution. PLN organizers canvassed the countryside, encouraging Costa Ricans to vote. At the same time, the opposition remained relatively weak. The only true threat to Figueres was Ulate, but the constitution prohibited him from running again. The opposition responded by nominating Fernando Castro, a wealthy landowner. The U.S. embassy emphasized that Castro had a colorless personality and relied on "a weak platform . . . based principally on anti-Figuerismo." The majority of Castro's support came from conservatives and some foreigners who feared Figueres's social and international policies. Somoza even donated $20,000 to Castro's campaign.[3]

As the July 1953 election approached, tensions rose. Figueres appeared comfortably in the lead. Even so, he publicly promised to accept the returns as long as the elections were honest.[4] Despite Figueres's guarantees, Ulate prepared for the worst. He organized a special force of fifteen men to serve as bodyguards for Castro in the event of an upset victory.[5]

The preparations proved unnecessary. Few problems arose during the balloting, and U.S. officials characterized the process as "an example of democratic education rarely seen in Latin America or elsewhere and a tribute to the country's history."[6] Figueres and the PLN won an overwhelming victory, garnering 65 percent of the vote and taking thirty of the forty-five congressional seats.[7] To explain the crushing defeat, the embassy blamed Castro's reliance on his negative tactics and Figueres's tireless and positive campaign.[8]

Various groups and individuals in the United States greeted the PLN victory enthusiastically. In addition to the Americans for Democratic Action, the Inter-American Association for Democracy and Freedom, and

Congress, officials in the Eisenhower administration also liked Figueres and the PLN. The president's brother, Milton Eisenhower, would later call Don Pepe "one of the real fighters for democratic freedom and social justice in Latin America."[9] The support of these people was important: when Figueres implemented several controversial policies in his first two years in office, they provided Costa Rica with a loyal following in Washington.

Public portrayals of the new president in the United States were also generally favorable. *Newsweek* characterized him as "a MIT-educated coffee planter, [who] led a popular revolt which in five weeks overthrew the politicians and their Red allies." "Figueres offered the voter a kind of Costa Rican New Deal," the magazine added, and "expressed friendship for the people of the United States."[10] *Time* highlighted experiments at Figueres's *finca* where he "set up a private welfare state for his workers. He built them clean bungalows, saw them well fed from a community vegetable farm and dairy that provided free milk for every child." The article emphasized that Figueres had modeled his administration on the middle-of-the-road socialist government of Denmark. "Our movement is not in any sense a Marxian revolution. . . . It is really a revolution of the middle class," Figueres was quoted as saying.[11]

While many Americans viewed Figueres and his associates positively, not all observers embraced the PLN victory optimistically. The first secretary of the embassy in San José, Alex Cohen, characterized Figueres as a political opportunist who was pro-United States when it served him.[12] Assistant Secretary of State John M. Cabot and the new U.S. ambassador to Costa Rica, Robert Hill, agreed that Figueres was "quick but not bright, full of contradictions, unscrupulous, ambitious, vain, vacillating."[13]

The State Department also appraised the new president's advisers in a memorandum, "The Men Around Figueres." The embassy characterized the most prominent members of the administration as middle-class reformers, emphasizing that "of the group now closest around Figueres, none carries the general reputation of an extremist nor of a dishonest character." The report added that "all profess pro–United States sentiments or at least, are not reputed as unfriendly to the United States." "No one rivals Figueres in formation of party policy and programs. . . . Figueres is a man who is still growing, with a mind continually at work with new concepts." Nevertheless, the report concluded, "in the writer's opinion, Figueres can be influenced considerably, when handled adroitly by persons of determined personality and convictions."[14]

The comparatively positive appraisals did not help assuage the fears of some U.S. diplomats who believed that Figueres might be a loose cannon. State Department officials noted that Figueres's resounding success allowed him to claim the "mandate of the people," and that the PLN control of the Legislative Assembly assured him a free hand to promote a legislative agenda. They warned that disputes might arise because his programs included the reduction of the profits of the United Fruit Company and the American and Foreign Power Company, the primary North American investors in Costa Rica.[15]

U.S. officials correctly perceived Figueres's determination to secure better concessions for his country from American companies, primarily UFCO. The bargaining went through several stages and began even before the elections. While visiting Washington in May 1953, Figueres met with Thomas Mann of the State Department. He referred in vague terms to several possible courses, including the nationalization of a UFCO operating subsidiary, stock ownership in the company by the Costa Rican government, or an increase in income taxes. When queried about the proposals, UFCO officials responded that a contract already existed and that government ownership of its stock was a bad idea, although they hinted that they might pay higher income taxes.[16]

Although Figueres concentrated on the elections during the summer, UFCO remained an important issue. He emphasized that if he won, his administration would prefer open and honest negotiations.[17] His associates emphasized that the negative reactions of the United States toward the UFCO controversy in Guatemala strongly influenced his responses. As a result, he downplayed critics' accusations that he was a dangerous leftist by denying any intent to nationalize foreign industries to subsidize new social programs.[18] "People in the United States are always saying something must be done about underdeveloped countries," Figueres declared, "but when someone comes along to do something, these same people draw back, afraid of change, simply because it represents a change in the old established order of things."[19] "We did not try to kill the goose which lays the golden eggs," Figueres would later state, "rather we say to it that she laid them here in our nest."[20] He repeatedly assured Ambassador Hill that he could be anti-UFCO while remaining pro-American and anti-Communist.[21]

Figueres started seriously negotiating with UFCO after winning the election. A shrewd bargainer, he initially demanded more than he expected. In a meeting with the president of UFCO, Kenneth Redmond, he proposed a 10 percent income tax increase and the expropriation of company holdings in the Quepos region as payment for back taxes. When Redmond protested that the existing contract would be valid for another twenty years, the president reminded him that conditions had changed and Costa Rica deserved a better agreement.[22]

UFCO officials immediately sought State Department intervention. In a meeting with Undersecretary of State Walter Bedell Smith, UFCO Chairman Thomas Jefferson Coolidge attacked Figueres. He produced an article written by Figueres in the *New Leader* that he argued demonstrated Don Pepe's belief that foreign capital was a short-term loan and not a permanent investment. The work contained some inflammatory language. "Foreign ownership of a large segment of a country's economy or territory constitutes 'economic occupation,' " Figueres had written. "This is no wild fancy. I know. I am a citizen of a 'banana republic,' " he continued.[23] Coolidge also denounced recent reports that Figueres planned work stoppages to force UFCO's submission. When Smith requested recommendations on possible action, the UFCO chairman asked the State Department to stress publicly the sanctity of contracts. Although he expressed distaste for the proposal as unneeded intervention, Smith agreed to act before Figueres's inauguration.[24]

Initially, many State Department personnel favored United Fruit. In September, Charles Burrows, director of the Office of Middle American Affairs, and Congressman Donald Jackson toured Central America and met with Figueres to emphasize contractual obligations and just compensation. Furthermore, in early October 1953, Assistant Secretary of State Cabot made speeches in Boston and Washington intended primarily for Figueres. In the speeches, Cabot emphasized the U.S. government's strong belief in the inviolability of contracts.[25]

The Costa Ricans closely monitored Cabot's speeches and other sources of U.S. opinion. The Foreign Ministry filed the October speeches, and the embassy in Washington also forwarded to San José copies of editorials and stories in important U.S. newspapers relating to Costa Rica and Latin America.[26] The Costa Rican network ranged very far. In January 1954, the Costa Rican embassy in Washington responded to an editorial in the Clarksville, Tennessee, *Leaf-Chronicle.* An embassy official denied the presence of a Communist plot to destroy coffee production in Costa Rica because the farmers of his country maintained prosperity and the Communists possessed no influence in areas where the people existed happily. At the bottom of the clipping the author wrote, "pretty small but this is the American heartland."[27] In addition, Figueres read the *New York Times* every day to ascertain American opinion toward his actions and those of other nationalists.[28] These materials provided the *figueristas* the insight to make more informed decisions in the negotiations and to anticipate their opponents' criticisms.

As the bargaining continued, State Department officials tempered their views toward Figueres. Already smarting from Latin American accusations of exerting undue influence in favor of UFCO in Guatemala, U.S. officials wanted to avoid additional charges of imperialism. In a meeting with Coolidge and other UFCO officials in November, Cabot warned, "it is better that they [UFCO] bend before they are broken, and I trust that they share this view."[29] He agreed that UFCO had a legitimate contract, but he feared intervening on the company's side. "Due to the deplorable public relations of the United Fruit Company," he stated, "we should not uphold the United Fruit Company in anything which appears abusive."[30]

The State Department privately urged UFCO officials to make concessions, but it continued pressing Figueres to reach a settlement. At the University of Florida and in Columbus, Ohio, Cabot made additional speeches that promoted the sanctity of contracts and private business, writing in his diary, "the Costa Rican newspapers 'got' my remarks at Columbus—all to good."[31] Figueres responded by publicly reiterating his belief in the importance of foreign capital to Costa Rica's development and emphasizing that his administration would rely on negotiation, although he never rejected using expropriation.[32]

Figueres's statements helped contribute to an eventual softening of the State Department's position. Although he publicly proposed a UFCO buyout, privately he supported a fifty-fifty split of profits and a guarantee of equality in pay and employment for Costa Rican workers. In November, Ambassador Hill traveled with Figueres on a three-day inspection of the Pacific banana-producing areas. After returning, he reported that Don Pepe was far from set on his course of action and if handled properly would agree to a mutually satisfactory arrangement.[33]

In the United States, various groups and individuals also portrayed Figueres and his associates as reasonable people. *Time* underscored his promise to provide equitable compensation and his assertion that he had proposed a simple plan of sale, not expropriation by violent, forceful seizure. The magazine declared that "when measured against the slam-bang attitude of Guatemala's Red-led land reformers, the Figueres approach practically reeked of sweet reasonableness."[34] Harry Kantor, a leading academic analyst of Central America, described Figueres as neither "a lawyer, a rich man's son, nor a professional soldier" like other presidents in Latin America, but a well-educated farmer with "tremendous energy and a great talent for organization."[35] "The new government is anti-Communist," he concluded, "and animated by a devotion to democratic procedure. It is a model other Latin American reformers could well follow."[36]

Figueres's approach also impressed members of the U.S. Congress. In early February, after attacking the Guatemalan government, Senator Fulbright praised the government of Costa Rica for "seeking an orderly and agreeable" settlement with United Fruit. He added that "both sides have respect for the sanctity of existing contracts, to which amendments can be made only by mutual agreement. . . . This should be the model course for solution of difficulties."[37] Even though Figueres posed a serious challenge to UFCO, positive perceptions such as these helped to prevent U.S. officials from overreacting to accusations leveled by his opponents.

Not everyone embraced Figueres and his programs so optimistically. Conservative congressmen, many with links to the Caribbean Basin dictators, tried undermining Don Pepe's position in the State Department and on Capitol Hill. Utilizing the *New Leader* article, "We Do Not Want Foreign Investments," several congressmen characterized Figueres as a Communist who threatened American businesses. They also underscored his ties with members of the democratic-left, such as the former Communist leader Betancourt.

In a meeting with Ambassador Hill, Figueres challenged their accusations. He produced a letter to the editors of the *New Leader* complaining that his title, "A Bold New Program," had been changed. He added that his country needed private investment and that any other policy was insane. Again addressing congressional criticism, he declared that "liberal governments such as his would always be criticized by conservative U.S. Congressmen" as long as his country promoted social programs and resisted U.S. business domination.[38] Finally, Figueres invited a congressional investigating committee to come to San José so that he could "set the boys straight on his economic policy."[39]

The Costa Ricans also launched a campaign in the United States to undermine their opponents' criticism. In Washington, Ambassador Antonio

Facio emphasized that his country's negotiations with UFCO were exclusively commercial and designed to create a just division of profits.[40] Speaking at the New England Pan American Society in Boston on 27 February 1954, Facio stressed his country's intention to maintain a positive relationship with the United States based on good faith and a firm grounding in international law.[41]

The Figueres administration's campaign successfully distanced the administration from charges of anti-Americanism and communism such as those leveled against Arbenz in Guatemala. The new assistant secretary of state for inter-American affairs, Henry Holland, declared in April 1954 that there was no evidence that Figueres was a Communist. He described Figueres's programs as nationalistic and added that, although socialistic, his party had consistently fought the Communists. Referring to Don Pepe's close association with prominent Caribbean exiles, Holland argued that "we should exercise caution against judging leftist leaders such as Betancourt and Figueres as Communists."[42]

Without State Department backing, UFCO proved more compliant in its negotiations with Costa Rica. After some heated discussions, both sides accepted a new contract on 4 June 1954. The agreement increased the tax on UFCO earnings from 15 to 30 percent. With land taxes and other dues, officials estimated the total tax rate was 42 percent. The company also agreed to pay customs duties on about half of its imported railway, harbor, and irrigation materials and accepted a new minimum wage law based on a cost-of-living formula. Finally, UFCO turned over to the government three major hospitals, forty-five dispensaries, and sixty-eight schools. Experts estimated that the thirty-four-year contract provided Costa Rica a net gain of more than $10 million per year in revenue.[43] The final settlement caused Daniel James to conclude, "The agreement was made possible because President José Figueres, while a hard bargainer and thoroughgoing nationalist, is a staunch anti-communist with whom one can do business."[44]

Figueres thus secured a major victory without damaging his credibility in either the United States or Costa Rica. The *figueristas* successfully negotiated a favorable contract by understanding the complexities of acceptable American business practices.[45] Although leftist leaders questioned the extent of the victory, the United States demonstrated in Guatemala and later in Cuba that it tolerated challenges to the existing economic system only within certain fixed limits. A more radical program would have been costly to Costa Rica both diplomatically and economically. The United States had a long-standing policy of overpowering challenges in the region, and it often would repeat the process unnecessarily in future instances.

Figueres clashed not only with American business interests but also with Washington over regional issues. In 1954, the United States called a meeting of the Organization of American States in Caracas. Spurred by intensified cold war clashes in Europe and Asia, U.S. policymakers, led by Secretary of State John Foster Dulles, designed the meeting primarily to pass a resolution calling for actions to curb communism in the western hemisphere, an obvious attack on Guatemala.[46] Responding to a request by the Venezuelan party, *Acción Democrática,* Figueres immediately announced that his country would boycott the Caracas Conference to protest the rule of the Venezuelan dictator, Marcos Pérez. Don Pepe insisted that he would attend only if Pérez released political prisoners and made democratic changes.[47] His country's absence, Figueres proclaimed, would be "the most eloquent cry, calling attention to the long-abandoned problem of internal democracy in Latin America." Figueres added, "I feel that Costa Rica is making a sacrifice for democracy . . . by not attending, and I am confident that even if we displease our democratic friends momentarily, the ultimate result of our heroic action will be encouragement for the democratic countries to fight hard for the good causes at the conference."[48]

The State Department immediately condemned Figueres's stance and encouraged him to rethink his position. It wanted a major democratic spokesman of Latin America present in Caracas to support its proposals. Ambassador Hill and other U.S. officials sought to entice Figueres into attending with promises of important discussions on economic assistance and the dispute between the United States and Guatemala.[49] Unswayed, Figueres protested that Washington's choice of sites legitimized Pérez's dictatorship.

The State Department tried other tactics. It drafted the former ambassador to Costa Rica and Figueres's good friend Nathaniel P. Davis to persuade Figueres to reconsider the action. Davis complied, urging the president to reconsider, arguing that Costa Rica could best protect democracy and self-determination by attending the conference.[50] The retired diplomat also reported to Figueres that Hill had expressed concern that Costa Rica's boycott would damage U.S.–Costa Rican relations, permitting Figueres's critics to attack him for refusing to support U.S. initiatives against Communist aggressors in the western hemisphere.[51]

Others in the United States, including Adolf Berle, also pressed Figueres and his advisers to attend the conference. At a dinner party in New York, Berle and Núñez clashed over the issue after the latter characterized the conference as a "ghastly caricature." Berle responded that the people of the region needed "to make pictures even if they were not wholly sincere and not wholly accurate," emphasizing that over time they could turn them into reality.[52]

Even some members of Figueres's own cabinet encouraged him to go to Caracas.[53] Ambassador Facio complained that Costa Rica's absence would hurt the Organization of American States, not Pérez. He stressed that the meeting would help ensure the peaceful settlement of disputes and create more dedication to democratic principles. "No one ever overcomes an enemy by staying away from the battlefield," he concluded.[54] At the last minute, even Betancourt tried persuading Don Pepe to send a delegation to Caracas, fearing that the boycott would cause Figueres additional problems with his opponents in the region and with the United States.[55]

The fears of Betancourt and Facio were not unfounded. Tensions from the boycott contributed to a cooling in relations between Ambassador Hill and Figueres. The conservative Republican from New Hampshire became increasingly critical of Don Pepe. He underscored that "Figuere's [*sic*] decision [was] partly idealistic but it also [was a] grandstand play for support of liberal elements in hemisphere. As sole nation not attending, he will get publicity far out [of] proportion to size [of the] country."[56] Later, Hill denounced Figueres for infiltrating the embassy and buying off staff members with prostitutes and drugs. He called the president a two-faced "chameleon" and a troublemaker in the region. In addition, he dragged out a January 1950 letter from Figueres to a Nicaraguan friend in which Figueres reportedly wrote that he could fool the Americans and establish a leftist government in Costa Rica.[57] Hill went so far as to accuse Figueres and Berle of conspiring to replace him with a more sympathetic ambassador.[58]

Despite the pressures from all sides, Figueres remained determined to protest the dictatorship of Pérez and remained true to his principles of opposing authoritarianism. He responded to his critics that "it was a matter of conscience for us in the Government to balance the merits of that [the State Department's] opinion, with the possible long-range benefits of our protest and non-assistance." "As to the immediate effects on public opinion," he continued, "I can say that, by and large, North American comments on our attitudes were unfavorable, while Latin American editorials and private statements were overwhelmingly favorable. Maybe this illustrates the difference in the two types of minds."[59]

Although dedicated to his beliefs, Figueres understood the need to counter his opponents' criticism that his action undercut U.S. policies against the Communists in Guatemala. He promised Costa Rican support of any resolution designed to extend democratic principles.[60] In an open letter, he declared, "We suffered the outrages of Communism and can testify that Communism is an attempt to destroy democratic institutions. . . . It is clear that Communism and Russian aggression are identical, and it is our duty to stand where the hemisphere stands."[61] Despite this statement, tensions remained high between Figueres and some State Department officials when Costa Rica boycotted the Caracas Conference. Nevertheless, Figueres's long record of anticommunism and moderate plan of economic nationalism helped ensure that most people in the State Department and the Eisenhower administration continued to support his regime when his enemies tried to overthrow him in early 1955.

Figueres solidified his anti-Communist reputation by working with Washington to find a solution for the perceived Guatemalan problem, although he differed markedly with the United States over methods to deal with the issue.[62] Earlier, the United States had pressured him to make a stand against the Guatemalans. Figueres always agreed on the seriousness of the Guatemalan situation, drawing many parallels between Guatemala in 1953 and Costa Rica before 1948. Nevertheless, he encouraged Washington to demonstrate restraint and denounced Somoza's proposal for unilateral action. Figueres expressed concern that Latin Americans would be incensed by U.S. intervention. Instead, he proposed encouraging liberal-democratic Guatemalans to regain control of the sidetracked revolution, but he sharply criticized direct military aid and the involvement of Somoza and other reactionaries.[63]

The U.S. role in assisting Castillo Armas in overthrowing Arbenz dismayed Figueres. He hated that Arbenz's replacement was an authoritarian who probably would ally himself with Somoza and the other dictators of the region. However, Figueres failed to criticize Washington's actions in Guatemala with the intensity of other Latin Americans.[64] To Figueres,

Arbenz had acted irresponsibly. Like Calderón and Picado in Costa Rica during the 1940s, he had become a Communist dupe and deserved removal. Figueres wanted a democratic rebellion in Guatemala like his own in Costa Rica, but such a revolution never occurred and he was powerless to change that fact.[65]

Figueres's anticommunism proved the deciding factor in helping him to maintain U.S. support as he sponsored nationalistic domestic and international policies. This point was very important. His opponents in the Caribbean Basin and the United States continued to portray him as a Communist because of his social programs and his aid to liberation movements in Nicaragua, Venezuela, and the Dominican Republic. Still, most Americans remained pro-Figueres, continually emphasizing that he was a nationalist reformer and not a Communist. The State Department's position proved significant. When the Caribbean dictators joined with Costa Rican exiles to try to depose Figueres, first in the summer of 1954 and later in January 1955, Washington responded quickly and assisted him in defeating a Somoza-inspired invasion.

The event that precipitated armed conflict between the two countries was an attempt by Nicaraguan exiles to assassinate Somoza in April 1954. Utilizing Costa Rican arms, the conspirators infiltrated Nicaragua with plans to murder the dictator. Somoza's agents uncovered the scheme and captured or killed all the plotters. Somoza personally tortured the captured plotters and secured confessions implicating Figueres. Managua immediately denounced San José's complicity and recalled its ambassador. Figueres denied the charges, but Somoza remained unappeased and a confrontation appeared imminent.[66]

The incident alarmed U.S. diplomats, and as Managua and San José issued charges and countercharges, they counseled restraint.[67] In July, Somoza dispatched his national guard to the Costa Rican border.[68] In response, embassy officials told Figueres that the United States would "step in" if Nicaragua invaded.[69] Washington also agreed to sell the Costa Ricans a significant quantity of arms for their civil guard.[70] On 9 July, Figueres asked Hill for direct military assistance. The ambassador urged negotiation between the two disputants, but instructed the chief of the U.S. military mission in Costa Rica, Col. Harry A. Welsch, to cooperate fully with the Figueres administration in defending San José.[71]

The State Department recognized the danger posed by Somoza's plot to replace Figueres with his crony, Calderón. State Department officials in

San José predicted widespread condemnation of the United States if it failed to respond, especially in light of recent events in Guatemala. They also warned that if the *calderonistas* again seized power the Communists might return to prominence in Costa Rica. As a result, U.S. diplomats questioned Somoza.[72] The Nicaraguan dictator denied the charges, but he warned that Figueres's meddling remained a sore spot with regional leaders. He accused Figueres of "crying wolf" to secure military equipment, especially fighter planes. He promised he would not launch a surprise attack, but he added that when he acted, "I will do it so fast Figueres won't even have time to put his pants on."[73]

The Venezuelan government joined Nicaragua in condemning Figueres and lobbying the State Department to withdraw support from him. The Venezuelans charged that he posed a serious threat to the stability and solidarity of the region because he provided aid to Betancourt and Juan Bosch. In response, Raymond Leddy, the State Department's officer in charge of Central American affairs, warned Venezuela's security minister, Pedro Estrada, that the Guatemalan situation remained the most important issue and that any actions against Figueres were unacceptable.[74] Despite a Venezuelan promise to do nothing, in a strange episode two weeks later a Venezuelan plane dropped leaflets on San José and Alajuela portraying Figueres and Betancourt as lovers.[75]

Ulate also attacked the administration after Figueres helped defeat a constitutional amendment that would have allowed Ulate to run for the presidency in 1957. The former president's editorials in the *Diario de Costa Rica* increasingly denounced the administration's corruption at home and recklessness abroad. On several occasions, Ulate's former ambassador to the United States, Rafael Oreamuno, visited the State Department and criticized Figueres, urging U.S. officials to create closer ties with his group.[76]

As the tensions increased, the State Department redoubled its efforts to defuse the situation. Secretary of State Dulles emphasized that the United States needed to prevent "adverse world reaction from overthrow of legitimately elected liberal democratic Costa Rican Government, for which the United States would be censured because of our predominant position in area and alleged role in recent change of government in Guatemala."[77] Dulles outlined "positive steps" to ease the problems. He ordered Assistant Secretary of State Holland to castigate Costa Rican and Nicaraguan officials for disturbing regional politics during the Guatemalan crisis. Hol-

El pájaro Figueres - El marico Betancourt

**Pájaro es el Presidente
y pájaro su asesor
de pájaros es el frente
qué pajarera, señor!!**

In 1954, Venezuelan planes dropped leaflets such as this one on the major cities in Costa Rica. This leaflet portrayed Betancourt and Figueres as homosexuals and criticized the relationship. U.S. embassy officials forwarded several copies to the State Department although they provided little comment on the incident.

land complied, and at a meeting with diplomats from both countries he emphasized that the United States expected Nicaragua to respect its OAS obligations and prevent any invasion from originating on its territory. He also advised Costa Rica to expel fifteen Nicaraguan exiles whom the Somoza government feared. Finally, he promised immediate delivery of

Costa Rica's recently purchased military equipment to offset Nicaraguan arms superiority.[78]

Despite U.S. attempts at mediation, the standoff persisted. In late July, Somoza sent additional troops to the border. "If Figueres Wants War," the Nicaraguan paper *La Prensa Libre* threatened, "He Can Have It."[79] As the bellicose language increased, the United States prepared for the worst. The State Department asked Brig. Gen. Russell L. Vittrup to ready plans for using American forces in Costa Rica's defense. It imposed several stipulations, including the limitation of objectives to military targets to prevent unnecessary civilian deaths and the confinement of military operations to Costa Rica. More important, only President Eisenhower could order the deployment of U.S. troops.[80]

For the moment, direct U.S. involvement was unnecessary. The pressures eased after Puerto Rico offered Betancourt and other exiles asylum.[81] Contented momentarily and recognizing the futility of challenging Costa Rica and the United States, Somoza withdrew his troops and the war of words subsided. Although a crisis appeared to have been averted, Hill urged Washington to insist that Figueres cease his adventurism, stressing that if he failed to comply the United States might not assist him the next time.[82]

For nearly four months tempers abated, but the problems persisted. In November 1954, rumors again circulated that Costa Rican exiles operating in Nicaragua were planning to overthrow Figueres.[83] Somoza continued providing arms and training to Calderón's forces, while the Venezuelan government funneled money and supplies to them. Learning from their summer failures, the plotters changed tactics. To undermine the ability of the United States and the Organization of American States to intervene under existing treaties, they planned an internal revolt without the appearance of foreign interference. They wanted to infiltrate Costa Rica, assassinate top officials, and attack military targets. Once the rebellion began, the insurgents believed that the disenchanted conservative landowning class and possibly even Ulate would rally to their side.[84]

The reports alarmed U.S. officials. Some feared that Calderón might win because of the political divisions in Costa Rica and because the rebels possessed a formidable air force of several P-47 fighter planes. Costa Rica could offer no aerial resistance, and U.S. diplomats understood the significance of airpower after Armas's coup in Guatemala. To offset the rebel advantage, Undersecretary of State Herbert Hoover, Jr., asked Secretary of

Defense Charles E. Wilson to send six interceptors to Panama with orders to protect Costa Rica in the event of hostilities.[85] *Time* seized on the concept, declaring that "with deadly U.S. jets only 30 minutes away, Tacho [Somoza] may find that there is not money enough in Nicaragua to tempt any air soldier of fortune to risk combat in a World War II propeller job."[86]

U.S. officials made other preparations to defend Costa Rica. The Joint Chiefs of Staff reported on 26 November that plans still existed for the "expeditious deployment" of U.S. ground and air forces in Costa Rica at Figueres's request and the authorization of Eisenhower. The Joint Chiefs added that the United States Air Force had scheduled a F-84 Thunderjet demonstration in the Canal Zone on 24 November and urged that the display be used to demonstrate U.S. capabilities in the region.[87] Finally, the Costa Ricans received 3,500 M-1 rifles, 500 Thompson submachine guns, several machine guns, rocket launchers, mortars, and ammunition from American sources.[88]

The Costa Ricans also moved to protect themselves. Figueres informed U.S. officials that any attempt to overthrow his government would result in a declaration of war on Nicaragua to force OAS action. In Washington, Facio requested that two U.S. destroyers be sent to Costa Rica as a deterrent. The State Department rejected the appeal and recommended OAS mediation. While Facio emphasized that only Washington could prevent bloodshed and that OAS machinery had proved slow and sometimes ineffective in the past, State Department officials insisted on OAS negotiations until they failed.[89]

As the rebels made preparations, Figueres's allies in the Caribbean Basin rallied to his side. On 27 November, a prominent member of the democratic left movement, Governor Luis Múñoz of Puerto Rico, petitioned Eisenhower to assist Figueres. He declared that Costa Rica "undoubtedly is one of the few countries in Latin America that measures up to the standards of a genuine democracy and Figueres is among the friends of the United States in the region pointedly because his friendship arises from common ideals of freedom." Múñoz denounced the "so-called revolutionaries" and proclaimed that Costa Rica's democracy could not fall into the hands of the regional dictators. He encouraged Eisenhower to employ any means necessary to protect the Costa Rican government.[90]

Throughout December, all the major participants prepared for the rebel attack. In Washington, intelligence reports were rather pessimistic and criticized Figueres. "His socialistic theories and international policies not only have alienated influential sectors of national opinion," the CIA asserted, "but have intensified old enmities with powerful foreign adversaries."[91] State Department sources underscored additional arms acquisitions by the rebels and Somoza and revealed the movement of pilots and airplanes from Guatemala. Finally, Somoza informed the U.S. ambassador to Nicaragua, Thomas Whelan, of impending internal problems in Costa Rica.[92] In response, the new U.S. ambassador to Costa Rica, Robert Woodward, emphasized that rebel air superiority posed a serious threat to Figueres and recommended that the State Department ask the NSC to determine whether to request that the OAS invoke the Rio Treaty if hostilities should begin.[93]

Activities had slowed during the Christmas holidays, but the long anticipated assault began on 11 January 1955 when a West Point graduate, Teodoro Picado, Jr., led five hundred rebel troops into northern Costa Rica.[94] That same day, rebel planes strafed San José, Cartago, and Liberia. A rebel radio station, identified as the "Voice of the Authentic Anti-Communist Revolutionary Army," compared Figueres to Arbenz and called on the Costa Rican people to rise up and expel the Communist *figueristas*.[95]

Rebel pleas for popular support fell on deaf ears; the Costa Rican people supported Figueres. While Picado remained in northern Costa Rica under the protection of Somoza, the Costa Rican civil guard and a hastily organized "minuteman" army moved northward to repulse the invasion. Civilians mobilized to fill the jobs vacated by soldiers. The San José boy scouts, for example, directed traffic so that policemen could join the army.[96]

In the United States, numerous groups and individuals rallied behind Figueres. On 12 January, Arthur M. Schlesinger, Jr., representing the ADA, exhorted Eisenhower to rush military supplies to the Costa Rican government to repel the unprovoked aggression.[97] In addition, Berle petitioned Dulles, Nelson A. Rockefeller, Jr., and other State Department officials to aid Figueres.[98] He also lined up support in the U.S. Congress and in the news agencies in Washington and Europe. A close associate of Berle, Senator Paul Douglas, encouraged Dulles to prevent Nicaragua from assisting the attack on Costa Rica. He characterized Figueres as a "genuine liberal" who deserved protection from the "highly reactionary dictatorships."[99] On the House floor, Rep. Albert Morano pleaded with Dulles to take "immediate and vigorous action" to end the hostilities.[100] The first vice-president of the AFL, Matthew Woll, issued a public statement entitled "Stop the War against Democratic Costa Rica! Preserve the Peace in

Central America!"[101] An overwhelming number of concerned Americans warned that if Costa Rica fell, political progress in Central America would suffer a tragic setback.[102]

With the assistance of the United States and the OAS, the Figueres administration moved quickly to defeat the insurgents. As early as 8 January, Costa Rica had requested OAS intervention to prevent bloodshed, but no action occurred. When the rebels crossed the border, however, the OAS Central Council convened and after some debate created an investigating committee. Representatives from the United States, Mexico, Brazil, Paraguay, and Ecuador immediately boarded USAF transports to make an on-the-spot investigation of the fighting in northern Costa Rica. The OAS also created an international aerial patrol to monitor outside interference.[103]

While the OAS organized for action, the State Department moved to end the hostilities. On 12 January, Dulles ordered Ambassador Whelan to warn Somoza that "public opinion and Congress here aroused by possibility that revolutionary forces [are] receiving air and ground facilities from sources outside Costa Rica."[104] That same day, the Costa Rican government received three thousand rounds of .50 caliber antiaircraft ammunition from the Canal Zone.[105] In an NSC meeting the following day, CIA Director Allen Dulles characterized the situation in Costa Rica as having taken on "a certain *opera bouffe* quality" after Somoza, the Nicaraguan pistol-shooting champion, challenged Figueres to a duel. Figueres declined, telling the Nicaraguan strongman to "grow up" and describing him as "crazy as a goat in the summer sun." Figueres agreed to accept the challenge, but only on the deck of the Soviet submarine Somoza reportedly had captured. Needless to say, the duel never occurred.[106] While the clash had comic episodes, Dulles and others recognized the seriousness of the situation and redoubled their attempts to end the conflict.[107]

While Allen Dulles appeared concerned with the events in Costa Rica, a difficult question surrounds the CIA role in the *calderonista* invasion. Figueres and several authors accused the CIA of assisting the rebels as repayment to Somoza for his role in the Guatemalan coup and to punish Figueres for his boycott of the Caracas Conference. The actual amount of assistance cannot be determined without greater access to CIA files. It does appear that the CIA at the least had advance knowledge of the attack and the insurgents' plans. During a courtesy call to Allen Dulles in November 1954, Ambassador Woodward recalled that one of the director's first remarks revolved around denying any responsibility for the attempts to overthrow Figueres. Despite the protests, many argued that the actions of the Costa Rican exiles too closely resembled the tactics employed in Guatemala and that much of the circumstantial evidence clearly indicated some CIA involvement. If the CIA had any role, the supporters of Figueres in the State Department clearly outmaneuvered the CIA operatives.[108]

The turning point occurred on 15 January when the investigating committee and U.S. officials in San José reported that rebel aircraft, operating from Nicaraguan bases, had bombed and strafed targets in Costa Rica. It also noted that USAF reconnaissance flights had uncovered supply lines running from Nicaragua to Picado's forces. To offset the rebels' air superiority and thwart Somoza's intervention, the committee recommended immediate OAS action.[109]

The United States and the Organization of American States reacted quickly. On 16 January, following a Costa Rican appeal, the OAS granted the United States permission to sell the Costa Ricans four P-51 Mustang fighter aircraft. Within a day, USAF pilots ferried the planes from National Guard bases in Texas to Costa Rica. American experts gave Costa Rican pilots a crash course in handling the aircraft and the next day, the newly formed Costa Rican air force flew sorties against the aggressors. The new aerial presence was pivotal, and within a week the rebel pilots surrendered to Nicaraguan officials.[110]

Somoza remained the last obstacle to a peaceful settlement. When the rebel movement foundered, he rushed his own forces to the border under the pretext of protecting his country against a perceived Costa Rican threat. The OAS responded quickly, fearing Somoza would fabricate an incident. On 20 January, the investigating committee created a neutral zone three miles on each side of the border and forbade Nicaraguan and Costa Rican troops from entering it until 25 January. In that period, the committee ordered the insurgents to leave the area or face extermination by the Costa Rican army. Sufficiently convinced of the futility of continuing, the rebels retreated across the border and surrendered to Nicaraguan officials. In addition, the Nicaraguans arrested Costa Rican exile leaders in Managua.[111]

The press in the United States generally favored the Costa Rican government and the *figueristas*. *Time* praised Figueres's "blue-jean militia armed with their own rifles and the pilots of the Mustangs who had no formal training in such technical aircraft. They beat Picado, the West Pointer, and a well-armed and trained rebel force." The article underscored that Figueres belittled Picado: "You can send them to school, but you can't give them brains," Figueres was quoted as saying.[112] A *New York Times* editorial commended the OAS and the United States for extending aid to Figueres and providing Somoza with "a lesson that he and other military dictators are unlikely to forget."[113] The lobbying of the Costa Ricans, Berle, and others clearly influenced the U.S. press, which in turn affected American perceptions of the conflict.

Commendations for the U.S. support of the Figueres administration came from all over the world. An editorial in *America* declared, "It cannot be said that the United States intervened on this occasion in support of a corrupt and dictatorial regime whose only claim for help is that it maintains order while suppressing communism." The editorialist added, "The Costa Rican episode suggests that in some cases at least, future upheavals can be handled with some degree of order in the name and in the interests of the entire hemisphere."[114] The London-based *World Today* also praised Washington's stand in favor of Don Pepe. "The U.S.A. appears so far to have acted wisely" in Costa Rica, the article stated, emphasizing that "the State Department is faced with a difficult situation in having to take a stand against countries such as Nicaragua which have been consistently cooperative with United States business interests and whose support in the United Nations is of value." The article concluded that "although the country under Figueres is a democracy it nevertheless embodies a spirit of nationalism to be found in almost all the countries of Central and Latin America today, but in Costa Rica's case it is tempered by good sense and moderation."[115]

By February, most of the fighting had ended and the majority of rebels had surrendered. At this point, OAS and State Department officials set out to reduce the potential for future disputes. Acting on the investigating committee's recommendations, the OAS blamed both Costa Rica and Nicaragua's meddling for the conflict and created a special commission to monitor and mediate future disagreements.[116] U.S. diplomats also stepped up their attempts to defuse the situation. During a visit to Central America in February 1955, Vice-President Richard M. Nixon met separately with Figueres and Somoza. He tried to arrange a meeting between the disputants, but Figueres adamantly refused to attend, arguing that any council between the two men legitimized Somoza's rule. Nixon secured a victory when each leader promised to issue a statement guaranteeing that he would not aid any more attempts to overthrow the other.[117]

Vice President Richard Nixon and President Figueres examine a banana tree during the American's visit to Costa Rica in 1955. (Photograph courtesy of the Richard Nixon Library)

Both sides continued issuing charges of plots and counterplots, but difficulties eventually abated.[118] In September 1955, the special OAS committee reviewed the situation and recommended the termination of the Rio Treaty because of the improvement in relations between the two countries.[119] Several weeks later, Costa Rica and Nicaragua signed a pact of amity pledging that they would not allow rebel forces to operate in their territories. The settlements proved fairly effective and tensions slowly subsided, especially after the death of Somoza in 1956.[120]

The relations between Figueres and the United States during the remainder of his term were uneventful compared to his first two years in office. Figueres concentrated on domestic questions, such as the economy. He continued lobbying U.S. officials to pass laws stabilizing prices and providing parity for Latin American products, arguing that higher prices would allow the region's workers to purchase more finished goods from the United States and reduce its reliance on U.S. grants and loans.[121]

In other areas, Figueres worked with the United States to develop Costa Rica's economy and infrastructure. In March 1955, the Export-Import Bank loaned $2.5 million to the Costa Rican National Power and Light Company to finance the purchase of U.S. machinery to upgrade its power systems.[122] A year later, the World Bank approved a $3 million loan for Costa Rica to encourage investment in light industry and agriculture.[123] Costa Rica also received large quantities of U.S. aid from various agencies for health care, education, and infrastructure.[124]

The most important issue in the last two years of his term was Figueres's handlng of a perceived Communist resurgence in Costa Rica. He preferred to allow a small Communist front organization to operate just above the surface, noting that his social programs had undermined the Communists' base of operations and that the Communists posed no threat to his country's internal security. Some State Department officials disagreed, but they could not challenge his successes in undermining Communist activity.[125] A leading analyst on the Communists in Latin America, Robert Alexander, emphasized in 1957 that Costa Rican communism was of "relatively minor importance," underscoring that Figueres's programs of social reform represented the "only sure way to defeat the Communists."[126]

San José and Washington also clashed when Figueres continued giving aid to the democratic revolutionaries in the region, although he provided less direct assistance. In 1956, he tried other tactics to change American attitudes and to end U.S. support for the dictators. Figueres attempted to create new ties with several European nations and in September took a two-month trip to the continent to create new economic opportunities and new political alliances, hoping to be able to point to future political and economic alternatives if the United States refused to adopt different policies.[127] These actions antagonized some U.S. officials, but they hardly constituted a major threat to U.S. hegemony. Figueres never moved too far away from the United States because of his country's continued political and economic reliance on the core power.

In the final year of Figueres's rule, U.S. diplomats worked closely with his administration in economic and political matters. To demonstrate the U.S. commitment to Costa Rican democracy, Undersecretary of State for Latin American Affairs Roy Rubottom visited the country. He praised Costa Rica's dedication to democratic principles and encouraged its people to remain vigilant against the Communist threat. Rubottom emphasized that the best way to defeat communism was to promote education, social justice, and peace, proposals wholeheartedly supported by Figueres.[128]

As the presidential election of 1958 drew near, U.S. officials tried to avoid interfering in Costa Rican affairs. The CIA predicted a tight race because the PLN had split into two factions. Figueres backed his close friend Francisco Orlich, while the younger members of the party rallied behind Jorge Rossi. The breakdown allowed the opposition candidate, Mario Echandi, to gain significant strength and threaten additional years of PLN rule. The CIA emphasized that elections would happen on schedule and that the "newly elected Costa Rican government will be somewhat more conservative than the present one."[129]

The election took place without incident. The members of the PLN divided their votes between Rossi and Orlich, allowing Echandi to win. As he had promised, Figueres accepted the results. In early 1958, he turned over control of government to his political opponent, temporarily ending his party's dominance of Costa Rica's political system. The transition brought to an end a decade of dramatic changes in Costa Rica's domestic and international affairs, although the process of change did not end in 1958.

Costa Rica during Figueres's first elected term provides an interesting case study of how one country and its leadership resisted complete domination by a stronger power even in the most adverse geopolitical conditions. The administration tried steering an independent course and adopting policies that best benefited Costa Rica. At times, its activities conflicted with the policies and goals of the U.S. government and American business interests. The *figueristas* promoted their own form of nationalism, one that challenged the hegemony of American companies. They expanded government control of the economy through various autonomous agencies and successfully negotiated a new contract with UFCO that significantly increased the country's revenues. In the leftists' view, the *figueristas* accommodated the capitalists too much, especially the United States. This economic policy developed, however, not because of U.S. coercion but because the Costa Ricans shared many American views on capitalism. The United States proved in Guatemala and later in Cuba that it would tolerate few radical challenges to its economic hegemony. Unlike some of their Latin American counterparts, the Costa Ricans skillfully imposed their own form of economic nationalism without alienating the United States.

In foreign affairs, the Figueres administration followed the same pattern. In boycotting the Caracas Conference and continuing to aid the democratic left, Costa Rica successfully resisted American pressure. In their stance on Guatemala, however, the *figueristas* accommodated the United States by failing to criticize harshly the U.S. use of the Guatemala reactionaries. They further blunted criticism by backing Washington in the struggle against international communism, although their allegiance developed in response to common concerns rather than fear. In return, the United States rewarded their loyalty by helping to defeat the *calderonistas* and sponsoring internal development projects.

While differences arose, they were not enough to destroy a traditionally cordial relationship. In the end, the United States maintained fairly consistent policies toward the Third World during the early part of the Eisenhower administration. Washington accepted nationalist policies that did not challenge the basic economic and political concepts that drove U.S. foreign policy. The Costa Ricans understood this pattern and successfully manipulated Washington within the comparatively narrow constraints placed on international relations by the tensions of the cold war.

While members of Figueres's party lost the election in 1958, they did not disappear from the limelight in Costa Rica. They would return after the next presidential contest to continue their plans. Figueres especially proved a prominent figure in Costa Rican politics until 1990. His legacy was not soon forgotten. He would continue promoting social programs and other changes designed to enhance the lives of many Costa Ricans, although the movement lost some impetus after the 1950s. Most important, he left a lasting imprint on Costa Rica's international policies, strongly influencing his successors to continue developing policies that resisted and accommodated the United States.

8

OFTENTIMES THE TAIL WAGS THE DOG
Trends in Relations between Costa Rica and the United States during the Rise of José Figueres

After leaving office in 1958, José Figueres and his associates remained important actors in domestic and regional politics. Even though Figueres no longer served as president, some U.S. diplomats and administration officials continued to court him. The disastrous Latin American trip of Richard Nixon in 1958 caused U.S. policymakers to direct more attention to their southern neighbors.[1] Led by Milton Eisenhower and Roy Rubottom, U.S. officials increasingly looked on Figueres and other democratic liberal leaders as political models.[2] Figueres recognized the opportunity and increasingly pushed for changes in U.S. policy. On the invitation of Congressman Charles Porter of Oregon, he testified to a congressional committee in 1958 that Latin America strongly supported the United States, but he questioned U.S. assistance to dictators. "If you talk human dignity to Russia," he queried, "why do you hesitate so much to talk human dignity to the Dominican Republic?"[3]

During the remainder of Eisenhower's tenure Figueres continued to challenge the administration's foreign policies, but he proved more compliant to U.S. pressure after Washington began assisting the democratic left. Agencies such as the CIA started funneling funds to the non-Communist liberal forces in the late 1950s. Figueres worked with a leading CIA operative, Sacha Volman, to found the Institute of Political Education outside San José. The CIA helped to build a central post for coordinating the political activities of the exiles and publishing a journal, *Combate*. Figueres recognized that the money came from possibly disreputable sources, but he rationalized that it helped achieve positive change.[4]

Through the late 1950s, Figueres remained at the forefront of the struggle for democracy in Latin America. At first, he backed Fidel Castro in

Cuba, but he grew estranged from the new regime when he concluded that Castro and his associates had moved too far to the left. At the invitation of the Cubans, he had the audacity to make a speech in Havana during a 1959 visit warning of the dangers of shifting toward a more radical anti-American policy. One of Castro's ministers rushed the platform and wrestled away the microphone. After some tense moments, the Cubans allowed him to finish. Following his departure he became a vocal critic of the Castro government.

During the administrations of John F. Kennedy and Lyndon B. Johnson, Figueres continued working for democratic change in Latin America. He visited Washington often to give advice on subjects ranging from the Alliance for Progress to the stabilization of prices for Latin American goods. Some problems developed after he broke with Sacha Volman in 1962 following a heated debate on the control of the Institute of Political Education. Other difficulties arose in 1965 when he cooperated with Betancourt and Múñoz to promote a peaceful settlement in the Dominican Republic by creating an OAS trusteeship to oversee elections. Rebuffed by the Johnson administration, which installed its own choice and supervised the elections, Figueres criticized the United States, although his attacks lacked the stridency of those of his earlier years.

Throughout his life, Figueres was an important Latin American leader in the eyes of many U.S. officials. He continued to advise the United States to change its policy toward Latin America, especially after he returned to the presidency in 1970, although his policies became less idealistic and lacked the activism of his earlier career. He promoted price supports for agricultural products and denounced U.S. assistance to authoritarian governments in Nicaragua and Chile. He continued to provide aid to Betancourt and assisted Nicaraguan rebels who ultimately overthrew the Somoza family dictatorship. His later life was plagued by personal problems linked to his association with Robert Vesco and purported financial irregularities during his second presidential term, but he played a role in the negotiations that produced the 1987 Central American peace accord, his last major diplomatic accomplishment.

Figueres also remained politically active at home. In 1961, the PLN regained control under President Francisco Orlich, although Figueres served as ideological and party leader. The PLN expanded Costa Rica's welfare state, providing more health care and educational opportunities and en-

Figueres and former president Harry S. Truman pose for a picture at the Truman Library during Figueres's visit to the United States in 1959. (Photograph courtesy of the Harry S. Truman Library)

suring the availability of relatively inexpensive public services. The pattern continued into the 1980s with prominent PLN members such as Daniel Oduber and Alberto Monge winning the presidency. By the mid-1980s, a younger group in the PLN led by Oscar Arias rose to power, reducing some of the influence of Figueres and his associates. Figueres passed away in 1990, but his legacy endures in the Costa Rican social and political system in the form of his son José Maria, the current Costa Rican president.

This account of U.S.–Costa Rican relations during Figueres's early career provides insights at several levels. As a binational investigation, it demonstrates the characteristics of the normal pattern of relations between the two countries, demonstrating how relations survived and flourished during a very unstable period. At the regional level, the story highlights continuities in U.S.–Latin American relations during an important era, one in which the United States grappled with its status as a world power. Finally, in a broader context, this study uncovers a model of nonviolent resistance and accommodation by a smaller country and some of the weapons available to nonindustrialized nations in their struggle against U.S. domination.

At the binational level, Figueres's rise to power provides several insights regarding the pattern of U.S.–Costa Rican relations. The era ranges the entire gamut from the most traditional form of relations with Ulate's presidency to the volatile civil war of 1948. It illuminates how both countries sustained the traditional model of relations established before 1940. The standard continued as San José supported Washington on major international issues while fighting for independence of action in domestic and regional affairs. The United States responded by treating the Costa Ricans better than it did their neighbors, never directly using force to protect its interests as it did in other nations of the region.

At one end of the spectrum was Ulate. He was the archetypal Costa Rican leader who focused on domestic affairs and chose moderate over radical change. The *ulatistas* backed the United States in international affairs and did not disturb the peace in the region. As president, Ulate promoted a moderate social program that relied more on individuals than government for control, and he refused to allow the Caribbean exiles to utilize Costa Rica as a base. Quarrels sometimes arose with U.S. officials over issues such as his refusal to drive the Communists underground. Nevertheless, the differences were minor, and cooperation characterized U.S.–Costa Rican relations during his rule. In fact, some U.S. officials preferred

Ulate to his immediate predecessors or successor, an opinion often stated before Ulate stepped down in 1953.

The civil war of 1948 marks the other end of the scale. The conflict arose at a time when the wartime alliance between Washington and Moscow had disintegrated and the United States had assumed the leadership of the western world. The onset of the cold war significantly altered the relationship between the United States and the coalition of Picado, Calderón, and Mora, undermining the traditional pattern of relations. As in the Tinoco years, the United States took a comparatively hard line against the government. It reacted against a perceived threat even though Calderón and Picado had supported most U.S. policies. Several U.S. policymakers identified a Communist threat in Costa Rica, and when the fighting began they moved toward favoring Figueres's forces. There was no premeditated plan to overthrow the Picado administration, but when the opportunity presented itself, U.S. officials aided the rebels by cutting off military supplies, stopping Somoza's intervention while turning a blind eye to Guatemala's role in the conflict, and bringing diplomatic pressure to bear on the president to help ensure an insurgent victory.

While U.S. activities were significant, as they had been in previous conflicts, the major factor in deciding the outcome of the fighting and reestablishing cordial relations was the Costa Ricans themselves. Their aversion to the extremes represented by the more radical elements of the Vanguard and their dedication to democratic principles proved vital. The opposition destroyed the perceived Communist influence before U.S. policymakers intervened through direct or covert methods to combat a security threat. Some U.S. policymakers clearly overestimated Communist influence in Costa Rica and its possible challenge to U.S. interests, but they never created an army such as the one employed in Guatemala in 1954. For the most part, Costa Ricans, not Americans, determined the outcome and allowed the traditional relationship to survive even under the most trying circumstances.

The civil war of 1948 also ushered into leadership a new group of Costa Ricans with a different approach to restructuring society, one that rested comfortably between the two extremes of Ulate's near total accommodation and the perceived radicalism of the Vanguard and its political allies. The *figueristas* promoted their own brand of nationalism, characterized by government ownership of major utilities and public service industries and an independent foreign policy in regional affairs that at times conflicted with the United States. At a time when Washington often associated nationalism with anti-Americanism and communism, the *figueristas* distanced themselves from these negative images through a variety of methods. Figueres proved especially skilled at a form of diplomatic brinkmanship, measuring his program against the perceived response of the United States. In this way, his policies conformed more with the flexible and pragmatic approaches of Jawaharlal Nehru, Gamel Nasser, and Víctor Paz Estenssoro.[5] In addition, they nicely corresponded with the traditional pattern of relations.

The period from 1942 to 1957 covered the entire spectrum of U.S.–Costa Rican relations. The larger pattern has remained relatively constant since the 1850s and helps explain the recent relations between the United States and Costa Rica. The successes of President Oscar Arias in the 1980s fit into the pattern. He brought fame to the country when he assisted in negotiating a peace settlement in Central America. The Reagan administration originally opposed the effort, fearing that it would legitimize the Sandinistas. Arias and others resisted pressures from U.S. officials to leave the Nicaraguans out of the process. They incorporated the Sandinistas into the peace negotiations, helping ensure a promising agreement.

The entire history of U.S.–Costa Rican relations is an interesting one. This admittedly unusual relationship is a rare case in which the United States and a smaller nation have developed and maintained essentially stable relations based on mutual respect and cooperation. By providing a close look at the example of relations between Figueres and the United States, this study has attempted to shed some light on the complex question of how Costa Rica has dealt successfully with the United States. It also suggests some clues on how peaceful coexistence can take place even in a region where conflict has been the norm and the United States has made some poor policy choices.

On the regional level, the study of U.S.–Costa Rican relations in the early cold war period provides some insights into the short-term and long-term pattern of U.S.–Latin American relations. It highlights the importance of the Communist issue, continuities between the Truman and Eisenhower administrations, and the complexities of bureaucratic battles in Washington. U.S. officials followed the established trend in U.S.–Latin American relations, devoting their energies elsewhere and responding to crises rather than formulating proactive, innovative policies for the area.

This pattern of neglect and inattention continued uninterrupted during most of the period.

As it affected diplomatic affairs in many parts of the world, the cold war significantly affected U.S.–Latin American relations during the rise of Figueres. In Costa Rica, the civil war of 1948 was an enlightening example of the influence of the Communist question on diplomatic affairs. It was an early test of the U.S. response to communism in the region. Most historians have ignored or downplayed the U.S. reaction in the fighting, focusing more on Washington's interventionism in Guatemala in 1954 and the Dominican Republic in 1965.[6] Nevertheless, Washington's policy toward the Picado administration marked a turning point in postwar relations between the United States and Latin America.[7] Some U.S. policymakers openly questioned their dedication to the principles of the "Good Neighbor" policy, a process already begun with Argentina during World War II. The United States never fully mobilized to deal with the Communists in Costa Rica, but the results closely paralleled those in Guatemala. The actions of U.S. representatives helped ensure the downfall of a reportedly Communist-infiltrated government. The U.S. response to the Costa Rican civil war, not the Guatemalan affair, marked the onset of the cold war in Latin America and continued the process of dismantling the "Good Neighbor" system. The removal of the Costa Rican Communists made it easier for officials in Washington to justify the later intervention in Guatemala. Although the methods changed in the Eisenhower administration, this episode demonstrated that the United States had begun to challenge indigenous Communist movements in Latin America well before 1954.

Examining the U.S. role in the Costa Rican revolution of 1948 also expands our understanding of relations between the United States and Latin America during the Truman administration. Although historians have recognized that American policymakers showed interest in Latin America in the postwar period, they have typically focused on aid programs, regional conferences, and the changes that took place in the latter part of the administration.[8] This episode, however, serves as an interesting test case for the early years of the cold war in Latin America. Growing U.S. concern with the Communists in Costa Rica closely mirrored the hardening of Washington's policies toward worldwide communism. The slow reaction occurred because of the legacy of friendly relations and the fact that the event occurred early in the cold war. Yet, when the fighting began, the

United States implemented policies that helped guarantee a rebel victory. A number of State Department officials involved in responding to the revolution served in different capacities during the Eisenhower administration, including Bennett, Newbegin, and Armour. These "cold warriors" cut their teeth with the Costa Rican situation. In many ways, then, the U.S. role in the civil war of 1948 demonstrates the continuities between Truman's and Eisenhower's policies in Latin America.

Another link between the two administrations was that neither made Latin America a priority, both focusing instead on Europe and Asia. The United States devoted little attention to Costa Rica and its neighbors. It responded only to crises and perceived Communist threats, failing to promote actively the progressive social, economic, and political agendas in a region that desperately needed change. It supported the status quo, never developing programs like the Marshall Plan for Latin America. Washington relied instead on loans that created future debt problems and grants that ensured only short-term and cosmetic alterations.[9] This inattention had explosive results as Latin Americans expressed their discontent during the Nixon trip in 1958 and through Fidel Castro's alliance with the Soviet Union.

The Truman and Eisenhower administration's lack of interest in Latin America, as highlighted by the Costa Rican example, makes another contribution to our understanding of U.S.–Latin American relations. U.S. policies toward Costa Rica and Latin America originated not in the White House but largely with U.S. officials in the field and in the lower levels of the State Department. Rarely did presidents or secretaries of state devote much energy to Latin America, except during crises, such as the perceived Communist infiltration of Guatemala and the Costa Rican–Nicaraguan clashes in 1948 and 1955. As a result, ambassadors, embassy officials, and the desk officers such as Johnson, Donnelly, Davis, Bennett, Cohen, Hill, Woodward, and assistant secretaries of state Armour, Cabot, and Holland played a significant role in the creation and implementation of policy. Of course, influences outside the State Department, including the FBI, CIA, Congress, nongovernmental organizations, and leaders of developing countries, added their voices. What resulted was a complicated process, marked by numerous competing interests and conflicting agendas. This view mitigates against a sometimes simplistic explanation of top-to-bottom policymaking. The onset of the cold war and the massive expansion of the size of the federal bureaucracy ensured a new level of complexity in decision making as the United States increased its involvement in world affairs.

The Truman and Eisenhower policies toward Costa Rica and Latin America did not differ dramatically from those of other periods, past and future, in U.S. history. The long-term pattern of U.S. policy toward Latin America has revolved around U.S. officials focusing on maintaining stability to guarantee prime investment conditions and to prevent foreign intrusion. This process continued during and after World War II. The United States lacked a sophisticated vision for regional development and integration. The Costa Ricans fared better than others, but as a whole Latin America remained underdeveloped and dependent on the core powers. After a limited attempt at assisting the area in the 1960s, the United States returned to the policy of intervention and neglect. For the most part, this has remained the pattern until today.[10]

In the larger context of U.S. relations with the nonindustrialized world, the example of Figueres and Costa Rica demonstrates that nations and their leaders actively shape relations with the United States. Differences exist in the responses of the nonindustrialized world to the United States. Some states such as Cuba and Vietnam have violently resisted American hegemony. In others cases, collaborating élites such as the Somozas and Trujillo have subordinated the best interests of a majority of their countrymen in return for remaining in power. In between these two extremes, Costa Rica under Figueres employed methods of resistance and accommodation to respond to the United States.

My readings on a variety of topics have influenced my understanding of this relationship. An especially influential set of works was Latin American and Asian development studies, primarily James Scott's *Weapons of the Weak: Everyday Forms of Peasant Resistance*. For many years, social scientists and historians emphasized the passive nature of peasants in adapting to modifications caused by the dramatic social, economic, and political changes of the nineteenth and twentieth centuries. During the 1970s and 1980s, however, scholars increasingly challenged the accepted concepts. They demonstrated that, although weaker when compared to external forces and the domestic élites, peasants actively molded transformations to serve their own interests. Employing a variety of methods that ranged from violent resistance to the more subtle and daily reactions stressed by Scott, peasants dramatically have influenced changes in their world.[11]

The struggle of the peasants bore a striking resemblance to that of the relationship between the more powerful industrialized states and the periphery. The United States represents the dominant power (economically, politically, militarily), but the subordinate states, like the peasants, have adopted measures that allow them actively to shape relations between the United States and themselves.[12] Examining these tactics of adaptation makes a significant contribution by including the important role of the nonindustrialized world in the formulation and implementation of policies, thus balancing the view of the dynamics of international relations.[13]

In the case of Figueres and the United States, Figueres faced the task of dealing with a country substantially more powerful than his own. At the time, other countries possessed a *comparative advantage* in their relationship with the United States. They had more military power, greater quantities of strategic raw materials, a larger industrial base, better strategic location, a longer history of equality in international relations, and historical ties to other core countries that could counteract the United States. In this way, countries such as India or Venezuela had more weapons to deploy against the United States. Each country had unique circumstances, but very few more unsymmetrical relationships existed than that between Costa Rica and the United States. That disproportion makes it even more interesting to understand why Figueres was as successful (if not more so) than some larger and more powerful peripheral nations in his relationship with the United States.

A major reason for that success was that Figueres and his associates made the most of the available diplomatic and economic weapons. First, they benefited from a historical legacy of comparatively cordial relations that prevented initial overreaction. Figueres also possessed an understanding of American culture, an ability to promote the convergence of political cultures between the PLN and American liberal democrats of the "vital center," and a comprehension of the changing geopolitical conditions. These weapons allowed resistance when possible and accommodation when perceived necessary. While the United States maintained superiority, a constant give and take characterized the relationship as the Costa Ricans struggled to maintain independence of action. While relatively monotonous at times, these ordinary forms of response compose the bulk of the relations that occurred between the United States and the nonindustrialized world.

An important weapon inherited by Figueres and his associates was the historical legacy of cordial relations between Washington and San José.

When Figueres entered politics in the 1940s, most U.S. officials looked upon Costa Rica as a stable democratic society. The positive perceptions of Costa Rica differed from the negative images most Americans had of the region. In American eyes, Costa Ricans were white, industrious, democratic, and more egalitarian than their neighbors. The historical record had reinforced these popular portrayals as Costa Ricans had maintained a comparatively stable society and typically supported Washington. To many U.S. diplomats, politicians, and the public, Costa Rica represented a model for Latin American development.

These positive images were firmly rooted in the American consciousness when Figueres rose to power. While more radical than his predecessors, he was the product of a political culture that emphasized moderation and popular political participation. U.S. officials often highlighted this point, stressing that Figueres represented a form of nationalism firmly rooted in Costa Rica's traditions. The historical legacy played a significant role in providing Figueres something of a "honeymoon period," preventing an initial overreaction when he was a relatively unknown actor who jumped into the spotlight. It also allowed the *figueristas* to identify common links and symbols to prevent misunderstanding and guarantee continued good relations.

The *figueristas* had other weapons with which to promote their agenda without provoking the United States. They understood American culture. Their travels and studies in the United States provided them with firsthand knowledge of how Americans viewed themselves and others. As a result, they knew which buttons to push and not to push. Figueres proved especially skilled in this regard. He could quote Jefferson one minute and joke about the lack of intelligence associated with American football players the next. He often put Americans at ease, reducing the cultural gap and preventing misinterpretations. In fact, to some Americans, Figueres and his associates were more "American" than many of their countrymen. Often a conscious effort, this ability to comprehend American culture constituted a weapon that allowed peripheral leaders to use American ethnocentrism and racism to their advantage.

The historical goodwill and understanding of American culture allowed the Costa Ricans to create effective political alliances in the United States. Figueres and his associates shared visions of the western hemisphere and the world with democratic liberals in the U.S. government and nongovernmental groups. They actively sought to strengthen ties with these influential organizations and individuals. These people assisted Figueres in a number of ways, providing up-to-date information on conditions in the United States, sponsoring forums to promote his ideas, and lobbying U.S. diplomats at important junctures. They contributed to the maintenance of good relations and prevented an overreaction to some of the nationalistic policies of the *figueristas.*

Important actors in foreign relations that have received more attention recently are nongovernmental organizations. In the case of this study, groups such as the Americans for Democratic Action, the Inter-American Association for Democracy and Freedom, and the American Federation of Labor were important. They had access to a variety of tools that allowed the *figueristas* to promote their policies in the United States. Members included prominent publishers and reporters from important news organizations that followed the progress of Figueres, constantly underscoring his democratic and anti-Communist credentials. They also allowed Figueres to use their papers and magazines to outline his ideas, giving him an opportunity to prevent any misrepresentation of his policies. Members of these organizations also had access to the corridors of power in Washington. Their rolls included members of Congress, government officials, and State Department and White House advisers, such as Romualdi and Berle. These contacts gave the organizations some power to lobby effectively for Figueres when American conservatives and Latin American authoritarians attacked him. Although they often worked outside the formal channels of diplomatic relations, the nongovernmental organizations were capable allies.

People in the government who respected Figueres also acted against the powerful conservative movement sweeping Washington during the early cold war period. Within the State Department, officials such as Bennett, Davis, and Woodward actively supported Figueres and his associates. They countered attempts by his opponents in the White House, State Department, and CIA to portray Figueres as a possible Communist or at least a dupe of Moscow. The pro-Figueres faction in the State Department received assistance from some persons in the CIA, White House, and, more important, Congress—where senators such as Paul Douglas, Wayne Morse, and J. William Fulbright backed democratic reformism in Latin America. In the end, the pro-Figueres faction often (although not always) won, owing much to the positive perceptions of the Costa Rican and Washington's desire to maintain the country as a democratic model.

Figueres and his associates actively cultivated friendships with influential segments of American society. The political culture they represented won adherents in the United States. The *figueristas* exploited these associations thoroughly, using the contacts to espouse economic and political changes in Latin America. As much as any other Costa Rican before or after, Figueres was a self-promoter who understood the importance of public relations. He established himself as a leading proponent of democratic reform along with Betancourt and Haya de la Torre. The alliance with democratic liberals in the United States was yet another weapon that assisted his efforts to promote his agenda without provoking a negative response by Washington.

Another weapon fully developed by the *figueristas* was their ability to recognize the fluid geopolitical conditions of the postwar era. Unlike Somoza and Trujillo, who supported U.S. policies against the Communists for self-serving purposes, Figueres and his friends genuinely shared the U.S. aversion for communism. They opposed communism as a Soviet-inspired totalitarian ideology that infringed on individual rights. In a period when the United States often identified nationalism with communism, Figueres held the same view of the issue.

Figueres skillfully used the Communist question to his benefit. His defeat of the Communist coalition in 1948 provided him with strong anti-Communist credentials. He reinforced this position with unwavering support for the United States in major international questions, such as recognition of Communist China. These actions were significant. Figueres's social programs and his refusal to follow U.S. policy toward regional dictators caused some U.S. officials and citizens to question his loyalty. When the American conservatives and Latin American totalitarians characterized his policies as Communist oriented, Figueres and his allies countered by highlighting his defeat of communism in 1948 and his continued effort to build a stable system that undermined any Communist appeal. This understanding of the importance of the Communist issue contributed to the successes of Figueres in domestic and regional affairs.

The comprehension of issues such as the Communist question extended into the economic sphere, where the *figueristas* sought to reduce their country's dependence on foreign interests and to improve the plight of the majority. The presence of a strong pro-labor element, as represented by Núñez and Monge, kept labor and economic issues at the forefront. The *figueristas* employed a variety of tactics including nationalization and negotiation to refine an overly exploitative system. The leaders sought to enhance economic independence through government ownership and increased revenues. These policies aggravated American businessmen and their allies, who often responded with vicious attacks—although the battles never reached the level of those in Guatemala in 1954 or Chile in 1973.

The most radical economic weapon employed by the *figueristas* was nationalization. In using this method, they followed established policies of other Latin American leaders, such as Lázaro Cárdenas in Mexico in 1938. In the case of the banking system, they seized public institutions when the bankers failed to cooperate with proposed reforms. They also promoted government ownership of public utilities to ensure that the industries provided affordable services for all Costa Ricans, especially the poor. In their negotiations with UFCO in 1953, the PLN used the threat of nationalization to secure concessions, although that threat was always accompanied by the promise of fair payment for the nationalized properties. To American conservatives, policies such as these reeked of socialism. Nevertheless, the *figueristas* used this method sparingly, in part accommodating interests in their country and the United States. They chose instead weapons that incited less negative reactions.

The most effective economic weapon was negotiation. Reliance on this tactic entailed considerably fewer risks of overreaction by American officials and economic interests. It appealed to the good sense of postwar liberals and moderates who believed in business regulation and more equitable distribution of profits. The *figueristas* proved effective negotiators, asking initially for more than they wanted and using the threat of nationalization and labor strikes as bargaining tools. From UFCO, they successfully secured significant increases in government revenues and guarantees for Costa Rican workers. In this way, they had more funds for social spending. They no doubt benefited from good timing. When dealing with UFCO, the State Department moved from a supportive position to one less so after Guatemala. As a weapon, negotiation provided a way to seek better agreements without some of the dangers inherent in nationalization. It was an integral part of the relationship between Costa Rica and American businesses before and after Figueres.

The Costa Ricans possessed comparatively few weapons when compared to other countries. Other nations have more bargaining power, especially nations that possess strategic materials. These states have tactics not available to Figueres, including the formation of economic cartels (such the Organization of Petroleum Exporting Countries), which give member states a greater ability to control a lucrative product on which the industrialized nations depend. OPEC members can use negotiation and boycotts to obtain better contracts and also promote political policies. Other economic weapons include promoting Import Substitution Industries and higher tariffs to protect domestic industries. Even an individual laborer often has the right to strike and to level lawsuits against U.S. companies. In these ways, the peripheral nations battle at numerous levels against dependence upon the United States, although the example differs from country to country.

The *figueristas* also developed tactics of resistance and accommodation regarding the discourse between the two nations. U.S. dominance extends beyond the material realm to the realm of ideals and symbols. In this area, the Costa Ricans worked hard to define the nature of the relationship. At times they utilized common ideals to their advantage, while at other points they rejected U.S. attempts to dictate the discourse and provided their own alternatives. What resulted was a tug-of-war to use idealism and symbolism to justify actions, constituting another part of the pattern of resistance and accommodation between the core and periphery.

In the political sphere, Figueres and his associates understood the significance of certain political images. In their speeches, interviews, books, and articles, they employed symbols deeply imbedded in the political lexicon of the United States. Over and over again, they characterized their country and party as representative of Jeffersonian republicanism, a nation of small yeomen farmers dedicated to democratic principles and egalitarianism. They also grafted more modern symbols onto the model, often underscoring similarities between the PLN agenda and the New Deal programs of Franklin Roosevelt. They emphasized parallels between the two political cultures, especially reformism and antitotalitarianism. Not all Americans admired Jefferson or Roosevelt, but the two presidents held near mythic positions in the eyes of many of their countrymen. Raising these symbols was important and assisted the *figueristas'* efforts to reinforce their bonds with the United States.

Yet not all of the Costa Ricans' attempts in the realm of discourse stressed shared ideas and symbols. In the economic sphere, Figueres and his associates refused to accept American and western European explanations for Latin American underdevelopment. Most Americans blamed the region's Spanish heritage for ensuring economic stagnation. Figueres and other Latin Americans, however, focused on different justifications. They defined the problem as grounded in the imbalance in international trade. The core powers set the prices, undervaluing raw materials such as coffee and bananas while charging high prices for finished materials. Figueres sought fair payment, arguing that if Latin Americans had more money they could purchase American goods. In other ways, he fought for just compensation from American companies and questioned the effectiveness of U.S. aid policies. Much like other nationalists in Latin America, such as Betancourt and Haya de la Torre, Figueres wanted to refine the system and refused to accept American definitions espoused by government and business officials.

Disputing the basic assumptions of U.S. economic policies, Figueres attempted to alter the debate and add new variables to the argument. Latin American intellectuals and politicians like Figueres refused to accept western European and American intellectual models. They developed alternative explanations for underdevelopment and proposed methods of development that ensured progress for all parties, not only the core powers and their allies. More radical challenges evolved afterward, many centered on Marxist thought and dependency theory. Nevertheless, all these models of thought were important examples of the intellectual challenge to U.S. hegemony that has continued in various forms since the establishment of relations.

In the political arena, Figueres used the channels of discourse to challenge U.S. policies. He aggravated Washington by constantly highlighting the hypocrisy of U.S. leaders who professed allegiance to democracy and social justice but aided Latin American authoritarians. He battled the United States with words, making numerous speeches and publishing articles and editorials that chastised the United States for its assistance to the dictators. He used common symbols to appeal to U.S. idealism, invoking terms firmly rooted in U.S. political culture, such as *democracy, justice,* and *human rights.* In this role, he and others acted as a conscience, appealing to the U.S. preoccupation with its image and credibility in the struggle with the Soviet Union. They kept the issue of democracy and human rights in the spotlight, a process accelerated by Nixon's trip to Latin America in 1958 and Fidel Castro's rise to power.

The intellectual challenges Figueres and his allies made to U.S. policy were important. Their refusal to accept American explanations for economic (non)development and for U.S. support of authoritarianism fueled Latin American nationalism. That refusal had unexpected benefits for Figueres. In one way, the *figueristas* played a game of being more democratic than the United States, although they always portrayed U.S. efforts as misguided rather than inherently evil. They benefited from this effort because more and more the United States viewed the Costa Ricans as a major democratic spokesman of Latin America. While this process had begun earlier, Figueres increased Costa Rica's exposure by actively promoting his country's dedication to democratic and humanitarian principles. American leaders from Kennedy to Reagan increasingly depicted Costa Rica as the model for Latin American development. In a way Costa Rica has become a symbol in U.S. foreign policy for peripheral development, guaranteeing U.S. backing for Costa Rican actions even during periods of disagreement.

The discourse between nations is an arena in which the developing world has become more aggressive since 1945. Battling the United States at this level does not entail the same dangers as material challenges because the direct damage caused by the war of words is difficult to quantify. Nevertheless, the United States tries to define the nature of relations between countries. It devotes time and energy to trying to render precisely the nature of the international system in American terms. It employs various weapons, such as the United States Information Agency, cultural missions, and educational exchanges to try to win the hearts and minds of the peoples of the developing world. These agencies and private exchanges extol the virtues of American society, often successfully. Nonindustrialized nations do not passively accept attempts to Americanize them, and they develop alternative explanations that often undermine U.S. hegemony. This phenomenon is an interesting area of study that forms part of the peripheral response to the United States.

The preceding discussion points out some but definitely not all of the "weapons of the weak." In the past, many historians and policymakers have downgraded the role of the nonindustrialized world to that of a passive actor. As this study suggests, the periphery has a number of nonviolent strategies with which to respond to the United States. These more routine forms of resistance and accommodation, when taken individually, may appear inconsequential as compared to the power of the core nation, but the aggregation of the acts multiplied tenfold or more creates over time (to borrow Scott's simile) an enormous social, political, and economic coral reef that often tears to shambles the policies formulated on the ships of states and the yachts of foreign economic interests. While there are problems of determining where resistance and accommodation end and compliance begins, the instincts of survival and "working the system . . . to their minimum disadvantage" are strong forces that affect international relations. The United States maintains the upper hand, but the study of the periphery provides several contributions to the understanding of U.S. foreign relations.

First, reviewing the more routine forms of peripheral responses to the United States helps to explain, in part, inconsistencies in U.S. policy. Although Washington's policies revolve around fundamental principles, all related to the protection of U.S. interests, the internal dynamics of other countries generate different responses from U.S. policymakers both in Washington and on location. The differences highlight the importance of examining the role of peripheral nations and their individual patterns of resistance and accommodation. The diversity of the reactions helps explain the successes and failures in U.S. relations with the developing world.

This study also makes a contribution by outlining a progression in the historiography of U.S. foreign relations. Critics have complained that the field remains too narrow and focuses ethnocentrically on Washington's role in international affairs at the expense of foreign nations and nongovernmental factors. This work has incorporated the peripheral nation, stressing its influence on the formulation and implementation of policies. Throughout their histories, the subordinate powers have developed methods of resistance and accommodation to respond to the core powers such as the United States, Great Britain, Japan, and the Soviet Union. Blending peripheral responses into our studies allows us to create more balance and understanding in the evaluation of relations between the core and periphery.[14]

This methodology also moves the historian toward complementing the study of those relationships marked by violent rejections of U.S. hegemony. While important, violent incidents constitute a comparatively small percentage of peripheral responses to the United States. In the majority of cases, relations between nations are peaceful and characterized by careful judgments by peripheral leaders as to the ramifications of their initiatives and responses. If historians fail to incorporate the studies of routine responses, they may miss an opportunity to provide a fuller comprehension of U.S. relations with the nonindustrialized world.

Emphasizing the "weapons of the weak" raises, I hope, some questions regarding the development of U.S. foreign relations. Many analysts and government leaders try to develop policies according to models of behavior in international relations. These paradigms often disregard the response of the nonindustrialized world. No matter what kind of policies are formulated in Washington or in the United Nations, the peripheral culture will provide a certain slant to the implementation. Many times, the United States has ignored the fact that differences exist even within regions. Even when Washington makes efforts to appreciate those differences, ethnocentrism clouds the lens and causes many blunders. Foreign relations is a complex process, one not dictated solely by U.S. presidents and advisers. As demonstrated in this book, there are numerous variables at work, creating a complicated mechanism that changes over time. Too often in the past, people have tried to simplify this phenomenon, leading to misunderstanding and critical errors on both sides.

This emphasis on the nonindustrialized world's responses also provides insights that not everyone may enjoy. An important one is peripheral responsibility. In the past, many analysts have emphasized the U.S. role in the underdevelopment of the periphery, frequently blaming most problems on core nations such as the United States. Incorporating the role of the nonindustrialized world makes it clearer that leaders in subordinate states must share the responsibility for the successes and failures of social, economic, and political policies promoted by the core powers. This tendency in many ways impairs the rhetoric of nationalists who have focused on the part of the outside powers while downplaying their own accountability.

This study, however, does not absolve the United States of its responsibility. By virtue of its military and economic strength, the dominant power still exerts greater influence in the relationship. While this case study has analyzed a relatively successful relationship between a developing nation and the United States, it must also note the consequences. Washington did not passively submit to Costa Rican initiatives. As with the other nations of the region, it tried to maintain its hegemony, limiting Costa Rican attempts at independence of action in regional affairs. In the late 1940s and throughout the 1950s the United States limited Figueres's assistance to the democratic left, rejecting democratic development in favor of stability and anticommunism. This pattern was part of a general postwar trend that had long-term effects. If the United States had allowed the democratic left movement to operate freely, Latin Americans might have removed the dictators and established democracies. The problem of Trujillo, Fulgencio Batista, and Somoza came back to haunt the United States.

More important, Washington interfered in domestic affairs. During the Picado presidency and the civil war, some U.S. diplomats undermined the Costa Rican government because they feared the growing prominence of the Communists. They violated the principle of nonintervention to protect the United States from a challenge by a group reportedly aligned with the Soviet Union. Afterward, the United States limited what the *figueristas* might have accomplished in Costa Rica. Several members of the PLN wanted more radical social and economic programs, but Figueres and others exercised caution because they feared the response of conservatives in their country and the United States. The threat, real or imagined, suppressed possible solutions and limited the initiative of the Costa Ricans. This fact is important because it points to a problem that has plagued U.S. foreign policy: an unwillingness to allow more radical policies that challenge accepted concepts of American leaders—even though those policies might benefit the needs of the people of the subordinate power.[15]

The history of U.S.–Costa Rica relations during the rise of Figueres provides an interesting and important case study that makes a number of contributions to the study of U.S. foreign relations. This admittedly unusual relationship is a rare instance in which the United States and a smaller nation have developed and maintained essentially stable relations based to a large extent on mutual respect and cooperation. It provides some understanding at a number of levels of analysis, highlighting a pattern of relations over the long term and presenting an account of a peripheral country that successfully employed a number of "weapons of the weak." By providing a close look at this example, this study sheds some light on the complex question of why some nations successfully resist subjugation and others fail to do so. This study also provides clues as to how peaceful coexistence can be possible even in a region where conflict has been the norm and the United States has made some poor policy choices.

NOTES

Preface

1. I utilize several defining terms in the text, including *nonindustrialized world.* I use this term to describe nations that rely primarily on the production of agricultural commodities and other raw materials and that maintain only a small industrial sector (although the size of that sector can differ from nation to nation). Such a country's population is predominantly rural. The term distinguishes most other nations from the United States, especially after 1870. I also utilize terms borrowed from world systems theory, a theory best articulated by Immanuel Wallerstein in *The Modern World-System: Capitalist Agriculture and the Origins of the European World-Economy in the Sixteenth Century* (New York: Academic Press, 1976). *Core* and *periphery* are terms that are useful in describing the relations between the industrialized and nonindustrialized world, especially in the context of the twentieth century.

2. *Hegemony* may be defined as "a preponderance of power of one state over other states." Hegemony can be economical, political, or cultural, although the degree of hegemony varies from one nation to another. Guy Poitras, *The Ordeal of Hegemony: The United States and Latin America* (Boulder, Colo.: Westview Press, 1990), 2.

3. This phrase is borrowed from a discussion of peasants and their response to the dominant social, economic, and political structure. Eric Hobsbawm, "Peasants and Politics," *Journal of Peasant Studies* 1, no. 1 (1973): 3–22.

4. Dissertations and Spanish-language works on Costa Rica include Jacobo Schifter-Sikora, "Origins of the Cold War in Central America: A Study of Diplomatic Relations between Costa Rica and the United States, 1940–1949" (Ph.D. diss., Columbia University, 1983); idem, *Las alianzas conflictivas: Las relaciones de Costa Rica y Estados Unidos de la Segunda Guerra Mundial a los inicios de la Guerra Civil* (San José: Libro Libre, 1986); Paul Atwood, "The United States and Costa Rica, 1945–1960: The Containment of Liberal Nationalism" (Ph.D. diss., Boston University, 1991); and a series of articles by Charles Stansifer, Thomas M. Leonard, and Richard V. Salisbury. General studies of the region include Walter LaFeber, *Inevitable Revolutions: The United States in Central America* (New York: W. W. Norton, 1984); Thomas M. Leonard, *The United States and Central America: The Search for Stability* (Athens: University of Georgia Press, 1991); and John E. Findling, *Close Neighbors, Distant Friends: United States–Central American Relations* (Westport, Conn.: Greenwood Press, 1987).

1. The Switzerland of the Americas: Costa Rica and the Foundations of Cordial Relations with the United States

1. Charles P. Howland, *American Relations in the Caribbean* (New Haven, Conn.: Yale University Press, 1929), 220.

2. Ricardo Fernández-Guardia, *Cartilla histórica de Costa Rica* (San José: Imprenta Lehmann, 1967), 20; John P. Augelli and Robert C. West, *Middle America: Its Lands and*

People (Englewood Cliffs, N.J.: Prentice-Hall, 1966), 449–51; Carolyn Hall, *Costa Rica: A Geographical Interpretation in Historical Perspective* (Boulder, Colo.: Westview Press, 1985), 3–23; Frederick Lange, "The Cultural Geography of Costa Rica," in *Prehistoric Settlement Patterns in Costa Rica,* ed. Frederick Lange and Lynette Norr (Urbana, Ill.: Journal of the Steward Anthropological Society, 1986); Luis Ferrero, *Costa Rica precolombina: Arqueología, etnologia, tecnologia, arte* (San José: Editorial Costa Rica, 1981); Jorge A. Lines, *Anthropological Bibliography of Aboriginal Costa Rica* (San José: Tropical Science Center, 1967); Jorge León, "Land Utilization in Costa Rica," *The Geographical Review* 38 (July 1948): 444–56.

3. Chester Lloyd Jones, *Costa Rica and Civilization in the Caribbean* (Madison: University of Wisconsin Press, 1935), 10–12; Hall, *Costa Rica,* 66.

4. Elizabeth Fonseca-Corrales, *Costa Rica colonial: la tierra y el hombre* (San José: Editorial Universidad Centroamérica, 1984), 107–45; Doris Zemurray-Stone, "Indians and Costa Rica," *Bulletin of the Pan American Union* 82 (February 1948): 64–67; idem, *Pre-Colombian Man in Costa Rica* (Cambridge, Mass.: Peabody Museum Press, 1977), 217–18. A whole issue of the journal *America Indígena* is dedicated to the Costa Rican Indians. Gonzalo Rubio-Orbe, ed., *America Indígena* 43 (April–June 1974): 291–559.

5. Carlos Meléndez-Chavarri, *Conquistadors y pobladores: Origines histórico-sociales de los costarricenses* (San José: Editorial Universidad Estatal a Distancia, 1982), 92–97; Mitchell Seligson, "Agrarian Policies in Dependent Societies: Costa Rica," *Journal of Interamerican Studies and World Affairs* 19 (May 1977): 203–4; Murdo J. MacLeod, *Spanish Central America: A Socioeconomic History, 1520–1720* (Berkeley: University of California Press, 1973), 300.

6. Cited in Miles L. Wortman, *Government and Society in Central America, 1680–1840* (New York: Columbia University Press, 1982), 77.

7. Wortman, *Government and Society in Central America,* 164; MacLeod, *Spanish Central America,* 334–40.

8. Cited in Michael D. Olien, "The Negro in Costa Rica: The Ethnohistory of an Ethnic Minority in a Complex Society" (Ph.D. diss., University of Oregon, 1967), 60.

9. Luis Barahona, "Tres notas sobre el carácter costarricense," in *Ensayistas costarricenses,* ed. Luis Ferrero (San José: Libreria Lehmann, 1971); John C. Morgan, "The Partido Nacional of Costa Rica: A Case Study of Myth and Political Culture" (Ph.D. diss., Louisiana State University, 1979), 57–61.

10. Elías Zamora-Acosta, *Etnografía histórica de Costa Rica, 1561–1615* (Seville: Imprenta Raimundo, 1980), 126–28; Ricardo Blanco-Segura, *Historia eclesiástica de Costa Rica: Del descubrimiento a la ereción de la Diocesis, 1502–1850* (San José: Editorial Costa Rica, 1967).

11. Philip J. Williams, *The Catholic Church and Politics in Nicaragua and Costa Rica* (Pittsburgh: University of Pittsburgh Press, 1989); Thomas Karnes, "The Origins of Costa Rican Federalism," *The Americas* 15 (June 1959): 251–52.

12. Samuel Z. Stone, *The Heritage of the Conquistadors: Ruling Classes in Central America from Conquest to the Sandinistas* (Lincoln: University of Nebraska Press, 1990).

13. Karen Biesanz, Mavis Biesanz, and Richard Biesanz, *Los costarricenses* (San José: Editorial Universidad Estatal a Distancia, 1979), 24; James Busey, *Notes on Costa Rican Democracy* (Boulder: University of Colorado Press, 1962), 58; Chalmers S. Brumbaugh, "Costa Rica: The Making of a Livable Society" (Ph.D. diss., University of Wisconsin, 1985). Despite the belief in the "leyenda blanca," the 1801 breakdown of the population was: Indians, 16 percent; whites, 9 percent; mestizos, 58 percent; mulattos, 17 percent. Hall, *Costa Rica,* 62.

14. Hall, *Costa Rica*, 70–72; R. N. Adams, "Cultural Components of Central America," *American Anthropologist* 58 (1956): 881–907; Mitchell Seligson, "La tesis de la 'sociedad dual': Una reexaminación del caso de Costa Rica," *Revista de Ciencias Sociales* 10 (1977): 33–47; Mary Allison, "A Survey of Literature and Culture of Costa Rica" (Ph.D. diss., University of Washington, 1952), 21–22.

15. A working definition of *political culture* is: "the beliefs about patterns of political interaction and political institutions." Sidney Verba, "Comparative Political Culture," in *Political Culture and Political Development*, ed. Sidney Verba and Lucien Pye (Princeton, N.J.: Princeton University Press, 1965), 526–27. Other good discussions of political culture are Gabriel Almond and Sidney Verba, *The Civic Culture* (Princeton, N.J.: Princeton University Press, 1963), and Lucian W. Pye, "Culture and Political Science: Problems in the Evolution of Political Culture," *Social Science Quarterly* 53 (September 1972): 285–96. Scholars have developed several critiques of Pye and Almond. One important critique is that each country has several political cultures, not a monolithic one. Elizabeth J. Perry, "Introduction: Chinese Political Culture Revisited," in *Popular Protest and Political Culture in Modern China*, ed. Elizabeth J. Perry and Jeffrey N. Wasserstrom (Boulder, Colo.: Westview Press, 1992), 1–13.

16. Stone, *Heritage of the Conquistadors*, 9–11.

17. Dana W. Murphy, "Costa Rica, 1953–1970: The Evolution of a Working Multiparty System in the Post-Revolutionary Era" (Ph.D. diss., University of Washington, 1976), 16–18.

18. John A. Booth, "Democracy and Citizen Action in Costa Rica: The Modes and Correlates of Popular Participation in Politics" (Ph.D. diss., University of Texas at Austin, 1975), 51–52; idem, "Costa Rica: The Roots of Democratic Stability," in *Democracy in Developing Countries: Latin America*, ed. Larry Diamond, Juan Linz, and Seymour Martin Lipset (Boulder, Colo.: Lynne Rienner, 1989): 388–89.

19. MacLeod, *Spanish Central America*, 334–37.

20. Karnes, "Origins of Costa Rican Federalism," 251–56; Wortman, *Government and Society in Central America*, 205.

21. Several political scientists have focused on the influence of the development of the political culture on foreign affairs in Latin America, including Roland Ebel and Raymond Taras, "Cultural Style and International Policy-making: The Latin American Tradition," in *Culture and International Relations*, ed. Jongsuk Chay (New York: Praeger, 1990): 191–206.

22. José Luis Vega-Carballo, "Parties, Political Development and Social Conflict in Honduras and Costa Rica: A Comparative Analysis," in *Sociology of Developing Nations: Central America*, ed. Jan L. Flora and Edelberto Torres-Rivas (New York: Monthly Review, 1989), 98–105.

23. Karen Biesanz, Mavis Biesanz, and Richard Biesanz, *The Costa Ricans* (Englewood Cliffs, N.J.: Prentice-Hall, 1982), 18–21; Rodolfo Cerdas-Cruz, *Formación del estado en Costa Rica* (San José: Editorial Universidad Costa Rica, 1967); Hernán G. Peralta, *Augustín de Iturbide y Costa Rica* (San José: Editorial Costa Rica, 1968); Eugenio Sancho-Riba, "Merchant-Planters and Modernization: Early Liberal Experiments in Costa Rica, 1849–1970" (Ph.D. diss., University of California, San Diego, 1982).

24. Carlos Monge-Alfro, *Geografía social y humana de Costa Rica* (San José: Imprenta Libreria Universal, 1942), 18–20; Cerdas-Cruz, *Formación del estado en Costa Rica*, 39–61; Rodrigo Facio-Brenes, *Estudio sobre economía costarricense* (San José: Editorial Costa Rica, 1975), 39–51; Allen M. Young, *Costa Rica: Nature, Prosperity and Peace on the Rich Coast* (Milwaukee: Interamerican Research Corporation, 1984), 3; Mitchell Seligson,

Peasants of Costa Rica and the Development of Agrarian Capitalism (Madison: University of Wisconsin Press, 1980), 207–16; Booth, "Costa Rica: The Roots of Democratic Stability," 389.

25. Lowell Gudmundson, *Costa Rica before Coffee: Society and Economy on the Eve of the Export Boom* (Baton Rouge: Louisiana State University Press, 1986), 20–23.

26. John A. Booth, "Costa Rica," in *Latin American Labor Organizations,* ed. Gerald Greenfield and Sheldon Maram (Westport, Conn.: Greenwood Press, 1987), 213.

27. Samuel Z. Stone, *La dinastía de los conquistadores: La crisis del poder en la Costa Rica contemporánea* (San José: Editorial Universitaria Centroamérica, 1982), 97–125; idem, "Production and Politics in Central American Convulsions," *Journal of Latin American Studies* 15 (November 1983): 462; Charles D. Ameringer, *Democracy in Costa Rica* (New York: Praeger, 1982), 3.

28. William P. Glade, *The Latin American Economies* (New York: American Books, 1969), 228.

29. Biesanz, Biesanz, and Biesanz, *The Costa Ricans,* 18–22; J. Fred Rippy, "Relations of the United States and Costa Rica during the Guardia Era," *Bulletin of the Pan American Union* 77 (February 1943): 61–68.

30. Theodore S. Creedman, "The Political Development of Costa Rica, 1936–1944: Politics of an Emerging Welfare State in a Patriarchial Society" (Ph.D. diss., University of Maryland, 1971), 27–35.

31. Wilton Nelson, *A History of Protestantism in Costa Rica* (Lucknow, England: Lucknow Publishing House, 1963), 23–27.

32. John H. Furbay, *Education in Costa Rica* (Washington, D.C.: U.S. Office of Education, 1946), 6–8; Luis Felipe González-Flores, *Evolución de la instrucción pública en Costa Rica* (San José: Imprenta Nacional, 1978); Samuel Rovinski, *Cultural Policy in Costa Rica* (Vendôme: Imprimerie des Presses Universitaires de France, 1977), 9; Edward D. Hernández, "Modernization and Dependency in Costa Rica during the Decade of the 1880s" (Ph.D. diss., University of California, Los Angeles, 1980); Busey, *Notes on Costa Rican Democracy,* 49.

33. Ricardo Jinesta and Carlos Jinesta, *La instrucción pública en Costa Rica* (San José: Imprenta Falco y Borrase, 1921), 33–38; Orlando Salazar-Mora, *El apogeo de la república liberal en Costa Rica, 1870–1914* (San José: Editorial de la Universidad de Costa Rica, 1990), 234.

34. Allison, "Survey of the Literature," 58–59. The educational reforms paid dividends. The illiteracy rate declined from 69 percent in 1892 to 23 percent by 1927. Chester Lloyd Jones, *The Caribbean Since 1900* (New York: Russell & Russell, 1936), 357.

35. Antonio Zelaya C., *Cien años de libertad de prensa en Costa Rica; 1843–1943* (San José: Editorial en homenajo al periodísmo nacional, 1943); Allison, "Survey of the Literature," 63.

36. John A. Booth, "Representative Constitutional Democracy in Costa Rica: Adaptation to Crisis in the Turbulent 1980s," in *Central America: Crisis and Adaptation,* ed. Steve C. Ropp and James A. Morris (Albuquerque: University of New Mexico Press, 1984), 162.

37. James L. Busey, "The Presidents of Costa Rica," *The Americas* 18 (January 1961): 55–70.

38. Booth, "Costa Rica: The Roots of Democratic Stability," 391–93; Booth, "Representative Constitutional Democracy," 162.

39. Mercedes Muñoz-Guillén, *El estado y la abolición del ejército, 1914–1949* (San José: Editorial Porvenir, 1990), 104.

40. Stone, *Heritage of the Conquistidors,* 76–86; Allison, "Survey of the Literature," 367.

41. Akira Iriye, *Power and Culture: The Japanese-American War, 1941–1945* (New York: Cambridge University Press, 1981); Frank Costigliola, *Awkward Dominion: American Political, Economic, and Cultural Relations with Europe, 1919–1933* (Ithaca, N.Y.: Cornell University Press, 1984); Emily Rosenberg, *Spreading the American Dream: American Cultural Expansion, 1890–1945* (New York: Hill & Wang, 1982); Frank Ninkovich, *The Diplomacy of Ideas: United States Foreign Policy and Cultural Relations, 1938–1950* (New York: Cambridge University Press, 1981), 2.

42. Akira Iriye, "Culture," *Journal of American History* 77 (June 1990): 100.

43. Franklin D. Parker, *Travels in Central America, 1821–1840* (Gainesville: University of Florida Press, 1970), 217.

44. Ibid., 283–97.

45. Hubert Howe Bancroft, *History of Central America,* vol. 3 (San Francisco: History Company, 1887), 596.

46. Ibid., 622, 634. Other interesting commentaries that emphasized the traditional perceptions were Ephraim Squier, *The States of Central America* (New York: Harper, 1858); idem, *Notes on Central America* (New York: Harper, 1855); William Curtis, "The Smallest of the American Republics," *Harper's Magazine* 75 (October 1887): 668–82; George Earl Church, "Costa Rica," *The Geographical Journal* 10 (July–December 1897): 56–84; Thomas Francis Meagher, "Holidays in Costa Rica," *Harper's Magazine* 20 (December 1859–May 1860): 18, 145, 304; Paul Biolley, *Costa Rica and Her Future* (Washington, D.C.: Judd & Detweiler, 1889); International Bureau of the American Republics, *Costa Rica: A Handbook* (Washington, D.C.: Government Printing Office, 1892); idem, *Commercial Directory of Costa Rica, Guatemala, Honduras, Nicaragua, Salvador* (Washington, D.C.: Government Printing Office, 1891).

47. Richard Villafranca-Carazo, *Costa Rica: The Gem of the America Republics: The Land, Its Resources and Its People* (New York: Sackett & Wilhems, 1895), 8.

48. Cited in J. S. Fuerst, "Central America's Forgotten Democracy," *Commonweal* 110 (20 May 1983): 302–3.

49. Francisco Montero-Barrantes, *Historia de Costa Rica* (San José: Tipografía Nacional, 1892); Joaquín Bernardo Calvo-Mora, *La República de Costa Rica* (New York: Rand, McNally, 1890); Mario Sancho, *Costa Rica: Suiza Centroamerica* (San José: Talleoces Tipográficos "La Tribuna," 1935).

50. Astrid Fischel-Volio, *Consenso y represión; una interpretación socio-política de la educación costarricense* (San José: Editorial Costa Rica, 1987).

51. Dana Munro, *The Five Republics of Central America* (New York, 1918), 139.

52. Ibid., 140.

53. Ibid., 148.

54. Ibid.

55. Hubert Herring, *Good Neighbors: Argentina, Brazil, Chile and Seventeen Other Countries* (New Haven, Conn.: Yale University Press, 1941), 302. Other examples of American views of Costa Rica at the time include: Chester Lloyd Jones, "The Costa Rican Attitude Toward the United States," *World Affairs* 96 (March 1933): 41–43; John Gunther, "Costa Rica, a True Democracy," *Current History and Forum* 52 (24 December 1940): 11–13; James Rippy, *The Caribbean Danger Zone* (New York: G. P. Putnam's Sons, 1940); Wallace Thompson, *Rainbow Countries of Central America* (New York: E. P. Dutton and Sons, 1926), 25; Leo Waibel, "White Settlement in Costa Rica," *Geographical Review* 24 (October 1939): 529–60.

56. Frederick B. Pike, *The United States and Latin America: Myths and Stereotypes of Civilization and Nature* (Austin: University of Texas Press, 1992), xiii–xvii.

57. This understanding was not true for the Costa Ricans. The élites especially knew of the democratic ideas of the United States. The Constitution of 1824 and subsequent constitutions were strongly patterned after the U.S. model. Other cultural exchanges influenced Costa Ricans. Americans were well respected in the fields of scientific investigation, particularly zoology and ornithology. Luis Felipe González-Flores, *Historia de la influencia extranjera en el desenvolvimiento educacional y científico de Costa Rica* (San José: Imprenta Nacional, 1921), 187–234; Harry Bernstein, *Origins of Inter-American Interest, 1700–1812* (New York: Russell & Russell, 1965), 12–18.

58. Thomas L. Karnes, *The Failure of Union: Central America, 1824–1975* (Tempe: Center for Latin American Studies, Arizona State University, 1976), 29–95; Mary Zygmunta Froncek, "Diplomatic Relations between [the] United States and Costa Rica, 1823–1882" (Ph.D. diss., Fordham University, 1959), 51–62; Walter LaFeber, *The Panama Canal: The Crisis in Historical Perspective* (New York: Oxford University Press, 1989); Kenneth Bourne, "The Clayton-Bulwer Treaty and the Decline of British Opposition to the Territorial Expansion of the United States, 1857–1860," *Journal of Modern History* 33 (Summer 1961): 281–97; Richard Van Alystne, "British Diplomacy and the Clayton-Bulwer Treaty," *Journal of Modern History* 11 (Spring 1939): 149–83.

59. Rafael Obregón-Loría, "Nuestras relaciones internacionales a mediados del siglo XIX," *Revista de la Universidad de Costa Rica* 14 (November 1956): 102–3.

60. Ibid., 137–38; Froncek, "Diplomatic Relations," 51–93.

61. Obregón-Loría, "Nuestras relaciones internacionales," 146–78.

62. David Healy, *Drive to Hegemony: The United States in the Caribbean, 1898–1917* (Madison: University of Wisconsin Press, 1988), 19–23.

63. Olien, "The Negro in Costa Rica"; Quince Duncan and Carlos Meléndez-Chavarri, *El negro en Costa Rica* (San José: Editorial Costa Rica, 1972).

64. Charles Brockett, *Land, Power and Poverty: Agrarian Transformation and Political Conflict in Central America* (Boston: Unwin-Hyman, 1988), 29–33.

65. Stacy May and Galo Plaza-Lasso, *The United Fruit Company in Latin America* (New York: Arno Press, 1958), 20.

66. Josef L. Kunz, "The Idea of 'Collective Security' in Pan-American Developments," *Western Political Quarterly* 6 (December 1953): 672–73; Thomas D. Schoonover, *The United States in Central America, 1860–1911: Episodes of Social Imperialism and Imperial Rivalry in the World System* (Durham, N.C.: Duke University Press, 1991), 28–45; Wilfrid Hardy Callcott, *The Caribbean Policy of the United States, 1890–1920* (New York: Octagon Books, 1966), 46; Thomas M. Leonard, *Central America and United States Policies, 1820s–1980s* (Claremont, Calif.: Regina Books, 1985), 42–47; Gordon Ireland, *Boundaries, Possessions and Conflicts in Central and North America and the Caribbean* (New York: Octagon Books, 1971), 20; Froncek, "Diplomatic Relations," 189–205.

67. Carlos José Gutiérrez, "Neutralidad e intervención: dirección y problemas de la política internacional costarricense durante el primer tercio del siglo XX," *Revista de la Universidad de Costa Rica* 13 (July 1956): 18–27; Karnes, *The Failure of Union*, 188; Charles L. Stansifer, "Application of the Tobar Doctrine to Central America," *The Americas* 23 (January 1967): 252–54.

68. Liane Llane Heggy, "The Development of Dependence in Costa Rica and the Role of the Soviet Union" (Ph.D. diss., University of Maryland, 1990), 57, 96; Callcott, *Caribbean Policy of the United States*, 254–91.

69. Armando Rodríguez-Porras, *Juan Rafael Mora-Porras y la guerra contra los filibus-*

teros (San José: Imprenta Las Americas, 1955); Albert Z. Carr, *The World and William Walker* (New York: Harper & Row, 1963); Findling, *Close Neighbors*, 26–33; William F. Slade, "The Federation of Central America" (Ph.D. diss., Clark University, 1917), 109–33.

70. Richard V. Salisbury, *Anti-Imperialism and International Competition in Central America, 1920–1929* (Wilmington, Del.: Scholarly Resources, 1989), 8–92; Bryce Wood, *The United States and the Latin American Wars, 1932–1942* (New York: Columbia University Press, 1966), 7; Suzanne O'Connor, "Costa Rica in the World Community of Nations, 1919–1939: A Case Study in Latin American Internationalism" (Ph.D. diss., Loyola University of Chicago, 1976), 233–34; Stansifer, "Application of the Tobar Doctrine," 260–62.

71. Callcott, *Caribbean Policy of the United States*, 385.

72. Jones, *The Caribbean since 1900*, 405–7.

73. Ibid., 359–64; Eduardo Oconitrillo-García, *Un siglo de política costarricense: Crónica de 32 campañas presidenciales* (San José: Editorial Universidad Estatal a Distancia, 1981), 59–64.

74. Rafael Obregón-Loría, *Hechos militares y políticos de Costa Rica* (Alajuela, Costa Rica: Museo Histórico Cultural Juan Santamaría, 1981), 263–84; Hugo Murillo-Jiménez, "Wilson and Tinoco: The U.S. and the Policy of Non-Recognition in Costa Rica, 1917–1919" (Ph.D. diss., University of California, San Diego, 1978) [published as *Tinoco y los Estados Unidos: Génesis y caída de un régimen* (San José: Editorial Universidad Estatal a Distancia, 1981)].

75. Murillo-Jiménez, "Wilson and Tinoco," 32–46.

76. Ibid., 32–90.

77. Ibid., 94–113, 148–71.

78. Richard V. Salisbury, "The Anti-Imperialist Career of Alejandro Alvarado Quirós," *Hispanic American Historical Review* 57 (November 1977): 590–94; idem, "Costa Rica and the 1920–1921 Union Movement: A Reassessment," *Journal of Interamerican Studies and World Affairs* 19 (August 1977): 393–418; idem, *Costa Rican Relations with Central America, 1900–1934* (Buffalo, N.Y.: Council on International Studies, 1975).

79. Salisbury, "The Anti-Imperialist Career of Alejandro Alvarado Quirós," 595–602.

80. Ibid., 603–12.

81. Victor Bulmer-Thomas, *The Political Economy of Central America since 1920* (New York: Cambridge University Press, 1987), 8–9.

82. Neale Ronning, "Intervention, International Law, and the Inter-American System," *Journal of Interamerican Affairs* 3 (April 1961): 250–54; Francis Wilcox, "The Monroe Doctrine and World War II," *American Political Science Review* 36 (June 1942): 433–53; John Mathews, "Roosevelt's Latin American Policy," *American Political Science Review* 29 (October 1935): 805–21.

83. Anne W. Lommel, "The United States' Efforts to Foster Peace and Stability in Central America, 1923–1954" (Ph.D. diss., University of Minnesota, 1967), 130–34.

2. Laying the Foundations of Change: The United States, President Rafael Angel Calderón, and the Rise of José Figueres, 1940–1944

1. Charles Morrow Wilson, *Challenge and Opportunity: Central America* (New York: Henry Holt, 1941), 92.

2. John P. Bell, *Crisis in Costa Rica: The 1948 Revolution* (Austin: University of Texas Press, 1971), 20.

3. Creedman, "Political Development of Costa Rica," 90.

4. Ibid., 89–91.

5. Rafael Angel Calderón-Guardia, *El gobernante y el hombre frente al problema social costarricense* (San José: Privately published, 1942), 11–13; Fernando Torres-Vinenzi, *Doctor Rafael Calderón-Guardia—esbozo biográfico* (San José: Imprenta Lehmann, 1940), 1–48; Jorge Mario Salazar-Mora, *Calderón-Guardia* (San José: Ministerio de Cultura, Juventud y Desportes, 1980), 25–27; Lillian Parker-Wallace, *Leo XIII and the Rise of Socialism* (Durham, N.C.: Duke University Press, 1966), 254–76; Harold Bonilla, *Los presidentes* (San José: Editorial Estatal a Distancia 1979), 371–424.

6. Helen Jacobstein, *The Process of Economic Development in Costa Rica, 1948–1970: Some Political Factors* (New York: Garland Publishers, 1987), 14; Brumbaugh, "Costa Rica," 268; Mario Carvajal-Herrera, "Ideologías en la política costarricense y sus resultados electorales," *Revista de Ciencias Sociales* 7 (April 1973): 8–12.

7. Bell, *Crisis in Costa Rica,* 29–31.

8. Jorge Mario Salazar-Mora, "Rafael Angel Calderón-Guardía, el funador," *Revista de Ciencias Sociales* 49–50 (September–December 1990): 7–11; Pan American Union, "Costa Rican National University Established," *Bulletin of the Pan American Union* 74 (December 1940): 844–45; John McCamant, *Development Assistance in Central America* (New York: Praeger, 1968), 195–96.

9. Pan American Union, "Costa Rican Housing Board," *Bulletin of the Pan American Union* 75 (May 1941): 314–15.

10. Mark Rosenberg, "The Politics of Health Care in Costa Rica, 1941–1975" (Ph.D. diss., University of Pittsburgh, 1976), 84–128; idem, "Social Reform in Costa Rica: Social Security and the Presidency of Rafael Angel Calderón," *Hispanic American Historical Review* 62 (May 1981): 278–96; idem, "Social Security Policymaking in Costa Rica: A Research Report," *Latin American Research Review* 14 (1979): 118–23.

11. Creedman, "Political Development of Costa Rica," 186.

12. James Dunkerley, *Power in the Isthmus* (New York: Verso, 1988), 126; Kenneth J. Mijeski, "The Executive-Legislative Policy Process in Costa Rica" (Ph.D. diss., University of North Carolina, 1971), 53–54.

13. Sheldon Liss, *Radical Thought in Central America* (Boulder, Colo.: Westview Press, 1991), 144–49; John Booth, "Costa Rica," 213–20; Ana María Botey and Rodolfo Cisneros, *La crisis del 1929 y la fundación del Partido Comunista de Costa Rica* (San José: Editorial Costa Rica, 1984); Clarence F. Jones and Paul C. Morison, "Evolution of the Banana Industry in Costa Rica," *Economic Geography* 28 (January 1952): 7–14.

14. Rosa Emilia Rodríguez-Stein, "Collective Actions in Peripheral Nations: A Comparative Analysis of Five Central American Countries" (Ph.D. diss., University of Arizona, 1989), 59–60; Charles D. Kepner, Jr., *Social Aspects of the Banana Industry* (New York: AMS Press, 1967), 188–90; Arthur A. Pollan, *The United Fruit Company in Middle America* (New York: privately published, 1944), 3–27; Brumbaugh, "Costa Rica," 200–201.

15. Charles D. Ameringer, *Don Pepe: A Political Biography of José Figueres of Costa Rica* (Albuquerque: University of New Mexico Press, 1978), 9.

16. Bell, *Crisis in Costa Rica,* 42.

17. Ibid., 110; Norma Stolz Chinchilla, "Class Struggles in Central America: Background and Overview," *Latin American Perspectives* 7 (Spring–Summer 1980): 2–23.

18. Williams, *The Catholic Church and Politics in Nicaragua and Costa Rica* (Pittsburgh: University of Pittsburgh Press, 1989), 111.

19. Oscar Aguilar-Bulgarelli, *Costa Rica y sus hechos políticos de 1948* (San José: Editorial Universitaria Centroamérica, 1974), 395–411; Alberto Cañas, *Los ocho años* (San José: Editorial Liberación Nacional, 1955), 49; Jacobstein, *The Process of Economic Development in Costa Rica, 1948–1970,* 62.

20. Williams, *The Catholic Church and Politics in Nicaragua and Costa Rica,* 110; Ricardo Blanco-Segura, *Monseñor Sanabria* (San José: Editorial Costa Rica, 1971), 19–55; Rodrigo Fernández-Vásquez, "Costa Rica: Interpretación histórica sobre reforma social y acción eclesiastica, 1940–1982," *Estudios Sociales Centroamericanos* 33 (September–December 1982): 224–25.

21. Bell, *Crisis in Costa Rica,* 31; Salazar-Mora, *Calderón-Guardia,* 55–93; Joseph McGovern, "The Costa Rican Labor Movement: A Study in Political Unionism," *Public and International Affairs* 4 (Spring 1966): 88–116.

22. Hanson H. Hathaway, "Costa Rica's Bloodless Revolution," *The Pan American* 5 (May 1944): 15–16; Pan American Union, "Message of the President of Costa Rica," *Bulletin of the Pan American Union* 77 (December 1943): 706–9; Pan American Union, "Message of the President of Costa Rica," *Bulletin of the Pan American Union* 78 (September 1944): 526–28.

23. Creedman, "Political Development of Costa Rica," 162–67.

24. Charles Proctor, "Political Systems," in *Turrialba: Social Systems and the Introduction of Change,* ed. Charles P. Loomis, et al. (Glencoe, Ill.: Free Press, 1953), 220–21; Bell, *Crisis in Costa Rica,* 46.

25. Ameringer, *Don Pepe,* 13–16.

26. Cañas, *Los ocho años,* 43–49. An interesting example of the Center's publications includes the pamphlet *El Partido Comunista de Costa Rica, enjuiciado por sus hechos* (San José: El Centro de Estudios de Problemas Nacionales, 1943).

27. Bell, *Crisis in Costa Rica,* 35–36, 81–82.

28. The bibliography of José Figueres is large and includes: Alberto Baeza-Flores, *La lucha sin fin* (Mexico City: Costa-Amic., 1969); Harold H. Bonilla, *Figueres and Costa Rica: An Unauthorized Political Biography* (San José: Editorial Texto Limitada, 1975); Arturo Castro-Esquivel, *José Figueres-Ferrer* (San José: Imprenta Tormo, 1955); Alfonso Chase, *José Figueres: Escritos y discursos, 1942–1962* (San José: Editorial Costa Rica, 1989); Tomás Guerra, *José Figueres: Una vida por la justicia social* (San José: 1987); Harry Kantor, *Bibliography of José Figueres* (Tempe: Center for Latin American Studies, Arizona State University, 1972); Hugo Navarro-Bolandi, *José Figueres en la evolución de Costa Rica* (Mexico City: Imprenta Quirós, 1953).

29. Figueres was conceived in Spain but born in Costa Rica after his parents emigrated to the country. His parents and relatives reportedly instilled in him values that characterized their native country more than Costa Rica, including a reliance on direct conflict to settle matters.

30. Robert Alexander, interiew with author, 15 June 1992, New Brunswick, New Jersey; Charles Ameringer, interview with author, 19 June 1993, Charlottesville, Virginia.

31. Schifter-Sikora, "Origins of the Cold War," 175–76; Ameriinger, *Don Pepe,* 17.

32. Third Secretary of Embassy in San José S. Roger Tyler to Secretary of State, 14 January 1944, National Archives of the United States, Record Group 59, 818.00/1916 [hereinafter cited by names of communicators, date, RG 59 and filing information];

Chargé d'Affaires Edward Trueblood to Secretary of State, 24 May 1944, RG 59, 818.00/2054.

33. Edgar S. Furniss, "American Wartime Objectives in Latin America," *World Politics* 7 (August 1950): 373–88.

34. Pan American Union, "The Washington Visit of the President-Elect of Costa Rica," *Bulletin of the Pan American Union* 14 (May 1940): 374.

35. Schifter-Sikora, "Origins of the Cold War," 77.

36. U.S. Army Commander DeCourcy Browne to the State Department, 26 March 1940, RG 59, 818.014/33.

37. Hornibrook to Secretary of State, 24 June 1940, *Foreign Relations of United States, 1940* (Washington, D.C.: Government Printing Office, 1961), 5:87–88 [hereinafter cited by names of communicators, date, *FRUS*, year, volume number, and page numbers].

38. U.S. Naval Attaché in Guatemala F. M. June to Navy Department, 16 July 1940, RG 59, 818.00-N/125.

39. A good example of the wartime military cooperation is outlined in *FRUS, 1942*, vol. 5, "Agreement Between the U.S. and Costa Rica Regarding Principles Applying to Mutual Aid in the Prosecution of the War," 16 January 1942, 235–38. Throughout the war, the Costa Rican army remained small. In 1943, it had 241 enlisted men and 46 officers. Federal Bureau of Investigation, "Totalitarian Activities in Costa Rica Today," September 1943, Private Papers of Harry L. Hopkins, FBI Reports, File #142, 118, Franklin D. Roosevelt Library, Hyde Park, New York [hereinafter FDR Library].

40. Hornibrook to Secretary of State, 1 March 1941, *FRUS, 1941* 7:82–83; Hornibrook to Secretary of State, 26 March 1941, *FRUS, 1941* 7:83–84; Hornibrook to Secretary of State, 27 March 1941, *FRUS, 1941* 7:84–85; Welles to Hornibrook, 28 March 1941, *FRUS, 1941* 7:86.

41. Hornibrook to Secretary of State, 30 March 1941, *FRUS, 1941* 7:86–87; Hornibrook to Secretary of State, 4 April 1941, *FRUS, 1941* 7:87; Hull to Hornibrook, 25 April 1941, *FRUS, 1941* 7:87–88.

42. Chargé in Costa Rica Edward Dwyre to Secretary of State, 26 April 1941, *FRUS, 1941* 7:88; Hull to Dwyre, 13 May 1941, *FRUS, 1941* 7:88; Dwyre to Secretary of State, 28 May 1941, *FRUS, 1941* 7:90–91; Dwyre to Secretary of State, 31 May 1941, *FRUS, 1941* 7:91; Hull to Dwyre, 5 June 1941, *FRUS, 1941* 7:91–92; Dwyre to Secretary of State, 6 June 1941, *FRUS, 1941* 7:92–94; Hull to Dwyre, 7 June 1941, *FRUS, 1941* 7:94; Dwyre to Secretary of State, 9 June 1941, *FRUS, 1941* 7:95.

43. *Diario de Costa Rica* (San José), 8 December 1941; Henry M. Howell, "Western Hemisphere Accord," *The South Atlantic Quarterly* 41 (July 1942): 250; Carlos Calvo-Gamboa, *Costa Rica en la segunda guerra mundial, 1939–1945* (San José: Editorial Universidad Estatal a Distancia, 1985). Paul Daniels, a prominent State Department official, declared, "One good thing about Costa Rica is that they declared war before anybody else on the Nazis. Arthur Lane was down there at the time and he was quite proud of that." Paul C. Daniels, interview with Richard D. McKinzie, 11 June 1974, transcript, Harry S. Truman Oral History Collection, Harry S. Truman Library, Independence, Kansas, 21 [hereinafter Truman Library].

44. C. Harvey Gardiner, "The Japanese and Central America," *Journal of Interamerican Studies* 14 (February 1972): 15–49.

45. Irving Child, "The Background of Public Opinion in Costa Rica," *Public Opinion Quarterly* 7 (Summer 1943): 244–47; Schifter-Sikora, "Origins of the Cold War," 52–70;

Glade, *Latin American Economies,* 223; Eugencio Herrera-Balharry, *Los alemanes y el estado cafetalero* (San José: Editorial Estatal a Distáncia, 1988), 1–230; J. Manuel Espinosa, *Inter-American Beginnings of U.S. Cultural Diplomacy, 1936–1948* (Washington, D.C.: Government Printing Office 1976), 255–56.

46. Memorandum by the Office of the Assistant Secretary of State, 5 January 1942, *FRUS, 1942* 5:280–81.

47. Scotten to Secretary of State, 16 July 1942, RG 59, 818.012/37; Edward Barnhart, "Citizenship and Political Tests in Latin American Republics in World War II," *Hispanic American Historical Review* 42 (August 1962): 301.

48. Ameringer, *Don Pepe,* 10–11.

49. "Morazan's Dream," *Time* 40 (21 September 1942): 35–36.

50. Joseph Thorning, "Costa Rica: A Rural Democracy," *World Affairs* 108 (September 1945): 178.

51. Child, "Background of Public Opinion," 243.

52. Lawrence Martin and Sylvia Martin, "Four Strong Men and a President," *Harper's Magazine* 185 (September 1942): 418–27.

53. U.S. Department of State, "Survey of the Elements of Instability in the Latin American Sector," 30 January 1942, Papers of Henry Wallace, Box 79, FDR Library.

54. Randall B. Woods, "Decision-making in Diplomacy: The Rio Conference of 1942," *Social Science Quarterly* 55 (1975): 901–18; Bryce Wood, *The Dismantling of the Good Neighbor Policy* (Austin: University of Texas Press, 1985), 1–4; Michael J. Francis, "The United States at Rio, 1942: The Strains of Pan Americanism," *Journal of Latin American Studies* 6 (May 1974): 77–95.

55. Acting Secretary of State Edward Stettinius to the Diplomatic Representatives in the United Kingdom and all the American Republics Except Argentina, 2 August 1944, *FRUS, 1944* 7:336–37.

56. Hull to Hornibrook, 25 September 1940, *FRUS, 1940* 5:736; Calderón to Roosevelt, 16 September 1943, Office Files 153, Box 1, FDR Library.

57. Welles to Roosevelt, 12 June 1942, Office Files 153, Box 1, FDR Library.

58. Hull to Scotten, 27 May 1942, *FRUS, 1942* 5:247.

59. Calderón first met Somoza when he went to Nicaragua in 1937 to serve as a commissioner to help settle a Nicaraguan-Honduran border problem. They developed a strong relationship that lasted for many years afterward. Creedman, "Political Development of Costa Rica," 162–67; Schifter-Sikora, "Origins of the Cold War," 211–13.

60. Robert J. Alexander, *Communism in Latin America* (New Brunswick, N.J.: Rutgers University Press, 1957), 24–27; Heggy, "Development of Dependence," 57, 96.

61. Scotten to Secretary of State, 23 July 1942, RG 59, 818.00B/123; Schifter-Sikora, "Origins of the Cold War," 197–204.

62. Des Portes to Secretary of State, 11 August 1943, RG 59, 818.00B/129.

63. J. Edgar Hoover to Major General Edwin M. Watson (secretary to the president), 27 November 1941, Office File 10b, File 998-A, FDR Library.

64. FBI, "Totalitarian Activities in Costa Rica Today," 118, FDR Library.

65. Ibid., 124.

66. Ibid., 129.

67. Embassy in Costa Rica to the War Department, 10 July 1942, Map Room File, Box 79, FDR Library.

68. Des Portes to Secretary of State, 20 October 1943, RG 59, 818.00/1891.

69. Bell, *Crisis in Costa Rica,* 43.

70. Scotten to Secretary of State, 20 March 1943, *FRUS, 1943* 6:61–62. After a meeting with Mora, Chargé d'Affaires Trueblood wrote that "Mora impressed me as an extremely serious minded individual with well defined views on many subjects and intensely interested in improving the labor and living conditions of the people of Costa Rica. His observations were almost entirely in a moderate vein." Trueblood to Secretary of State, 1 February 1944, RG 59, 818.00/1940.

71. Trueblood to State Department, 24 September 1943, RG 59, 818.00/1830.

72. Thorning, "Costa Rica," 171–80; "Dangerous Election," *Time* 63 (14 February 1944): 38; Hathaway, "Costa Rica's Bloodless Revolution," 13–16; Ameringer, *Don Pepe,* 25–27; Cañas, *Los ocho años,* 49–62; *New York Times,* 8 February 1944. Calderón further angered members of the opposition in the last months of his presidency. He declared an amnesty for members of his party accused of electoral offenses and fiscal corruption. Although the Supreme Court overturned the decree, to many the act demonstrated "the President's inclination to misuse executive power." Bell, *Crisis in Costa Rica,* 72.

3. The Times Are a-Changing: The Emergence of Problems between the Picado Administration and the United States, 1944–1948

1. Joseph Thorning, "The Costa Rican Story," *World Affairs* 112 (Summer 1949): 49.

2. Reynold E. Carlson, "Economic Development in Central America," *Inter-American Economic Affairs* 2 (Autumn 1948): 5–30.

3. Picado had problems with the Catholic Church resulting from a divorce, and his ties with the Church were never as close as Calderón's.

4. Pan American Union, "Message of the President of Costa Rica," *Bulletin of the Pan American Union* 79 (August 1945): 470–71; Bell, *Crisis in Costa Rica,* 26.

5. Bonilla, *Los presidentes,* 425–59.

6. Federico Gonzalo Vargas, "The Income Tax in a Developing Nation: The Costa Rican Case" (Ph.D. diss., University of Colorado, 1973); Pan American Union, "Income Tax in Costa Rica," *Bulletin of the Pan American Union* 81 (August 1947): 455.

7. Pan American Union, "Visit of the President-Elect of Costa Rica to Washington," *Bulletin of the Pan American Union* 78 (July 1944): 361–64.

8. Trueblood to Secretary of State, 15 January 1944, National Archives of the United States, Record Group 59, 818.00/1-927.

9. Ibid.; Des Portes to Secretary of State, 16 February 1944, RG 59, 818.00/1985.

10. Johnson to Costa Rican Foreign Minister Julio Acosta, 13 August 1945, Archivo Nacional de Costa Rica, Relaciones Exteriories, Estados Unidos, Packet 1070 [hereinafter cited by names of communicators, date, A.N.C.R., country name, and filing information].

11. J. Garry Clifford, "Bureaucratic Politics," in *Explaining the History of American Foreign Relations,* ed. Michael J. Hogan and Thomas G. Paterson (New York: Cambridge University Press, 1991), 141–50.

12. Johnson to Secretary of State, 27 February 1945, RG 59, 818.00/2–2745.

13. Johnson to Secretary of State, 6 March 1945, RG 59, 818.00/3–645.

14. *Diario de Costa Rica,* 2 March 1945.

15. Johnson to Secretary of State, 26 April 1945, RG 59, 818.00/4–2645.

16. Ibid.

17. Mora to Truman, 7 July 1945, Official Files (OF) #153-Misc, Truman Library.

18. Johnson to Secretary of State, 12 April 1945, RG 59, 818.00/4–1245.

19. Ibid.

20. Cited in David Green, *The Containment of Latin America: A History of the Myths and Realities of the Good Neighbor Policy* (Chicago: Quadrangle Books, 1971), 181.

21. FBI Director J. Edgar Hoover to Assistant Secretary of State Adolf A. Berle, Jr., 23 November 1944, RG 59, 818.00B/11–2344. Earlier, Hoover reported to Berle that a secret anti-Communist organization had been organized in Costa Rica to combat the Vanguard by creating a spy network and shock troops to challenge the Communists. Hoover to Berle, 2 September 1944, RG 59, 818.00B/9–244.

22. Hoover to Frederick Lyon, Department of State Chief of the Division of Foreign Activity Correlation, 1 August 1945, RG 59, 818.00/8–145.

23. José Luis Torres-Rodríguez, *Otílio Ulate: Su partido y sus luchas* (San José: Editorial Costa Rica, 1985), 14–15, 49; John W. Gardner, "The Costa Rican Junta of 1948–1949" (Ph.D. diss., St. John's University, 1971), 105–6.

24. Memorandum of conversation between Murray Wise and Francisco Gutiérrez, 1 May 1946, RG 59, 818.00/5–146; Schifter-Sikora, "Origins of the Cold War," 234–36; Espinosa, *Inter-American Beginnings*, 288; Mario Solera-Castro, Lowell Gudmundson, and Jacobo Schifter-Sikora, *El judío en Costa Rica* (San José: Editorial Estatal a Distancia, 1979), 172.

25. Father Benjamín Núñez, interview with author, 28 June 1991, San José, Costa Rica.

26. Fernández-Vásquez, "Costa Rica," 221–48; James Backer, *La iglesia y el sindicalismo en Costa Rica* (San José: Editorial Costa Rica, 1974), 99–107; McGovern, "Costa Rican Labor Movement," 103; Labor Attaché in Costa Rica Daniel Valdés to the Secretary of State, 4 June 1946, RG 59, 818.504/6–446.

27. Johnson to Secretary of State, 10 May 1945, RG 59, 818.00/5–1045.

28. Al Weinrub, *The AFL-CIO in Central America: A Look at the American Institute for Free Labor Development* (Oakland, Calif.: Labor Network on Central America, 1987), 7; Schifter-Sikora, "Origins of the Cold War," 237–40.

29. Ameringer, *Don Pepe*, 29–31; Bell, *Crisis in Costa Rica*, 43.

30. Johnson to Secretary of State, 15 March 1945, RG 59, 818.00/3–1545.

31. Obregón-Loría, *Hechos militares y políticos*, 315; Chargé d'Affaires Raleigh Gibson to Secretary of State, 26 June 1946, RG 59, 818.00/6–2646; Hoover to Lyon, 13 December 1945, RG 59, 818.00/12–345; Third Secretary of the Embassy Livingston Watrous to the Secretary of State, 31 December 1945, RG 59, 818.00/12–3145; Johnson to the Secretary of State, 12 April 1946, RG 59, 818.00/4–246.

32. *Ultima Hora* (San José), 9 November 1946.

33. Johnson to Secretary of State, 14 November 1946, RG 59, 818.00/11–1446; Johnson to the Secretary of State, 30 October 1946, RG 59, 818.00/19–3046.

34. Johnson to the Secretary of State, 20 February 1946, RG 59, 818.00/2–2046.

35. Johnson to Secretary of State, 22 March 1946, *FRUS, 1946* 9:693.

36. Ibid., 693–94.

37. U.S. Embassy to the Costa Rican Government, 12 March 1946, A.N.C.R., Estados Unidos, Packet 1070; Memorandum from the Costa Rican Government to the U.S. Government relating to Argentina, 16 March 1946, A.N.C.R., Estados Unidos, Packet 1070; Johnson to the Secretary of State, 20 February 1946, *FRUS, 1946* 9:692; Johnson to the Secretary of State, 3 April 1946, *FRUS, 1946* 9:12–13; Johnson to Secretary of State, 25 October 1946, *FRUS, 1946* 9:697; J. Tillapaugh, "Closed Hemisphere

and Open World? The Dispute Over Regional Security at the U.N. Conference, 1945," *Diplomatic History* 2 (Winter 1977): 25–42.

38. Johnson to Secretary of State, 25 October 1946, *FRUS, 1946* 9:697.

39. Gibson to the Secretary of State, 12 July 1946, *FRUS, 1946* 9:683–84.

40. Johnson to Acosta, 30 October 1946, A.N.C.R., Estados Unidos, Packet 1070; Acosta to Johnson, 1 November 1946, A.N.C.R., Estados Unidos, Packet 1070; U.S. Embassy to Acosta, 12 September 1946, A.N.C.R., Estados Unidos, Packet 1373. The Costa Ricans also supported the United States and its efforts to create a nation-state for the Jews. Solera-Castro, Gudmundson, and Schifter-Sikora, *El judío en Costa Rica,* 364–70.

41. Johnson to Secretary of State, 22 March 1946, *FRUS, 1946* 9:693.

42. Ibid.

43. Ibid.

44. Johnson to Secretary of State, 1 April 1946, RG 59, 818.00/4–146.

45. Johnson to Secretary of State, 4 May 1946, RG 59, 818.00/5–446.

46. Johnson to Secretary of State, 12 April 1946, RG 59, 818.00/4–1246.

47. Johnson to the Secretary of State, 29 October 1946, RG 59, 818.00/10–2946.

48. The literature on the origins of the Cold War is endless. Some very good works include: Walter LaFeber, *America, Russia, and the Cold War, 1945–1992,* 7th ed. (New York: McGraw-Hill, 1992); Lloyd Gardner, *Architects of Illusion: Men and Ideas in American Foreign Policy, 1941–1949* (Chicago: Quadrangle Books, 1970); Adam Ulam, *The Rivals: America and Russia since World War II* (New York: Viking Press, 1971); Thomas G. Paterson, *Soviet-American Confrontation* (Baltimore: Johns Hopkins Press, 1973); Richard Freeland, *The Truman Doctrine and the Origins of McCarthyism* (New York: Knopf, 1972); John L. Gaddis, *The United States and the Origins of the Cold War* (New York: Columbia University Press, 1972).

49. Hoover to Lyon, 10 June 1946, RG 59, 818.00/6–1046; Alexander, *Communism in Latin America,* 40. The CIA described the Congress as Communist controlled. It stated: "The head of the Confederation is Vicente Lombardo Toledano, who despite his assertion that he is not a Communist, is regarded throughout the area as the Communists' spokesman in labor affairs." Central Intelligence Agency, "Soviet Objectives in Latin America," 10 April 1947, Personal Secretary's Files (PSF), Intelligence Files, Box 254, Truman Library.

50. Hoover to Lyon, 3 July 1946, RG 59, 818.00/7–346.

51. Hoover to Lyon, 19 April 1946, RG 59, 818.00 B/4–1946.

52. Schifter-Sikora, "Origins of the Cold War," 249–51.

53. William T. Bennett, Jr., letter to author, 11 January 1992. Bennett developed a reputation as a virulent anti-Communist during his service in the State Department. He worked in the Eisenhower administration during the Guatemalan intervention in 1954 and later served as U.S. ambassador to the Dominican Republic during the crisis in 1965 and as ambassador to the North Atlantic Treaty Organization.

54. Johnson to Secretary of State, 25 November 1945, *FRUS, 1945* 9:884–85.

55. Acting Secretary of State Dean Acheson to Johnson, 21 August 1946, *FRUS, 1946* 9:684–85; Acheson to Johnson, 12 December 1946, *FRUS, 1946* 9:689–90; Memorandum of conversation between Gutiérrez and Wise, 21 March 1947, RG 59, 818.00/3–2147.

56. State Department to the Embassy in Costa Rica, 14 February 1947, RG 59, 818.00/2–1347; Johnson to State Department, 13 February 1947, RG 59, 818.00/2–1347.

57. *La Tribuna* (San José), 2 July 1946.

58. Memorandum of conversation between Calderón, Gutiérrez, Braden, and Wise, 5 June 1946, RG 59, 818.00/6–546.

59. *La Tribuna,* 1 December 1946.

60. Johnson to Secretary of State, 28 March 1947, RG 59, 818.00/3–2847.

61. Memorandum from Bennett to Wise, Ellis Briggs, and Robert Woodward, 7 April 1947, RG 59, 818.00/3–2747.

62. Cañas, *Los ocho años,* 85.

63. Ameringer, *Don Pepe,* 33.

64. Bennett to Braden, 17 February 1947, RG 59, 818.00/2–1747.

65. Johnson to Truman, March 20, 1947, OF #731, Truman Library. Later, Truman's secretary, Charles G. Ross, in a response to a letter from Johnson, stated: "Here is another cry of anguish from Hallet Johnson." Ross to Acheson, 16 April 1947, OF #731, Truman Library. The opposition highlighted Johnson's removal. In a cruel irony, the paper *La Hora* published a section entitled "Jokes and Hoaxes," which included a segment about the existing efforts to remove Communists from the State Department. It immediately followed the announcement of Johnson's reassignment. *La Hora* (San José), 25 March 1947.

66. Another motive for Johnson's removal may have been to unseat a pro-Braden supporter, part of an overall move against the secretary of state in early 1947.

67. Johnson to Secretary of State, 14 April 1947, RG 59, 818.00/4–1447.

68. Ibid.

69. Thomas M. Leonard, "The United States and Costa Rica, 1944–1949: Perceptions of Political Dynamics," *SECOLAS Annals* 13 (1982): 24.

70. Lester to Bennett, 22 May 1947, RG 59, 818.00/5–2247.

71. Teodoro Picado-Lara (the president's son) letter to the author, 13 September 1991.

72. U.S. Ambassador to Costa Rica Walter Donnelly to Secretary of State, 7 July 1947, RG 59, 818.00/7–747.

73. Ibid. Donnelly presented his credentials on 27 June 1947.

74. William Krehm, *Democracies and Tyrannies of the Caribbean* (Westport, Conn.: Lawrence Hill, 1984), 122–25; Leonard, *The United States and Central America,* 137–49; William Berman, *Under the Big Stick: Nicaragua and the United States since 1848* (Boston: South End Press, 1986); 236–37; Paul Coe Clark, *The United States and Somoza, 1933 1956: A Revisionist Look* (New York: Praeger, 1992), 162–74.

75. Memorandum of discussion of the Nicaraguan political situation between Chief of the Division of Central America and Panama Affairs Robert Newbegin and Nicaraguan Ambassador Guillermo Sevilla-Sacasa, 5 June 1947, *Foreign Relations: Memoranda of Conversation of Secretary of State, 1947–1952* (Washington, D.C.: Government Printing Office, 1988) [microfiche], no. 36 [hereinafter cited by names of communicators, date, *Memoranda of Conversation of Secretary of State, 1947–1952,* and number]; Marshall to American Diplomatic Representatives in the American Republics, 12 January 1948, *FRUS, 1948* 9:99.

76. Embassy in San José to War Department, 30 September 1944, Map Room File, Box 79, FDR Library; Washington to Secretary of State, 29 September 1944, RG 59, 818.00/9–2944; Obregón-Loría, *Hechos militares y politicos,* 313–15; "Revolt Against Nothing," *Newsweek* 24 (23 October 1944): 67.

77. Donnelly to Secretary of State, 20 September 1947, *FRUS, 1947* 8:872–74.

78. First Secretary of the Embassy John Carrigan to Secretary of State, 25 November 1947, *FRUS, 1947* 8:877.

79. Schifter-Sikora, "Origins of the Cold War," 290–91.

80. John D. Martz, *Central America* (Chapel Hill: University of North Carolina Press, 1959), 212–14; Obregón-Loría, *Hechos militares y políticos,* 315–18; "Freedom to Campaign," *Newsweek* 30 (4 August 1947): 52; "Costa Rican Revolt," *Life* 23 (25 August 1947): 36; *La Tribuna,* 26 July 1947; *Ultima Hora,* 26 July 1947.

81. Memorandum of conversation between Carrigan and Wise, 29 July 1947, RG 59, 818.00/7–2947; Memorandum of conversation between Carrigan, Wise, and Donnelly, 29 July 1947, *FRUS, 1947* 8:582–83.

82. Ameringer, *Don Pepe,* 36–37; Pan American Union, "Costa Rican Election Law," *Bulletin of the Pan American Union* 81 (January 1947): 49–50; *La Gaceta* (San José), 27 March 1946.

83. Charles D. Ameringer, *The Democratic Left in Exile: The Antidictatorial Struggle in the Caribbean, 1945–1959* (Coral Gables, Fla.: University of Miami Press, 1974), 63–75; Aguilar-Bulgarelli, *Costa Rica y sus hechos políticos,* 245–61.

84. Wise to Newbegin and Trueblood, 3 October 1946, RG 59, 818.00/9–1946.

85. Johnson to Secretary of State, 3 April 1947, RG 59, 818.00/4–347.

86. Carrigan to Secretary of State, 10 July 1947, RG 59, 818.00/7–1047.

87. Donnelly to Secretary of State, 9 October 1947, RG 59, 818.00/10–947.

88. Ibid.

89. The FBI began turning over intelligence operations in Latin America in August 1946. Arthur B. Darling, *The Central Intelligence Agency: An Instrument of Government to 1950* (University Park: Pennsylvania State University Press, 1990), 120–21.

90. Central Intelligence Agency, "Soviet Objectives in Latin America," 1 November 1947, PSF, Intelligence File, Box 254, Truman Library.

91. Ibid.

92. Ibid.

4. The First Latin American Battleground of the Cold War: The U.S. Response to the Costa Rican Civil War of 1948

1. Taken partially from the title of an address Figueres presented at Rollins College in 1951.

2. *New York Times,* 22 March 1948.

3. Bell, *Crisis in Costa Rica,* 122; Vice-consul Alex Cohen to Secretary of State, 12 January 1948, RG 59, 818.00/1–1248.

4. *Diario de Costa Rica,* 16 January 1948; First Secretary of the Embassy Andrew Donovan to Secretary of State, 20 January 1948, RG 59, 818.00/1–2048; Memorandum from Bennett to Newbegin and the director of the Office of American Republic Affairs, Paul Daniels, 20 January 1948, RG 59, 818.00/1–2048.

5. Bell, *Crisis in Costa Rica,* 60.

6. Memorandum from Bennett to Newbegin, Robert Woodward, and Daniels, 28 January 1948, RG 59, 818.00/1–2148.

7. Ibid.

8. Carrigan to Secretary of State, 8 January 1948, RG 59, 818.00/1–848.

9. Cohen to Secretary of State, 27 January 1948, RG 59, 818.00/1–2748.

10. *La Estrella de Panamá* (Panama City), 8 February 1948.
11. Ibid.
12. Aguilar-Bulgarelli, *Costa Rica y sus hechos políticos,* 479.
13. *La Tribuna* (San José), 11 February 1948.
14. *La Estrella de Panamá,* 10 February 1948.
15. Gardner, "Costa Rican Junta," 44–45.
16. *La Tribuna,* 13 February 1948; *La Estrella de Panamá,* 14 February 1948.
17. *La Hora* (San José), 21 February 1948; *La Tribuna,* 22 February 1948.
18. Davis to Secretary of State, 12 February 1948, RG 59, 818.00/2–1248.
19. Davis to Secretary of State, 18 February 1948, RG 59, 818.00/2–1148.
20. Davis to Secretary of State, 26 February 1948, RG 59, 818.00/2–2648; Davis to Secretary of State, 27 February 1948, RG 59, 818.00/2–2748.
21. *La Estrella de Panamá,* 29 February 1948. The National Republican charges of fraud centered on the director of the electoral tribunal, Benjamín Odio. They accused him of not including voters on the lists from areas supportive of the Vanguard and National Republicans. The charges carried some weight; Odio left San José immediately after the announcement and joined the rebel forces. Ameringer, *Don Pepe,* 43–44.
22. *La Gaceta* (San José), 3 March 1948.
23. Bell, *Crisis in Costa Rica,* 128.
24. Ibid., 129.
25. Diary of Nathaniel Davis, 1 March 1948, Private Papers of Nathaniel P. Davis, Box 1, Truman Library [hereinafter Davis Diary].
26. Bonilla to Davis, 3 March 1948, A.N.C.R., Estados Unidos, Packet 1549; Davis Diary, 2 March 1948; *The Times* [London], 4 March 1948; Davis to Secretary of State, 2 March 1948, *FRUS, 1948* 9:488–89; Davis to Secretary of State, 3 March 1948, *FRUS, 1948* 9:489–91.
27. *La Estrella de Panamá,* 4 March 1948; Davis Diary, 3 March 1948.
28. Davis Diary, 5 March 1948.
29. Ibid.; Davis to Secretary of State, 5 March 1948, RG 59, 818.00/3–548.
30. Memorandum of conversation between Gutiérrez, Newbegin, and Daniels, 5 March 1948, RG 59, 818.00/3–548.
31. *La Estrella de Panamá,* 7 March 1948; John D. Martz, *Central America: The Crisis and the Challenge* (Chapel Hill: University of North Carolina Press, 1959), 218.
32. Ameringer, *Don Pepe,* 31–32.
33. Harry B. Murkland, "Costa Rica: Fortunate Society," *Current History* 22 (March 1952): 144.
34. Obregón-Loría, *Hechos militares y políticos,*322–32; Ameringer, *Democratic Left,* 76.
35. Central Intelligence Agency, "The Caribbean Legion," 17 March 1949, PSF, Intelligence Files, Box 256, Truman Library; Harry Murkland, "The Complicated Caribbean," *Current History* 18 (January 1950): 9.
36. Ameringer, *Don Pepe,* 51.
37. Jesús Aranda-Barrantes, *Los excombatientes de 1948–55* (San José: Imprenta Lehmann, 1984); Davis Diary, 14 March 1948; *La Estrella de Panamá,* 14 March 1948.
38. Davis Diary, 14 March 1948.
39. Davis to Bonilla, 18 March 1948, A.N.C.R., Estados Unidos, Packet 1549; Davis Diary, 18 March 1948.
40. Davis Diary, 17 March 1948; Davis to Secretary of State, 19 March 1948, RG 59, 818.00/3–1948.

41. Ameringer, *Don Pepe,* 48–54.

42. Davis Diary, 21 March 1948.

43. Davis to Secretary of State, 24 March 1948, RG 59, 818.00/3–1448.

44. Cited in Thomas Paterson, *On Every Front: The Making of the Cold War* (New York: W. W. Norton, 1979), 63.

45. *Public Papers of the President: Harry S. Truman, 1948* (Washington, D.C.: Government Printing Office, 1964), 180–81.

46. Gonzalo Facio, interview with author, 22 October 1991, Washington, D.C. [hereinafter Facio interview].

47. Memorandum of conversation between Gutiérrez, Facio, Norman Armour (special assistant to the Secretary of State), and Bennett, 11 March 1948, RG 59, 818.00/3–1148.

48. Ibid.

49. Facio interview.

50. William T. Bennett, Jr., letter to the author, 11 January 1992 [hereinafter Bennett letter].

51. Ameringer, *Don Pepe,* 56.

52. Memorandum of conversation between Bennett and representatives from Senator Caperhart's office, 16 March 1948, RG 59, 818.00/3–1648.

53. Hocking to the State Department, 19 March 1948, RG 59, 818.00/3–1948.

54. *La Estrella de Panamá,* 25 March 1948.

55. Ibid., 19 March 1948.

56. *New York Times,* 22 March 1948.

57. Memorandum by Bennett, 26 March 1948, *FRUS, 1948* 9:502–3. Bennett later stated that the propaganda of the league had been effective. "Their propaganda, including such actions as demonstrations with anti-Communist placards outside the USSR mission to the United Nations in New York, was quite effective. Costa Rica enjoyed—and enjoys today—a high reputation in American public opinion as a geniune democracy—one of very few at the time in Latin America. As such, their anti-Communist efforts were taken seriously," he concluded. Bennett letter.

58. Bell, *Crisis in Costa Rica,* 140–41; Chargé d'Affaires in Honduras Harold Montamat to Secretary of State, 18 March 1948, RG 59, 818.00/3–1848.

59. Memorandum of conversation by Newbegin, 19 March 1948, *FRUS, 1948* 9:496–97.

60. Bernbaum to Secretary of State, 18 March 1948, RG 59, 818.00/3–1848; *La Estrella de Panamá,* 16 March 1948.

61. Marshall to Embassy in Managua, 16 March 1948, RG 59, 818.00/3–1548.

62. Davis Diary, 20 March 1948.

63. Memorandum of conversation between Bernbaum and Newbegin, 22 March 1948, RG 59, FW 818.00/3–2248; Newbegin to Bernbaum, 23 March 1948, RG 59, 818.00/3–2248. It was fairly clear that Somoza recorded the conversation because Ambassador Sevilla discussed the first part of it with U.S. officials even before Bernbaum met with Somoza.

64. Davis Diary, 5 March 1948. *Time* reported that Somoza interfered to protect a lucrative cattle and trading business with Calderón, ventures that would be threatened if the rebels emerged victorious. "Everybody's War," *Time* 51 (29 March 1948): 42.

65. Bernbaum to Secretary of State, 22 March 1948, RG 59, 818.00/3–2248.

66. Ibid.

67. Marshall to the Diplomatic Representatives in the American Republics, 22 March 1948, *FRUS, 1948* 9:499.

68. Davis Diary, 18 March 1948.

69. Ibid.

70. Alberto Martén, Figueres's second in command, interview with author, 3 March 1992, San José, Costa Rica. Another lieutenant, Bruce Masis, substantiated Martén's claim. Bruce Masis, interview with author, 4 March 1992, San José, Costa Rica.

71. Memorandum of conversation by Newbegin, 19 March 1948, RG 59, 818.00/3–1948.

72. Ibid.

73. Bernbaum to Secretary of State, 20 March 1948, RG 59, 818.00/3–2048.

74. Ibid.

75. Kyle to Secretary of State, 24 March 1948, *FRUS, 1948* 9:499.

76. Memorandum of conversation between González, Daniels, and Newbegin, 23 March 1948, RG 59, 818.00/3–2348.

77. *La Estrella de Panamá*, 1 April 1948.

78. Cohen to Secretary of State, 2 April 1948, RG 59, 818.00/4–248.

79. Davis to Secretary of State, 4 April 1948, RG 59, 818.00/4–448.

80. *The Panama American* (Panama City), 1 April 1948.

81. "The President Is Sick," *Time* 51 (5 April 1948): 38.

82. "Neighborhood Squabble," *Newsweek* 31 (5 April 1948): 44.

83. *Excelsior* (Mexico City), 7 April 1948.

84. Davis to Secretary of State, 1 April 1948, RG 59, 818.00/4–148.

85. *Costa Rican Information Bulletin*, 31 March 1948, 8 April 1948, Papers of Robert J. Alexander, File-Costa Rica (General), Rutgers University, New Brunswick, New Jersey [hereinafter Alexander Papers].

86. National Security Council, "The Position of the United States With Respect to Soviet-Directed World Communism," 3 June 1948 (originally prepared 30 March 1948), PSF, NSC Meeting File, Box 203, Truman Library; Roger R. Trask, "The Impact of the Cold War on United States–Latin American Relations, 1945–1949," *Diplomatic History* 1 (Summer 1977): 279–81.

87. National Security Council, "U.S. Policy Regarding Anti-Communist Measures Which Could Be Planned and Carried Out within the Inter American System," 28 June 1948 (originally prepared 22 March 1948), PSF, Subject File, Box 198, Truman Library.

88. NSC, "U.S. Policy Regarding Anti-Communist Measures Which Could Be Planned and Carried Out within the Inter-American System," 28 June 1948.

89. On April 8, the CIA produced a review of world events for the NSC. It concluded that the "civil conflict in Costa Rica is significant chiefly because of its bearing on emergent balance of power alignments in the Caribbean. . . . The existence of such antagonistic intrarregional alignments is prejudicial to Hemisphere solidarity." National Security Council, "Review of the World Situation As It Relates to the Security of the United States," 22 April 1948, PSF, NSC Meeting Files, Box 203, Truman Library.

90. "Bogotá Berserk," *Newsweek* 31 (19 April 1948): 48–49; Alberto Lleras-Camargo, "The Bogotá Conference," *Bulletin of the Pan American Union* 52 (June 1948): 301–11.

91. R. Roy Rubottom, letter to author, 15 December 1991; Darling, *Central Intelligence Agency*, 241–42.

92. Ameringer, *Don Pepe*, 56.

93. Davis Diary, 11 April 1948.

94. Ibid.

95. Ibid., 12 April 1948.

96. Gardner, "Costa Rican Junta," 56; Davis Diary, 13 March 1948; Bell, *Crisis in Costa Rica*, 145; Ameringer, *Don Pepe*, 59–61.

97. Davis Diary, 14 April 1948; Bell, *Crisis in Costa Rica*, 145.

98. José Figueres-Ferrer, *El espíritu del 48* (San José: Editorial Costa Rica, 1987), 258; Davis Diary, 15 April 1948.

99. Ameringer, *Don Pepe*, 61–63.

100. Bell, *Crisis in Costa Rica*, 149.

101. Bernbaum to Secretary of State, 17 April 1948, *FRUS, 1948* 9:517.

102. Davis Diary, 16 April 1948.

103. Davis to Secretary of State, 17 April 1948, RG 59, 818.00/4–1748.

104. Davis to Secretary of State, 19 April 1948, *FRUS, 1948* 9:520; Davis Diary, 18 April 1948. Davis and U.S. officials in Managua later learned that Picado had requested Somoza's assistance. Bernbaum to Secretary of State, 20 April 1948, RG 59, 818.00/4–2048; Davis Diary, 21 April 1948.

105. Memorandum of conversation by Newbegin, 19 April 1948, *FRUS, 1948* 9:519–20.

106. Memorandum of conversation between Daniels and Woodward, 19 April 1948, *Memoranda of Conversation of Secretary of State, 1947–1952*, no. 503.

107. Memorandum of conversation between Woodward and Brigadier General and Special Assistant to the Secretary of State Marshall S. Carter, 20 April 1948, *Memoranda of Conversation of Secretary of State, 1947–1952*, no. 522.

108. Bernbaum to Secretary of State, 20 April 1948, *FRUS, 1948* 9:522.

109. Marshall to the American Diplomatic Officers in the American Republics except Nicaragua, 30 April 1948, *FRUS, 1948* 9:108; *Department of State Bulletin*, 30 May 1948, 716.

110. Davis Diary, 19 April 1948.

111. "Commissar in San José," *Time* 51 (19 April 1948): 39–40; Bell, *Crisis in Costa Rica*, 146.

112. Aguilar-Bulgarelli, *Costa Rica y sus hechos políticos*, 310–14; Ameringer, *Don Pepe*, 63–64.

113. Bell, *Crisis in Costa Rica*, 150. U.S. commanders in the Canal Zone placed troops on alert on 20 April 1948 during the passage of several Soviet ships through the canal. Whether the timing of the U.S. action was deliberate is hard to ascertain. Even if coincidental, the opposition and possibly even U.S. officials used the event to intimidate Picado into stepping down. *New York Times*, 21 April 1948.

114. Davis Diary, 19 April 1948; Aguilar-Bulgarelli, *Costa Rica y sus hechos políticos*, 318.

115. Davis Diary, 19 April 1948; "Farewell to Arms," *Newsweek* 31 (10 May 1948): 38.

116. *La Estrella de Panamá*, 21 April 1948; Davis Diary, 20 April 1948; Davis to Secretary of State, 24 April 1948, RG 59, 818.00/4–2448.

117. Aguilar-Bulgarelli, *Costa Rica y sus hechos políticos*, 326–27.

118. Cohen to Secretary of State, 29 April 1948, RG 59, 818.00/4–2948.

119. Teodoro Picado-Michalski, *El pacto de la Embajada de Mexico, su incumpluimento* (Managua: Privately published, 1950), 5–6.

5. The First Time Around: The Costa Rican Junta and the United States, 1948–1949

1. Cited in Leonard, "United States and Costa Rica," 27.

2. J. E. Webb, "U.S. Expresses Gratification with New Costa Rican Government," *Department of State Bulletin* 21 (28 November 1949): 833.

3. Martén attended Pace Institute and Cathedral College, while Facio studied at New York University. Núñez went to Catholic University, while Esquivel studied law at Harvard.

4. Gardner, "Costa Rican Junta," 79–102.

5. Ibid., 108–11; Charles W. Anderson, "Politics and Development Policy in Central America," *Midwest Journal of Political Science* 5 (November 1961): 332–50; Judy Oliver-Milner, "Political Thought of José Figueres," *South Eastern Latin Americanist* 17 (June 1973): 1–4.

6. Gardner, "Costa Rican Junta," 67.

7. Anthony Winson, *Coffee and Democracy in Modern Costa Rica* (Toronto: Between the Lines, 1989), 50–76; Bell, *Crisis in Costa Rica*, 159; Gardner, "Costa Rican Junta," 358.

8. Judy Oliver-Milner, "Otílio Ulate and the Traditional Response to Contemporary Change in Costa Rica" (Ph.D. diss., Louisiana State University, 1977), 88–89; Charles Denton, "The Politics of Development in Costa Rica" (Ph.D. diss., University of Texas at Austin, 1969), 51–266; Anthony Winson, "One Road to Democracy with Development: José Figueres and the Social Democratic Project after 1948," in *Central America: Democracy, Development, and Change*, ed. John M. Kirk and George W. Schuyler (New York: Praeger, 1988), 89; Alberto Martén, interview with author, 3 March 1992, San José, Costa Rica [hereinafter Martén interview]; José Figueres, interview with Robert Alexander, 18 April 1951, Alexander Papers.

9. Davis to Secretary of State, 24 June 1948, RG 59, 818.00/6–2448.

10. Booth, "Democracy and Citizen Action," 58; Michael Olien, "Negro in Costa Rica," 125, 160; Martz, *Central America*, 225.

11. Davis to Secretary of State, 21 June 1948, RG 59, 818.00/6–2148.

12. *La Gaceta*, 20 July 1948; *La Prensa Libre*, 19 July 1948; Robert J. Alexander, "The Latin American Aprista Parties," *The Political Quarterly* 20 (July–September 1949): 239; Padre Núñez, interview with Robert Alexander, 28 July 1948, Alexander Papers; Gonzalo Facio, interview with Robert Alexander, 29 July 1948, Alexander Papers.

13. Memorandum from Wise to Newbegin, Woodward, and Daniels, 20 May 1948, RG 59, 818.00/5–2048.

14. Memorandum from Wise to Newbegin, Woodward, Daniels, 11 May 1948, RG 59, 818.00/5–1148.

15. Cohen to Secretary of State, 19 July 1948, RG 59, 818.00/7–1948.

16. Cited in Paul Ellman, "A Troubled Oasis of Peace," *Maclean's* 97 (18 June 1984): 10.

17. Memorandum of conversation between Daniels and Calderón, 24 May 1948, RG 59, 818.00/5–2448.

18. Bernbaum to Secretary of State, 16 June 1948, RG 59, 818.00/6–1648.

19. Marshall to the Embassy in Costa Rica, 3 May 1948, *FRUS, 1948;* Marshall to Embassy in Costa Rica, 5 May 1948, *FRUS, 1948* 9:525.

20. Memorandum from Wise to Newbegin, Woodward, Daniels, 20 May 1948, RG 59, 818.00/5–2048.

21. Davis to Secretary of State, 11 June 1948, RG 59, 818.00/6–1148.

22. Cohen to Secretary of State, 19 August 1948, RG 59, 818.00/8–1948.

23. Martz, *Central America,* 226.

24. First Secretary of the Embassy in Costa Rica Andrew Donovan to Secretary of State, 4 January 1950, RG 59, 718.00/1–450.

25. Esquivel to Marshall, 9 October 1948, A.N.C.R., Relaciones Exteriores, Estados Unidos, Packet 1562.

26. *Diario de Costa Rica,* 26 May 1948.

27. Cohen to Secretary of State, 3 September 1948, RG 59, 818.00/9–348; Bennett to Daniels, 13 October 1948, RG 59, FW 818.00/10–548.

28. Ameringer, *Democratic Left,* 80–85; Davis to Secretary of State, 2 May 1948, RG 59, 818.00/5–248.

29. Murkland, "Complicated Caribbean," 9; Davis to Secretary of State, 10 May 1948, RG 59, 818.00/5–1048.

30. Memorandum of conversation between Marshall and the Ambassador of the Dominican Republic to the United States, Luis Thinon, 8 June 1948, *Memoranda of Conversation of Secretary of State, 1947–1952,* no. 588.

31. Memorandum of conversation between Newbegin and Sevilla, 29 June 1948, *FRUS, 1948* 9:531.

32. Ibid.

33. Ameringer, *Democratic Left,* 80–85; Donovan to Secretary of State, 6 August 1948, RG 59, 818.00/8–648. During one meeting of the junta, a majority tried pressuring Figueres to abandon the legion. Disgusted, he left the meeting, threatening to resign and join his friends in Guatemala. The crisis was averted when the junta members backed down and Figueres continued as president. Father Benjamín Núñez, interview with author, 28 June 1991, San José, Costa Rica [hereinafter Núñez interview]; Facio interview.

34. Marshall to U.S. Embassy in Panama, 27 August 1948, RG 59, 818.00/8–2048.

35. Bennett to Daniels, 28 September 1948, RG 59, FW 818.00/9–2848.

36. Cohen to Secretary of State, 22 September 1948, RG 59, 818.00/9–2248.

37. Bernbaum to Secretary of State, 12 June 1948, RG 59, 818.00/6–1248; Martz, *Central America,* 225.

38. Bernbaum to Secretary of State, 27 June 1948, RG 59, 818.00/6–2748.

39. Memorandum of conversation between Bennett and Esquivel, 20 July 1948, *FRUS, 1948* 9:532–33.

40. Memorandum of conversation between Bennett and Esquivel, 10 August 1948, *FRUS, 1948* 9:533.

41. Since the reestablishment of relations in May, Washington had moved closer to the Nicaraguan dictator, a process that continued as the cold war intensified and Washington put aside its earlier opposition to authoritarianism in return for allegiance in the struggle against the Soviet Union.

42. Bennett to Daniels, 12 October 1948, RG 59, 818.00/10–1248.

43. Davis to Secretary of State, 29 November 1948, *FRUS, 1948* 9:535–36.

44. Ana Luisa Cerdas-Albertazzi, *La abolición del ejército en Costa Rica* (San José: Nacional de Commenoraciones Históricas, 1988); Leonard Bird, *Costa Rica: The Unarmed Democracy* (London: Sheppard Press, 1984), 89–103; Robert D. Putnam, "Research Note: Toward Explaining Military Intervention in Latin American Politics," *World Politics* 20 (October 1967): 108; "Farewell to Arms," *Newsweek* 32 (13 December 1948): 42;

James L. Busey, "Foundations of Contrast: Costa Rica and Nicaragua," *Western Political Quarterly* 11 (September 1958): 649.

45. Davis to Secretary of State, 2 December 1948, RG 59, 818.00/12–248.

46. Ambassador George Shaw to Secretary of State, 3 December 1948, RG 59, 818.00/12–348.

47. Shaw to Secretary of State and Embassy in San José, 5 December 1948, RG 59, 818.00/12–548.

48. Second Secretary of the Embassy in Managua Philip Williams to Secretary of State, 10 December 1948, RG 59, 818.00/12–1048.

49. "Spark in the Tinder," *Newsweek* 32 (20 December 1948): 38.

50. Salazar-Mora, *Calderón Guardia,* 119–20.

51. Davis to Secretary of State, 11 December 1948, *FRUS, 1948* 9:536–37.

52. Davis Diary, 11 December 1948.

53. Williams to Secretary of State, 11 December 1948, RG 59, 818.00/12–1148; "Uneasy Guests," *Time* 52 (27 December 1948): 30–31.

54. Shaw to Secretary of State, 12 December 1948, *FRUS, 1948* 9:539; Sevilla to Marshall, 13 December 1948, RG 59, 818.00/12–1348.

55. Davis Diary, 13 December 1948.

56. "Spark in the Tinder," 38.

57. "Sneak Punch," *Time* 52 (20 December 1948): 34.

58. Olive Holmes, "Costa Rican Crisis Exposes Central American Feuds," *Foreign Policy Bulletin* 28 (24 December 1948): 2–3; Memorandum of conversation between Bennett and Armand Berard, French Minister to the United States, 13 December 1948, RG 59, 818.00/12–1348; State Department to the Diplomatic Representatives in the American Republics, 13 December 1948, *FRUS, 1948* 9:540.

59. Gardner, "Costa Rican Junta," 146–48; Salazar-Mora, *Calderón Guardia,* 120.

60. Shaw to Secretary of State, 14 December 1948, RG 59, 818.00/12–1448.

61. Davis Diary, 14 December 1948; Shaw to Secretary of State, 14 December 1948, RG 59, 818.00/12–1448.

62. State Department to the Diplomatic Representatives in the American Republics, 14 December 1948, *FRUS, 1948* 9:541.

63. Paul C. Daniels, "Influence of Inter-American Relations on U.S. Foreign Policy," *Department of State Bulletin* 20 (10 April 1949): 460–63; Carmen Cortés, "The Costa Rican Invasion-Revolt," *The Pan American* 9 (January 1949): 8–11; M. Margaret Ball, *The OAS in Transition* (Durham, N.C.: Duke University Press, 1969), 442–46; Jerome Slater, *The OAS and United States Foreign Policy* (Columbus: Ohio State University Press, 1967), 69–71.

64. "Treaty on Trial," *Newsweek* 32 (27 December 1948): 34.

65. Davis Diary, 15 December 1948.

66. William T. Bennett, Jr., "The Costa Rican–Nicaraguan Incident: Effective International Action in Keeping Peace," *Department of State Bulletin* 20 (5 June 1949): 709. Unbeknownst to Bennett, several hundred policemen in civilian clothes were in the crowd, and boy scouts had managed traffic. Davis Diary, 17 December 1948.

67. Cohen to Secretary of State, 22 December 1948, RG 59, 818.00/12–2248.

68. Cohen to Secretary of State, 21 December 1948, RG 59, 818.00/12–2148; *Diario de Costa Rica,* 19 December 1948.

69. Davis to Secretary of State, 21 December 1948, RG 59, 818.00/12–2138.

70. Hernan Tavares de Sá, "Test Tube for Peace: Costa Rica and Nicaragua," *Ameri-*

cas 1 (March 1949): 4; Holmes, "Costa Rican Crisis," 2–3; Lommel, "United States' Efforts," 141–47.

71. Letter from Enrique V. Corominas of the OAS Committee to Investigate the Conflict in Costa Rica to the Inter-American Commission of Military Investigators, 28 December 1948, A.N.C.R., OEA, Packet 2892-BIS; Edgar S. Furniss, "The Inter-American System and Recent Caribbean Disputes," *International Organization* 4 (November 1950): 589; "Blow at the Legion," *Newsweek* 33 (3 January 1949): 34; Daniels, "Influence of Inter-American Relations," 462–63; Ameringer, *Don Pepe,* 81–83. Bennett reported that "the U.S. Representative, Paul Daniels, would have supported a report that named names and called a spade a spade. But the Mexican member of the Committee . . . worked hard and successfully for a bland report that fudged the issues." Bennett, letter to author, 11 January 1992.

72. Shaw to Secretary of State, 26 December 1948, RG 59, 818.00/12–2648.

73. Davis Diary, 27 December 1948.

74. Shaw to Secretary of State, 31 December 1948, RG 59, 818.00/12–3148.

75. Esquivel to the *Washington Post,* 4 January 1949, A.N.C.R., OEA, Packet 1178.

76. Ibid.

77. Special Meeting of the OAS, 21 April 1949, A.N.C.R., OEA, Packet 3677; United Nations, "Costa Rican–Nicaraguan Incident," *United Nations Bulletin* 6 (15 April 1949): 384; Bennett, "Costa Rican–Nicaraguan Incident," 711–12.

78. Central Intelligence Agency, "Review of the World Situation," 19 January 1949, PSF, Intelligence File, Box 250, Truman Library.

79. Juan Andres Petersen, "Somoza Versus the Americas," *Nation* 168 (15 January 1949): 66.

80. "Clouds on the Border," *Newsweek* 33 (28 February 1949): 40.

81. Davis to Secretary of State, 17 March 1949, RG 59, 818.00/3–1749; *La Prensa Libre* (San José), 27 May 1949. Davis remained a firm supporter of Figueres even after his departure for his new assignment in May 1949 as U.S. ambassador to Hungary. They developed a strong friendship that continued until Davis's death.

82. Bennett to Woodward, William Barber (deputy assistant secretary of state for American republic affairs), and Daniels, 13 December 1948, RG 59, FW 818.00/12–1048.

83. Ameringer, *Don Pepe,* 84–86.

84. Figueres-Ferrer, *El espíritu del 48,* 327–28; "Battle for San José," *Time* 53 (11 April 1949): 43; Obregón-Loría, *Hechos militares y políticos,* 347; Davis Diary, 3 April 1948.

85. Daniels to Dean Rusk, 4 April 1949, RG 59, 818.00/4–449.

86. "Big Two," *Newsweek* 33 (2 May 1949): 38–40; "Priests and Politics," *Newsweek* 33 (30 May 1949): 42.

87. Kenneth J. Mijeski, "The Executive-Legislative Policy Process in Costa Rica" (Ph.D. diss., University of North Carolina, 1971), 54–55; Christopher Baker, "Costa Rican Legislative Behavior in Perspective" (Ph.D. diss., University of Florida, 1973); Busey, *Notes on Costa Rican Democracy,* 12–16; Paul G. Stephenson, "Costa Rican Government and Politics" (Ph.D. diss., Emory University, 1965), 74–107.

88. Ameringer, *Don Pepe,* 90.

89. Joaquín Garro, *Viente años de historia chica* (San José: Imprenta Vargas, 1967), 32–42; Ruth Brownlow Blanford, "The Women's Vote in Costa Rica," *Américas* 7 (June 1955): 3–7; Mark Rosenberg, "State Intervention and Presidential Control in Costa

Rica: The Role of the Partido Liberación Nacional," *SECOLAS Annals* 10 (March 1979): 99; Ameringer, *Democracy in Costa Rica,* 33–37. U.S. officials had watched the meetings carefully but refused to take any stance on the document. Cohen to Secretary of State, 13 April 1949, RG 59, 818.00/4–1359.

90. Memorandum of conversation by Bennett, 9 June 1949, *FRUS, 1949* 2:446–47.

91. Ameringer, *Democratic Left,* 88–89.

92. Ibid., 90.

93. R. D. Muir, Acting Chief of Protocol, to Matthew Connelly, Secretary to the President, 15 June 1949, Official Files, File #432, Truman Library; U.S. Ambassador in Venezuela Walter Donnelly to Secretary of State, 27 June 1949, *FRUS, 1949* 2:449–50; Marshall to Embassy in Venezuela, 30 June 1949, *FRUS, 1949* 2:450.

94. Central Intelligence Agency, "Review of World Situation," 20 July 1949, PSF, Intelligence File, Box 250, Truman Library.

95. Memorandum of conversation between Edward Miller, Bennett, Esquivel, and Daniel Oduber, 20 July 1949, RG 59, 818.00/7–2049.

96. Donovan to Secretary of State, 23 July 1949, RG 59, 818.00/7–2349; Donovan to Secretary of State, 26 July 1949, RG 59, 818.00/7–2649.

97. Cohen to Secretary of State, 28 July 1949, RG 59, 818.00/7–2849.

98. Memorandum by Ernest Siracusa to Barber, Daniels, and Assistant Chief of the Division of Caribbean Affairs Leonard H. Price, 4 August 1949, *FRUS, 1949* 2:454–57; Ameringer, *Democratic Left,* 98–99.

99. Memorandum by Assistant Chief of the Division of Special Inter-American Affairs Edward A. Jaminson, 5 September 1949, *FRUS, 1949* 2:459.

100. Dean Acheson, "Waging Peace in the Americas," *Department of State Bulletin* 21 (26 September 1949): 462–66; Olive Holmes, "Acheson Clarifies U.S. Policy in Latin America," *Foreign Policy Bulletin* 28 (7 October 1949): 3.

101. Memorandum of conversation between Dominican Ambassador to the United States Dr. Luis Thomen, Barber, and Charles Hauch, 29 September 1949, RG 59, 818.00/9–2949.

102. "Pepe's Choice," *Time* 54 (8 August 1949): 24; "Rift Widens," *Newsweek* 34 (8 August 1949): 32.

103. "Ultimatum Heeded," *Newsweek* 34 (7 November 1949): 42; "Toward Peace and Quiet," *Newsweek* 34 (17 October 1949): 48; Flack to Secretary of State, 27 October 1949, RG 59, 818.00/10–2749; Donovan to Secretary of State, 28 October 1949, RG 59, 818.00/10–2849.

104. "Democracy's Return," *Newsweek* 34 (21 November 1949): 48.

105. Acheson to Truman, 18 October 1949, OF, Box 153, Truman Library.

106. Webb, "U.S. Expresses Gratification," 833.

6. The Calm before the Storm: The Presidency of Otílio Ulate and the Rise of the Partido Liberación Nacional, 1949–1953

1. Murkland, "Costa Rica: Fortunate Society," 144.

2. Ibid., 141.

3. Oliver-Milner, "Otílio Ulate," 96–100; John D. Martz, *Central America,* 232; Robert D. Tomasek, "Costa Rica," in *Political Forces in Latin America: Dimensions of the*

Quest for Stability, ed. Ben G. Burnett and Kenneth Johnson (Belmont, Calif.: Wadsworth Publishing, 1968), 140–41.

4. "Vaccinated and Feeling Fine," *Time* 55 (23 January 1950): 25.

5. *Hispanic American Review,* May 1951, 14; Oliver-Milner, "Otílio Ulate," 122–42.

6. Oliver-Milner, "Otílio Ulate," 132–42.

7. Ibid., 143–49; McCamant, *Development Assistance,* 181–83.

8. Central Intelligence Agency, "Soviet Capabilities and Intentions in Latin America," 14 November 1950, PSF, Intelligence Files, Box 250, Truman Library.

9. Oliver-Milner, "Otílio Ulate," 102–4.

10. Otílio Ulate-Blanco, "Responsible Freedom in the Americas: The Individual and the States," *Vital Speeches* 21 (15 January 1955): 970.

11. Bennett to Wise, 12 September 1949, RG 59, FW 818.00/9–149; Embassy to Secretary of State, 19 January 1950, RG 59, 718.00/1–450. Before Mora left Mexico, several friends and associates gave him a farewell dinner. The party included Lombardo Toledano, who criticized the imperialism and warlike nature of the United States. Second Secretary of U.S. Embassy in Mexico William R. Laidlaw to the Secretary of State, 6 March 1950, RG 59, 718.00/3–650.

12. *Hispanic American Report,* September 1950, 14; Cohen to the State Department, 15 November 1950, RG 59, 718.00/11–1550.

13. Costa Rican Ambassador to the United States Rafael Oreamuno to Echandi, 24 April 1951, A.N.C.R., Nicaragua, Packet 1170-BIS; *Hispanic American Report,* April 1950, 23.

14. *Hispanic American Report,* May 1951, 14.

15. Oliver-Milner, "Otílio Ulate," 163–66.

16. *La Gaceta,* 24 July 1953; series of letters by Oreamuno and Don Fernando Lara, February 1953, A.N.C.R., Estados Unidos, Packet 1321.

17. Echandi to Rafael Angel Ulloa, 27 June 1950, A.N.C.R. Estados Unidos, Packet 1163.

18. Ulate to Truman, 28 June 1950, A.N.C.R., Estados Unidos, Packet 7878.

19. Echandi to Acheson, 1 August 1950, A.N.C.R., Estados Unidos, Packet 1167; Oreamuno to Echandi, 30 November 1950, A.N.C.R., Estados Unidos, Packet 1160; Oreamuno to Echandi, 4 December 1950, A.N.C.R., Estados Unidos, Packet 1168; Oreamuno to Lara, 27 October 1952, A.N.C.R., Naciones Unidas, Packet 1231.

20. Oreamuno to Echandi, 11 December 1950, A.N.C.R., Estados Unidos, Packet 1169-BIS.

21. Oreamuno to Echandi, 26 April 1951, A.N.C.R., Estados Unidos, Packet 1349-BIS.

22. A. Volio, "Lighting the Path to a Better World," *United Nations Bulletin* 13 (1 December 1952): 504.

23. Oreamuno to Lara, 16 July 1952, A.N.C.R., Naciones Unidas, Packet 1081-BIS.

24. "Ley battle y bloqueo económico a las países communistas," 21 December 1951, A.N.C.R., Estados Unidos, Packet 1053.

25. Oliver-Milner, "Otílio Ulate," 160; Policy Statement prepared in the Department of State, 3 March 1951, *FRUS, 1951,* 2:1317–18.

26. Unsigned memorandum of the undersecretary's meeting, 2 June 1950, *FRUS, 1950* 2:901–2.

27. Chargé d'Affaires in Guatemala Milton Wells to Secretary of State, 6 September 1950, *FRUS, 1950* 2:911.

28. Oreamuno to Lara, 24 July 1952, A.N.C.R., Guatemala, Packet 1081-BIS.

29. "Views Within the Department of State Regarding United States Policy Toward the American Republics As a Group," unsigned draft memorandum prepared for the Department of State, 4 January 1950, *FRUS, 1950* 2:592–96; "Policy Statement Prepared in the Department of State: Costa Rica," 3 March 1951, *FRUS, 1951* 2:1319.

30. Central Intelligence Agency, "Costa Rica," 20 February 1950, PSF, Box 254, Truman Library.

31. Ibid.

32. Speech by Oreamuno to the Third Conference on World Economic Development of the Institute for Inter-American Study and Research at the University of Delaware, 25 April 1952, A.N.C.R., Estados Unidos, Packet 1081-BIS.

33. Embassy to Secretary of State, 19 January 1950, RG 59, 718.00/1–450; memorandum by Deputy Undersecretary of State H. Freeman Matthews to the Executive Secretary of the National Security Council, James S. Lay, 20 April 1951, *FRUS, 1951* 2:1011–12; Oreamuno to Lara, 14 September 1953, A.N.C.R., Estados Unidos, Packet 1236.

34. Policy Statement Prepared in the Department of State: Costa Rica, 3 March 1951, *FRUS, 1951* 2:1315.

35. Ibid, 2:1318.

36. Oreamuno to Echandi, 9 January 1951, A.N.C.R., Estados Unidos, Packet 1349-BIS.

37. Edward Miller, chairman of the United States delegation to the special meeting of the Inter-American Economic and Social Council, to Secretary of State, 20 June 1950, *FRUS, 1950* 2:678.

38. Flack to Ricardo Toledo, sub-secretary of the Ministry of Foreign Relations, 18 September 1950, A.N.C.R., Estados Unidos, Packet 3312; U.S. Department of State, "Point 4 Agreement with Costa Rica," *Department of State Bulletin* 24 (22 January 1951): 151.

39. "Acuerdo general sobre Punto Cuatro para cooperación técnica entre Costa Rica y Estados Unidos," 11 January 1951, A.N.C.R., Convenios y Tratados, Packet 572; memorandum by Louis J. Halle, Jr., regional planning adviser of the Bureau of Inter-American Affairs, to Miller, 2 May 1951, *FRUS, 1951* 2:1061–62.

40. "Acuerdo para un programa cooperativo de salud e higiene público," 20 May 1951, A.N.C.R., Convenios y Tratados, Packet 571.

41. Williams to Echandi, 7 August 1951, A.N.C.R., Estados Unidos, Packet 3312.

42. Williams to Echandi, 8 November 1951, A.N.C.R., Estados Unidos, Packet 1213.

43. Oreamuno to Bonilla, 9 December 1952, A.N.C.R., Estados Unidos, Packet 1101-BIS; *International Financial News Survey,* 9 October 1953.

44. John Martz, "Costa Rica Electoral Trends, 1953–1966," *Western Political Quarterly* 20 (December 1967): 888–909; Carlos Araya-Ponchet, *Liberación Nacional en la historia política de Costa Rica, 1940–1980* (San José: Editorial Nacional de Textos, 1982), 13–48; Proctor, "Political Systems," 220–22.

45. Burt H. English, *Liberación Nacional in Costa Rica: The Development of a Political Party in a Transitional Society* (Gainesville: University of Florida Press, 1971); Suzanne Jonas Bodenheimer, "The Social Democratic Ideology in Latin America: The Case of Costa Rica's Partido Liberación Nacional," *Caribbean Studies* 10 (October 1970): 50; Charles W. Anderson, "Political Ideology and the Revolution of Rising Expectations in Central America, 1944–1958" (Ph.D. diss., University of Wisconsin–Madison, 1960), 99–149; Guerra, *José Figueres.*

46. Bodenheimer, "Social Democratic Ideology," 51.

47. Ibid.

48. Anderson, "Politics and Development Policy," 335; Oliver-Milner, "Political Thought of José Figueres," 3.

49. Denton, "Politics of Development in Costa Rica," 43–44; idem, "Bureaucracy in an Immobilist Society: The Case of Costa Rica," *Administrative Science Quarterly* 14 (September 1969): 420–22.

50. Anderson, "Political Ideology," 113.

51. Ameringer, *Don Pepe*, 95–96.

52. José Figueres-Ferrer, "Blunting Point Four," *Commonweal* 59 (1 January 1954): 322.

53. Ibid.

54. Michael Scully, "Don Pepe's Private War against Communism," *Reader's Digest* 56 (June 1950): 112.

55. Castro-Esquivel, *José Figueres-Ferrer*, 249–50. Figueres believed the struggle extended outside of Latin America. He strongly identified with the efforts of the Israelis to establish their anti-Communist and social democratic state. José Figueres-Ferrer, "Not to Have Dreamed in Vain," *Congress Weekly* 19 (October 1953): 8–9; Edy Kaufman, Yoram Shapira, and Joel Barromi, *Israel-Latin American Relations* (New Brunswick, N.J.: Transaction Books, 1979), 70.

56. Figueres-Ferrer, "Blunting Point Four," 324.

57. Ibid.

58. Chargé d'Affaires Andrew Donovan to Secretary of State, 4 January 1950, RG 59, 718.00/1–450; U.S. Ambassador to El Salvador George Shaw to Secretary of State, 9 June 1950, RG 59, 718.00/6–950; Donovan to Secretary of State, 28 November 1950, RG 59, 718.00/11–2850.

59. Anderson, "Political Ideology," 119–20.

60. Some good works on the importance of nongovernmental organizations include: Lowell Livezey, *Nongovernmental Organizations and the Idea of Human Rights* (Princeton, N.J.: Princeton University Press, 1987); Eugene Linden, *The Alms Race: The Impact of American Voluntary Aid Abroad* (New York: Random House, 1976); Lawrence T. Woods, *Asia-Pacific Diplomacy: Nongovernmental Organizations and International Relations* (Vancouver: UBC Press, 1993).

61. For more information on the "vital center" movement, see Steven M. Gillon, *Politics and Vision: The ADA and American Liberalism, 1947–1985* (New York: Oxford University Press, 1987), 16–22; Mary Sperling McAuliffe, *Crisis on the Left: Cold War Politics and American Liberals, 1947–1954* (Amherst: University of Massachusetts Press, 1978).

62. Figueres's publications and interviews include: *Palabras gastadas* (San José: Imprenta Española, Soley y Valverde, 1943); *Cartas a un cuidadano* (San José: Imprenta Nacional, 1956); "Blunting Point Four," 322; "Latin American Aspirations," *New Republic* 131 (13 December 1954): 8; "The Problems of Democracy in Latin America," *Journal of International Affairs* 9, no. 1 (1955): 17; "Not to Have Dreamed in Vain," 8–9; as well as Scully, "Don Pepe's Private War," 112.

63. Arthur M. Schlesinger, Jr., letter to author, 18 November 1991. Figueres and Schlesinger first met at the IADF meeting in Havana in 1950. Several years later Schlesinger visited Figueres at the president's request, "an experience which further strengthened my faith in a progressive democratic solution in the hemisphere." Arthur M. Schlesinger, Jr., *A Thousand Days: John F. Kennedy in the White House* (Boston: Houghton Mifflin, 1965), 173–74.

64. Trujillo's agents later described the IADF as "a small, obscure group [with]

tremendous power." Cited in Ameringer, *Democratic Left,* 225. Ameringer found the description in CARIB, report no. 8 (July 1958), p. 42. The CARIB report was distributed by Trujillo's forces in the Domincan Republic.

65. Rúben Esquivel, Costa Rican delegate to the United Nations, to the Foreign Ministry, undateed, A.N.C.R., Naciones Unidas, Packet 3193.

66. Ameringer, *Democratic Left,* 228.

67. Private Papers of Frances Grant, Box 8, Rutgers University Library, New Brunswick, New Jersey [hereinafter Grant Papers].

68. Strongly opposed to communism, the AFL had watched the Communists use popular front methods to gain increased power during World War II. The AFL leadership also expressed concern that the only unified hemispheric organization was the Communist-backed confederation, *Confederación de Trabajadores de Latin América* (CTAL). In response, the AFL commissioned Serafino Romualdi, an experienced anti-Communist organizer, to work in Latin America. Serafino Romualdi, *Presidents and Peons: Recollections of a Labor Ambassador in Latin America* (New York: Funk and Wagnalls, 1967), 27–35.

69. "Latin American Liberal Lauds U.S. Labor Aims," *AFL-CIO Free Labor News* 16 (February 1961): 1; Bodenheimer, "Social Democratic Ideology," 83; Alexander, *Communism in Latin America,* 12.

70. John Ohmans of the Office of Middle American Affairs to Williams, 16 September 1953, RG 59, 718.00/9–1653. Alexander interview.

71. Diary of Adolf A. Berle, Jr., 31 March 1953, Private Papers of Adolf A. Berle, Jr., Box 218, FDR Library [hereinafter Berle Diary]. President Eisenhower had created a special committee chaired by William Jackson, former deputy director of the CIA, to make recommendations on possible strategies for challenging the Russians. Berle headed the Central American section, whose main function was providing a plan for challenging the Communists in Guatemala. Thomas M. Leonard, *Central America and the United States: The Search for Stability* (Athens: University of Georgia Press, 1991), 138–39; Richard Immerman, *The CIA in Guatemala: The Foreign Policy of Intervention* (Austin: University of Texas Press, 1982), 130.

72. Berle Diary, 31 March 1953.

73. Ibid.

74. Ibid., 1 April 1953.

75. Bonilla, *Figueres and Costa Rica,* xxviii xxix.

76. Cohen to Secretary of State, 14 March 1951, RG 59, 718.00/3–1451.

77. Williams to Secretary of State, 6 August 1951, RG 59, 718.00/8–651.

78. Earnest Siracusa to Albert Nufer, Thomas Mann, and Miller, 24 March 1952, RG 59, 718.00/3–2452.

79. Williams to Costa Rican Desk Officer, Fred Heins, 21 June 1951, RG 59, 718.00/6–2151.

80. Cohen to Secretary of State, 2 June 1952, RG 59, 718.00/6–6521.

81. Figueres, interview with Robert Alexander, 1 August 1978, Alexander Papers.

82. Williams, interview with Robert Alexander, 29 August 1952, Alexander Papers.

83. *Washington Post,* 9 January 1953; William Blum, *The CIA: A Forgotten History; U.S. Global Interventions since World War 2* (London: Zed Books, 1986), 91.

84. Williams to Secretary of State, 3 November 1952, RG 59, 718.00/11–352.

85. Ambassador to Costa Rica Philip Fleming to Secretary of State, 4 February 1952, RG 59, 718.00/2–452.

86. Crume to Secretary of State, 7 May 1953, RG 59, 718.00/5–753.

7. Resistance and Accommodation: The United States and the Nationalism of José Figueres, 1953–1957

1. *Octubre*, 6 August 1953.

2. Robert Johnson, "Facts Behind the Figueres-Somoza Feud," *American Mercury* 81 (September 1955): 91–95.

3. John Ohmans to Robert Woodward, 14 July 1953, RG 59, 718.00/7–1453; First Secretary of the Embassy in Managua Rolland Welch to Secretary of State John Foster Dulles, 23 July 1953, RG 59, 718.00/7–2353.

4. *La República* (San José), 22 July 1953.

5. Fleming to Secretary of State, 22 July 1953, RG 59, 718.00/7–2253.

6. Williams to Secretary of State, 28 July 1953, RG 59, 718.00/7–2853.

7. Araya-Ponchet, *Liberación Nacional;* Harry Kantor, *The Costa Rican Election of 1953: A Case Study* (Gainesville: University of Florida Press, 1958).

8. Cohen to Secretary of State, 30 July 1953, RG 59, 718.00/7–3053.

9. Milton Eisenhower, *The Wine Is Bitter* (New York: Doubleday, 1961): 218.

10. "Don Pepe's Victory," *Newsweek* 42 (3 August 1953): 40.

11. "Middle Class Reformer," *Time* 62 (10 August 1953): 35.

12. Cohen to Ohmans, 22 September 1953, RG 59, 718.00/9–2253.

13. Diary of John M. Cabot, 15 January 1954, Diplomatic Papers of John Moors Cabot, Tufts University Library, Medford, Massachusetts, microfilm, [hereinafter Cabot Diary].

14. Secretary of the Embassy in San José Charles Stewart to Secretary of State, 16 November 1953, RG 59, 718.00/11–1653.

15. Memorandum by Raymond G. Leddy, officer in charge of Central American affairs, to Cabot, 6 August 1953, *FRUS, 1952–1954*, 4:827–28. Walter Bedell Smith reportedly characterized Figueres as "a peculiar fellow who's just become President of Costa Rica." Robert C. Hill, interview by John T. Mason, Jr., 19 October 1972, Dwight D. Eisenhower Oral History Collection, Dwight D. Eisenhower Library, Abilene, Kansas [hereinafter DDE Library].

16. Memorandum of conversation between Sam Baggett, vice-president of UFCO, Thomas Mann, and John Fisher, Guatemalan desk officer, 22 May 1953, RG 59811.05118/5–2253.

17. *La República*, 26 May 1953.

18. Facio interview; Núñez interview; Bruce Masis, interview with author, San José, 4 March 1992 [hereinafter Masis interview]; Karen Olsen-Beck de Figueres, interview with author, San José, 14 March 1992 [hereinafter Olsen-Beck interview].

19. "Costa Rica Victor Invites U.S. Capital," *New York Times*, 29 July 1953.

20. Ameringer, *Don Pepe*, 114–15.

21. Memorandum from Leddy to Cabot and Charles Burrows, director of the Office of Middle American Affairs, 6 August 1953, RG 59, 718.00/8–653.

22. Memorandum of conversation between Burrows, Smith, Coolidge, Kenneth Redmond, president of UFCO, and Joseph Montgomery, vice-president of UFCO, 4 September 1953, *FRUS, 1952–1954* 4:829–30. The embassy correctly underscored that Figueres was "deadly serious" but willing to compromise. Leddy to Ohmans, 27 August 1953, RG 59, 811.05118/4–2753.

23. José Figueres-Ferrer, "We Don't Want Foreign Investments," *New Leader* 36 (31 August 1953): 2–4.

24. Leddy to Ohmans, 27 August 1953, RG 59, 811.05118/4–2753.

25. Memorandum from Cabot to Smith, 17 September 1953, RG 59, 818.2376/9–1753.

26. There is a series of reports on the United States. A.N.C.R., Relaciones Exteriores Países, Estados Unidos, Packet 1512.

27. Jorge Hazera to the *Leaf-Chronicle*, 7 January 1954, A.N.C.R., Estados Unidos, Packet 1064.

28. Figueres, interview with Joan P. Alexander, San José, 5 August 1954, Alexander Papers; Burrows to Cabot, 26 October 1953, RG 59, 811.05115/10–2653.

29. Memorandum from Cabot to Deputy Assistant Secretary of State for Inter-American Affairs Robert F. Woodward, 18 November 1953, RG 59, 811.05118/11–1653.

30. Ibid.

31. Cabot Diary, 20 December 1953; *Diario de Costa Rica*, 4 December 1953.

32. *La Nación*, 20 December 1953.

33. Hill to Secretary of State, 28 December 1953, RG 59, 811.05118/12–2853.

34. "Buy United Fruit," *Time* 63 (4 January 1954): 26; "Fruit Company for Sale?" *Business Week* (2 January 1954): 56–57; "Costa Rica," *Hispanic American Report* 7 (January 1954): 15–16.

35. Harry Kantor, "A 'New Deal' Government for Costa Rica," *World Affairs* 117 (Spring 1954): 12.

36. Ibid., 11.

37. *Congressional Record*, 83rd Cong., 2d sess., 1 February 1954, vol. 100, pt. 1:1073.

38. Memorandum by Stewart to Secretary of State, 6 February 1954, *FRUS, 1952–1954* 4:836.

39. Memorandum by Stewart to Secretary of State, 6 February 1954, *FRUS, 1952–1954* 4:837. At a 9 February meeting, Hill stated that Figueres seemed willing to conform his attitudes to the realities of U.S. policies. Hill to Secretary of State, 9 February 1954, 811.95118/2–954.

40. *La República*, 23 February 1954.

41. Facio to Esquivel, 1 March 1954, RG 59, A.N.C.R., Estados Unidos, Packet 1064.

42. Holland to U.S. Representative to the United Nations Henry Cabot Lodge, Jr., 12 April 1954, *FRUS, 1952–1954* 4:840–41.

43. *New York Times*, 5 June 1954; "Banana Politics," *The Economist* 174 (29 January 1955): 374.

44. Daniel James, *Red Design for the Americas* (New York: John Day Company, 1954), 170.

45. José Figueres-Ferrer, "Costa Rica Welcomes Foreign Investments," *Central America and Mexico* 2 (December 1954): 37–40; *Diario Nacional* (San José), 12 December 1954.

46. Stephen Rabe, *Eisenhower and Latin America: The Foreign Policy of Anticommunism* (Chapel Hill: University of North Carolina Press, 1988), 49–85; Samuel Guy Inman, *Inter-American Conferences, 1826–1954* (Washington, D.C.: University Press of Washington, 1965), 257–70.

47. Robert J. Alexander, *Rómulo Betancourt and the Transformation of Venezuela* (New Brunswick, N.J.: Transaction Books, 1982), 374–75; *Diario de Costa Rica*, 12 November 1953; Stewart to Jack Neal, deputy director of the Office of Middle American Affairs/Bureau of Inter-American Affairs, 15 December 1953, RG 59, 718.00/12–1553.

48. Memorandum by Stewart to Secretary of State, 6 February 1954, *FRUS, 1952–1954* 4:836–39; "Costa Rica," *Hispanic American Report* 7 (February 1954): 16.

49. Memorandum by Stewart to Secretary of State, February 6, 1954, *FRUS, 1952–1954* 4:836–39. Later, when talking about the Caracas Conference, R. Roy Rubottom stated, "of course, we were embarrassed by the fact that the Costa Ricans did not go there." R. Roy Rubottom, interview with Richard D. Challener, 12 June 1966, transcript, John Foster Dulles Oral History Collection, Princeton University Library, Princeton, New Jersey.

50. Davis Diary, 22 February 1954.

51. Ibid., 1 March 1954.

52. Berle Diary, 9 April 1954.

53. Facio interview; Olsen-Beck interview.

54. Facio to the Foreign Ministry, 1 March 1954, A.N.C.R., Estados Unidos, Packet 1964.

55. Hill to Secretary of State, 18 February 1954, RG 59, 718.00/2–1854.

56. Hill to Secretary of State, 19 February 1954, RG 59, 718.00/2–1954.

57. Interview with Robert Hill, 14–22, Robert Hill Collection, Box 112, Folder 71, Herbert Hoover Institution Library, Stanford, California [hereinafter Hoover Institution].

58. Ibid.

59. Davis Diary, 3 April 1954. U.S. officials recognized that the Costa Ricans despised not only the choice of sites but also Washington's alliance with the military dictators. In a report on the Caracas Conference the NSC stated, "Democratic Uruguay entertained feelings of hostility for dictatorships like Venezuela at least as strong as those it felt for Communism." National Security Council, Notes of 189th Meeting of the NSC, 18 March 1954, Whitman Files, NSC Series, Box 5, DDE Library.

60. "Boletín del Ministerio de Relaciones Exteriores de Costa Rica sobre el comunismo," 6 April 1954, A.N.C.R., Estados Unidos, Packet 7878; release of the Embassy of Costa Rica, 26 May 1954, RG 59, A.N.C.R., Estados Unidos, Packet 1151.

61. "The Stay-Away Vote," *Time* 63 (5 April 1954): 40. An interesting sidelight on Figueres's understanding of North Americans occurred in a meeting with Hill, Stewart, and other embassy officials. When discussing Bolivian politics, Figueres described Juan Lechin's lack of intelligence by commenting, "He's just a football player." The statement secured "big laughs from a couple of broken-down U.S. athletes." Memorandum by Stewart, 6 February 1953, *FRUS, 1952–1954* 4:839.

62. Immerman, *CIA in Guatemala,* 129–30.

63. Berle Diary, 31 March 1953.

64. The Costa Ricans had watched the Communist situation in Guatemala closely. They monitored the ties between Guatemalan Ambassador to Costa Rica Ismael González and the Costa Rican Communists. Francisco Castro, chief of Costa Rican Intelligence, to the Ministry of Public Safety, 9 March 1954, A.N.C.R., Guatemala, Packet 1988; Participation of the Guatemalan Ambassador in a Communist Meeting, March 1954, A.N.C.R., Guatemala, Packet 1988. Other memorandums and clippings regarding the arms purchases in Guatemala can be found in "Armas sovieticas en Guatemala," 1954, A.N.C.R., Guatemala, Packet 1912.

65. Figueres-Ferrer, "Problems of Democracy in Latin America," 17.

66. Ameringer, *Democratic Left,* 206–10.

67. Nicaraguan Minister of Foreign Relations Oscar Sevilla to Esquivel, May 1954, A.N.C.R., Nicaragua, Packet 2622; *La República,* 28 April 1954; *Diario de Costa Rica,* 7 May 1954; *Novedades,* 4 June 1954.

68. *Novedades,* 7 July 1954; *La Prensa,* 6 July 1954.

69. Stewart to Secretary of State, 1 July 1954, RG 59, 718.00/7–154.

70. Ohmans to Hill, 7 July 1954, RG 59, 718.5614/7–754.

71. Memorandum of telephone conversation by Holland, 9 July 1954, RG 59, 617.18/7–954.

72. Ibid.

73. Ambassador to Nicaragua Thomas Whelan to Secretary of State, 9 July 1954, RG 59, 617.18/7–954.

74. Memorandum of Conversation between Leddy, Colombian Ambassador to the United States Don Eduardo Zuleta, and Venezeualan Ambassador to the United States César González, 9 June 1954, RG 59, 718.00/6–954.

75. Stewart to Secretary of State, 22 June 1954, RG 59, 718.00/6–2254.

76. Otílio Ulate-Blanco, *Hacia dónde lleva a Costa Rica el Señor Presidente Figueres?* (San José: Imprenta Universal, 1955), 6–35; Memorandum of conversation between Rafael Oreamuno and Woodward, 7 July 1954, RG 59, FW718.00/7–654.

77. Dulles to the Embassy in Guatemala, 9 July 1954, RG 59, 718.00/7–954.

78. Ibid.

79. Memorandum of conversation between Holland and Hill, 29 July 1954, RG 59, 617.18/7–2954; *Expressen,* 31 July 1954.

80. Holland to Secretary of the Army Robert T. Stevens, 4 August 1954, RG 59, 718.5/8–454.

81. *La República,* 15 July 1954. Betancourt left for Puerto Rico on 26 July.

82. Hill to Secretary of State, 6 August 1954, RG 59, 617.18/8–654; "Grimaces at the Border," *Newsweek* 44 (16 August 1954): 50; "Border Bluster," *Time* 64 (9 August 1954): 38.

83. *El Nacional,* 1 November 1954; *La Prensa Libre,* 17 November 1954.

84. Memorandum by Leddy to Holland, 18 November 1954, *FRUS, 1952–1954* 4:858–60.

85. Hoover to Wilson, 20 November 1954, RG 59, 718.5/11–2054; Memorandum by Leddy to Holland, 18 November 1954, *FRUS, 1952–1954* 4:858–60.

86. "By the Dark of the Moon," *Time* 64 (29 November 1954): 27.

87. Memorandum by the Chairman of the Joint Chiefs of Staff Arthur Radford to Wilson, 26 November 1954, RG 59, 718.5/12–1054.

88. National Security Council, Memorandum by special Costa Rican working group, 31 May 1956, NSC Staff: Papers, 1948–1961, OCB Central Files Series, Costa Rica, Box 28, DDE Library.

89. Memorandum by Deputy Assistant Secretary of State for Inter-American Affairs Edward J. Sparks to Secretary of State, 22 November 1954, *FRUS, 1952–1954* 4:861–62; Memorandum of conversation by Director of the Office of Middle American Affairs Robert Newbegin, 26 November 1954, *FRUS, 1952–1954* 4:864.

90. Múñoz to Eisenhower, 27 November 1954, Office File, White House Central Files, Box 857, DDE Library.

91. Memorandum by the special assistant to the Secretary for Intelligence, W. Park Armstrong, Jr., to Hoover, 6 December 1954, RG 59, 718.00/12–654.

92. Deputy Director of Intelligence Robert Amory, Jr., to Holland, 23 December 1954, RG 59, 718.00/12–2354. Somoza had purchased twenty-five P-51 Mustangs from Sweden. *The Christian Science Monitor,* 21 December 1954.

93. Woodward to Secretary of State, 3 January 1955, RG 59, 718.00/1–355. The

United States recommended that the Costa Ricans carry their case to the OAS. Woodward to Secretary of State, 7 January 1955, RG 59, 718.00/1–755.

94. The United States possessed advance notice of the rebel movements. Somoza informed Whelan that a "100 percent Costa Rican" rebellion would take place within the week. Whelan to Holland, 10 January 1955, *FRUS, 1955–1957* 6:586; Whelan to Secretary of State, 11 January 1955, RG 59, 718.00/1–1155.

95. Teodoro Picado, Jr., letter to the author, 13 September 1991; Ameringer, *Democratic Left,* 212–13; "Cloak and Dagger" *Business Week* (15 January 1955): 129–30; "Clash of Ideas . . . Clash of Arms," *U.S. News and World Report* 38 (21 January 1955): 78–81.

96. "Costa Rica," *Hispanic American Report* 8 (January 1955): 14–17; "Invasion," *Time* 65 (24 January 1955): 32.

97. Schlesinger to Eisenhower, 12 January 1955, OF, White House Central Files, Box 122, DDE Library.

98. Berle to Nelson Rockefeller, Jr., 12 January 1955, Private Papers of Adolf A. Berle, Jr., Box 218, FDR Library [hereinafter Berle Papers]; Berle to Dulles, 12 January 1955, Berle Papers.

99. Douglas to Dulles, 12 January 1955, RG 59, 718.00/1–1255.

100. *Congressional Record,* 84th Cong., 1st sess., 13 January 1955, vol. 101, pt. 1:329–30.

101. Romualdi to Holland, 14 January 1955, RG 59, FW 718.00/1–1455; *AFL News Reporter,* 21 January 1955.

102. "New Danger in Central America," *Economist* 174 (15 January 1955): 176; *Daily Worker,* 21 January 1955; *The Sun* (Baltimore), 22 January 1955; J. Alvarez del Vayo, "Costa Rican Crisis," *Nation* 180 (22 January 1955): 63–64; Harry Kantor, "The Struggle for Democracy in Costa Rica," *The South Atlantic Quarterly* 60 (January 1956): 12–18.

103. Holland to Wilson, 12 January 1955, *FRUS, 1955–1957* 6:591–92; Henry F. Holland, "OAS Action in Costa Rican Conflict," *Department of State Bulletin* 32 (31 January 1955): 178–80.

104. Dulles to Embassy in Nicaragua, 12 January 1955, RG 59, 718.00/1–1255; Whelan to Secretary of State, 12 January 1955, RG 59, 718.00/1–1255; Embassy in Caracas to Secretary of State, 12 January 1955, RG 59, 718.00/1–1255; *Novedades,* 12 January 1955.

105. Woodward to Secretary of State, 14 January 1955, *FRUS, 1955–1957* 6:587; National Security Council, Daily Intelligence Abstract, 13 January 1955, NSC Council Staff: Papers, 1948–1961, OCB Central Files Series, Box 111, no. 293, DDE Library.

106. Peter Calvert and Susan Calvert, *Latin America in the Twentieth Century* (New York: St. Martin's Press, 1993), 155.

107. National Security Council, Review of the 231st Meeting of the NSC, 13 January 1955, Whitman Files, NSC Series, Box 6, DDE Library.

108. Robert Woodward, letter to author, 13 December 1991 [hereinafter Woodward letter]; Ken Bode, "Don Pepe," *The New Republic* 23 (April 1977): 13–15; Ameringer, *Democratic Left,* 205–6; idem, *U.S. Foreign Intelligence: The Secret Side of American History* (Lexington, Mass.: Lexington Books, 1990); Blum, *The CIA,* 89–90; Thomas Ross and David Wise, *The Invisible Government* (New York: Random House, 1969), 119–20.

109. Luis Quintanilla to José A. Mora, president of OEA, 16 January 1955, A.N.C.R., Organización de Estados Americas (OEA); Woodward to Holland and John

Dreier, U.S. representative to the OAS, 15 January 1955, RG 59, 718.00/1–1555; Holland, "OAS Action," 180–81.

110. Woodward letter; Woodward to Secretary of State, 15 January 1955, *FRUS, 1955–1957* 6:597–99; U.S. Department of State, "Sale of Four U.S. Aircraft to Government of Costa Rica," *Department of State Bulletin* 32 (31 January 1955): 182.

111. Memorandum of Costa Rican Government to the OAS Investigating Committee, 25 January 1955, A.N.C.R., OEA, Packet 3251; Woodward to Secretary of State, 20 January 1955, *FRUS, 1955–1957* 6:602–3.

112. "Attack that Failed," *Time* 65 (31 January 1955): 29; "Costa Rican Revolt, or Is It an Invasion," *Life* 38 (24 January 1955): 39–42; "Lively 'Ghosts,' " *Newsweek* 45 (24 January 1955): 50.

113. *New York Times,* 29 January 1955.

114. "Costa Rican 'invasion,' " *America* 93 (29 January 1955): 443; "Atlantic Report on the World Today," *Atlantic Monthly* 195 (March 1955): 10–15; "A Problem for Us," *Newsweek* 45 (21 February 1955): 50.

115. "Costa Rica and the Invasion: Difficulties of a Central American Democracy," *World Today* 11 (March 1955): 129–38; del Vayo, "Costa Rican Crisis," 63–64.

116. "The Boiling Pot," *Newsweek* 45 (31 January 1955): 49.

117. Memorandum of discussion at the 240th meeting of the National Security Council, 10 March 1955, *FRUS, 1955–1957* 6:614–16. There is a series of memorandums on the vice-president's visit from early 1955, A.N.C.R., Estados Unidos, Packet 1544; "Goodwill and Good Deed," *Life* 38 (7 March 1955): 48.

118. *Información* (Havana), 6 July 1955; *El Comercio* (Lima), 6 July 1955. In July Somoza accused Figueres of conspiring to assassinate him. Reportedly, the Costa Ricans had allowed a convicted murderer, Carlos Jiménez, to escape from prison. With the help of Frank Marshall, a close associate of Figueres, Jiménez flew to Honduras and crossed into Nicaragua with orders to kill the Nicaraguan dictator. Before he could accomplish his mission, Nicaraguan police arrested him. He supposedly confessed to the plot and implicated the Figueres government, reporting that it had given him $10,000 to shoot Somoza. The Costa Ricans denied the accusations and responded by closing their borders and ordering their citizens to refrain from visiting Nicaragua. After some prodding by U.S. officials, representatives of the two governments met in Washington and discussed the dispute. *New York Times,* 21 July 1955.

119. Memorandum from Robert S. Folsom of the Office of Regional American Affairs to Holland, 2 September 1955, *FRUS, 1955–1957* 6:619–20.

120. Facio to the OAS Committee, 24 February 1955, A.N.C.R., OEA, Packet 1078; U.S. State Department, "Costa Rica and Nicaragua Sign Friendship Agreements," *Department of State Bulletin* 34 (27 February 1956): 339–40. Figueres appeared to have played no role in the assassination of Somoza.

121. Figueres to Senator George Smathers of Florida, 27 June 1956, Alexander Papers; Esquivel to Minister of Economy Jorge Rossi, 4 May 1956, A.N.C.R., Naciones Unidas, Packet 3396.

122. U.S. Department of State, "Eximbank Extends Credit to Costa Rican Power Company," *Department of State Bulletin* 31 (11 April 1955): 604.

123. U.S. Department of State, "$3 Million World Bank Loan to Costa Rica," *Department of State Bulletin* 13 (8 October 1956): 559–60.

124. Phillip P. Boucher, "U.S. Foreign Aid to Latin America: Hypothesis and Patterns in Historical Statistics, 1934–1974" (Ph.D. diss., University of California, Berkeley, 1979), 207–10.

125. National Security Council Staff, memorandum by Special Costa Rica working group, 31 May 1956, NSC Staff: Papers 1948–1961, OCB Central Files, OCB 091, Box 28, DDE Library; Woodward to Secretary of State, OCB Central Files 091, Box 28, 11 December 1956, DDE Library.

126. Alexander, *Communism in Latin America,* 383.

127. Ameringer, *Don Pepe,* 134–35.

128. *La República,* 29 June 1957.

129. Political Stability in Central America and the Caribbean through 1958, 23 April 1957, *FRUS, 1955–1957* 6:629.

8. Oftentimes the Tail Wags the Dog: Trends in Relations between Costa Rica and the United States during the Rise of José Figueres

1. Marvin R. Zahniser and W. Michael Weis, "A Diplomatic Pearl Harbor? Richard Nixon's Goodwill Mission to Latin America in 1958," *Diplomatic History* 13 (Spring 1989): 163–90.

2. Statement of Milton Eisenhower upon arriving in San José, Costa Rica, 18 July 1958, Papers of Milton Eisenhower, 1938–1973, Central American Speeches, 1958, Box 7, DDE Library; Roy R. Rubottom, letter to the author, 11 December 1991.

3. Ameringer, *U.S. Foreign Intelligence,* 255–56.

4. Ibid., 256.

5. Dennis Merrill, *Bread and the Ballot: The United States and India's Economic Development, 1947–1963* (Chapel Hill: University of North Carolina Press, 1990); Robert J. MacMahon, *The Cold War on the Periphery: The United States, India and Pakistan* (New York: Columbia University Press, 1994); Peter Hahn, *The United States, Great Britain, and Egypt, 1945–1956: Strategy and Diplomacy in the Early Cold War* (Chapel Hill: University of North Carolina Press, 1991); and Nick Cullather, *Illusions of Influence: The Political Economy of United States–Phillipines Relations, 1942–1960* (Palo Alto, Calif.: Stanford University Press, 1994) are a few good studies that analyze cases in which U.S. leaders accepted nationalism even when it conflicted with their goals and priorities. The authors have created interesting studies that note geopolitical conditions, regional differences, and foreign countries' roles in shaping U.S. formulation and implementation of policies, thus expanding our knowledge of how the United States responded to more neutralist and less partisan policies.

6. Wood, *Dismantling of the Good Neighbor System;* Cole Blasier, *The Hovering Giant: U.S. Responses to Revolutionary Change in Latin America* (Pittsburgh: University of Pittsburgh Press, 1976). One need only look at the literature on the U.S. role in the revolution and compare it to the large quantity of work on the U.S. role in Guatemala to see that the Costa Rican episode has been downplayed as rather insignificant. There is also an absence of specific works in either article or monograph form on the role of the United States in the Costa Rican civil war of 1948. Although Thomas Leonard, Walter LaFeber, and others have covered the event in their general studies of Central America, the most comprehensive studies remain unpublished dissertations: Schifter-Sikora, "Origins of the Cold War," and Atwood, "The United States and Costa Rica."

7. Other historians have questioned whether the United States intervened in the struggle, most notably Thomas Leonard and Marcia Quirós. Leonard, *The United States and Central America;* idem, *Central America and the United States;* Marcia Quirós, "The

United States and the Costa Rican Civil War of 1948: The Case Against Intervention," paper presented at the 18th Annual Conference of the Society for Historians of American Foreign Relations, Hyde Park, New York, June 1992. Part of the problem revolves around defining intervention. Some historians believe intervention is direct or covert military activity, but that definition is too narrow. In Latin America, Washington has utilized a variety of diplomatic and military weapons to defeat challenges to its hegemony, such as the use of diplomatic recognition and plotting by U.S. officials with the opposition. The forms that intervention takes can be more than hitting the Latin Americans over the head with a bat, but they still constitute intervention.

8. A very good example is Green, *Containment of Latin America.*

9. Dulles told Cabot in 1953, "Now, I want you to come up with an imaginative program, but I don't want you to spend any money." At the same time, Cabot complained that the United States spent as much money on trains for India as it did on all of Latin America. John Moors Cabot, interview with Philip A. Crowl, 15 November 1965, transcript, John Foster Dulles Oral History Collection, Princeton University Library, Princeton, N.J.

10. Robert A. Pastor, *Whirlpool: U.S. Foreign Policy Toward Latin America and the Caribbean* (Princeton, N.J.: Princeton University Press, 1992), xi–xiv.

11. Influential works on the roles of peasants include: James C. Scott, *Weapons of the Weak: Everyday Forms of Peasant Resistance* (New Haven, Conn.: Yale University Press, 1985); Eric R. Wolf, *Peasants* (Englewood Cliffs, N.J.: Prentice-Hall, 1966); Samuel L. Popkin, *The Rational Peasant: The Political Economy of Rural Society in Vietnam* (Berkeley: University of California Press, 1979); Florencia E. Mallon, *The Defense of Community in Peru's Central Highlands: Peasant Struggle and Capitalist Transition, 1860–1940* (Princeton, N.J.: Princeton University Press, 1983); Friedrich Katz, ed., *Riot, Rebellion, and Revolution: Rural-Social Conflict in Mexico* (Princeton, N.J.: Princeton University Press, 1988); Steve J. Stern, ed., *Resistance, Rebellion, and Consciousness in the Andean Peasant World* (Madison: University of Wisconsin Press, 1987).

12. Other works outside the field of U.S. foreign relations also have influenced this study, including Steve J. Stern, "Feudalism, Capitalism, and the World-System in the Perspective of Latin America and the Caribbean," *American Historical Review* 93 (October 1988): 829–72; Wallerstein, *The Modern World-System;* Jan R. Triska, ed., *Dominant Powers and Subordinate States: The United States in Latin America and the Soviet Union in Eastern Europe* (Durham, N.C.: Duke University Press, 1986); and Ronald Robinson, "Non-European Foundations of European Imperialism: Sketch for a Theory of Collaboration," in *Imperialism: The Robinson and Gallagher Controversy,* ed. William Roger Louis (New York: New Viewpoints, 1976), 128–51.

13. Kyle Longley, "Resisting Domination: The Relationship between the United States and José Figueres," *South Eastern Latin Americanist* 36 (Winter 1993): 7.

14. Thomas G. Paterson, "Introduction: Explaining the History of American Foreign Relations," *Journal of American History* 77 (June 1990): 93–98; Michael H. Hunt, "Internationalizing U.S. Diplomatic History: A Practical Agenda," *Diplomatic History* 15 (Winter 1991): 1–12; Louis A. Pérez, Jr., "Dependency," in *Explaining the History of American Foreign Relations,* ed. Michael J. Hogan and Thomas G. Paterson (New York: Cambridge University Press, 1991), 108–9; Thomas J. McCormick, "World Systems," in *Explaining the History of American Foreign Relations,* ed. Michael J. Hogan and Thomas G. Paterson (New York: Cambridge University Press, 1991), 92.

15. I have been strongly influenced by authors calling for more analysis of the con-

sequences of U.S. actions on the Latin American nations, including Stephen Rabe, "Marching Ahead (Slowly): The Historiography of Inter-American Relations," *Diplomatic History* 13 (Summer 1989): 297–316. A good overview of the state of the field and the radical perspective is presented by Mark T. Gilderhus in "An Emerging Synthesis? U.S.–Latin American Relations since World War II," *Diplomatic History* 16 (Summer 1992): 429–52.

BIBLIOGRAPHY

Acheson, Dean. "Waging Peace in the Americas." *Department of State Bulletin* 21 (26 September 1949): 462–66.

Acuna, Miguel. *El 48.* San José: Imprenta Lehmann, 1974.

Adams, R. N. "Cultural Components of Central America." *American Anthropologist* 58 (1956): 881–907.

Aguilar-Bulgarelli, Oscar. *Costa Rica y sus hechos políticos de 1948.* San José: Editorial Universitaria Centroamérica, 1974.

———. *La Constitución de 1949: Antecedentes y proyecciones.* San José: Editorial Costa Rica, 1973.

Alexander, Robert J. *Communism in Latin America.* New Brunswick, N.J.: Rutgers University Press, 1957.

———. *Rómulo Betancourt and the Transformation of Venezuela.* New Brunswick, N.J.: Transaction Books, 1982.

———. "The Latin American Aprista Parties." *The Political Quarterly* 20 (July–September 1949): 236–47.

Allison, Mary Clara. "A Survey of the Literature and Culture of Costa Rica." Ph.D. diss., University of Washington, 1952.

Almond, Gabriel. "Comparative Political Systems." *Journal of Politics* 18 (August 1956): 391–409.

Ameringer, Charles D. *The Democratic Left in Exile: The Antidictatorial Struggle in the Caribbean, 1945–1959.* Coral Gables, Fla.: University of Miami Press, 1974.

———. *Democracy in Costa Rica.* New York: Praeger, 1982.

———. *Don Pepe: A Political Biography of José Figueres of Costa Rica.* Albuquerque: University of New Mexico Press, 1978.

———. *U.S. Foreign Intelligence: The Secret Side of American History.* Lexington, Mass.: Lexington Books, 1990.

Anderson, Charles W. "Political Ideology and the Revolution of Rising Expectations in Central America, 1944–1958." Ph.D. diss., University of Wisconsin-Madison, 1960.

———. "Politics and Development Policy in Central America." *Midwest Journal of Political Science* 5 (November 1961): 332–50.

Aranda-Barrantes, Jesús. *Los excombatientes de 1948–55.* San José: Imprenta Lehmann, 1984.

Araya-Pochet, Carlos. *Liberación Nacional en la historia política de Costa Rica, 1940–1980.* San José: Editorial Nacional de Textos, 1982.

"Atlantic Report on the World Today." *Atlantic Monthly* 195 (March 1955): 10–15.

Atwood, Paul L. "The United States and Costa Rica, 1945–1960: The Containment of Liberal Nationalism." Ph.D. diss., Boston University, 1991.

Augelli, John P., and Robert C. West. *Middle America: Its Lands and Peoples.* Englewood Cliffs, N.J.: Prentice-Hall, 1966.

Backer, James. *La iglesia y el sindicalismo en Costa Rica.* San José: Editorial Costa Rica, 1974.

Baeza-Flores, Alberto. *La Lucha Sin Fin.* Mexico City: Costa-Amic., 1969.

Baker, Christopher. "Costa Rican Legislative Behavior in Perspective." Ph.D. diss., University of Florida, 1973.

Baker, George W., Jr. "Woodrow Wilson's Use of the Non-Recognition Policy in Costa Rica." *The Americas* 22 (July 1965): 3–21.

Ball, M. Margaret. *The OAS in Transition.* Durham: Duke University Press, 1969.

"Banana Politics." *Economist* 174 (29 January 1955): 374.

Bancroft, Hubert Howe. *History of Central America,* vol. 3. San Francisco: The History Company, 1887.

Barahona, Luis. "Tres notas sobre el carácter costarricense." In *Ensayistas costarricenses,* ed. Luis Ferrero. San José: Libreria Lehmann, 1971.

Barnhart, Edward N. "Citizenship and Political Tests in Latin American Republics in World War II." *Hispanic American Historical Review* 42 (August 1962): 297–333.

Bell, John Patrick. *Crisis in Costa Rica: The 1948 Revolution.* Austin: University of Texas Press, 1971.

———. "Political Power in Contemporary Costa Rica." *Journal of Interamerican Studies and World Affairs* 20 (November 1978): 443–54.

Bennett, William Tapley, Jr. "The Costa Rican–Nicaraguan Incident: Effective International Action in Keeping Peace." *Department of State Bulletin* 20 (5 June 1949): 707–12.

Berle, Adolf A., Jr. *Latin America: Diplomacy and Reality.* New York: Harper and Row, 1962.

Berman, Karl. *Under the Big Stick: Nicaragua and the United States since 1848.* Boston: South End Press, 1986.

Bernstein, Harry. *Origins of Inter-American Interest, 1700–1812.* New York: Russell and Russell, 1965.

Biesanz, Karen, Richard Biesanz, and Mavis Biesanz. *Los costarricense.* San José: Editorial Universidad Estatal a Distancia, 1979.

———. *The Costa Ricans.* Englewood Cliffs, N.J.: Prentice-Hall, 1982.

Biolley, Paul. *Costa Rica and Her Future.* Washington, D.C.: Judd and Detweiler, 1889.

Bird, Leonard. *Costa Rica: A Country without an Army.* Leeds, England: Leeds Community Press, 1979.

———. *Costa Rica: The Unarmed Democracy.* London: Sheppard Press, 1984.

Bishop-Berle, Beatrice, and Travis Beal Jacobs, eds. *Navigating the Rapids, 1918–1971: From the Papers of Adolf A. Berle.* New York: Harcourt Brace Jovanovich, 1973.

Blanco-Segura, Ricardo. *Historia eclesiástica de Costa Rica: Del descubrimiento a la erección de la Diocesis, 1502–1850.* San José: Editorial Costa Rica, 1967.

———. *Monseñor Sanabria.* San José: Editorial Costa Rica, 1971.

Blanford, Ruth Brownlow. "The Women's Vote in Costa Rica." *Américas* 7 (June 1955): 3–7.

Blasier, Cole. *The Hovering Giant: The U.S. Response to Revolutionary Change in Latin America.* Pittsburgh: University of Pittsburgh Press, 1976.

Blum, William. *The CIA: A Forgotten History: U.S. Global Interventions since World War 2.* London: Zed Books, 1986.

Bode, Ken. "Don Pepe." *The New Republic* 23 (April 1977): 13–15.

Bodenheimer, Suzanne. "The Social Democratic Ideology in Latin America: The Case of Costa Rica's Partido Liberación Nacional." *Caribbean Studies* 10 (October 1970): 49–96.

Bonilla, Harold H. *Figueres and Costa Rica: An Unauthorized Political Biography.* San José: Editorial Texto Limitada, 1975.

———. *Los presidentes.* San José: Editorial Estatal a Distancia, 1979.

Booth, John A. "Costa Rica." In *Latin American Labor Organization,* ed. Gerald Greenfield and Sheldon Maram, 213–42. Westport, Conn.: Greenwood Press, 1987.

———. "Costa Rica: The Roots of Democratic Stability." In *Democracy in Developing Countries,* ed. Larry Diamond, Juan Linz, and Seymour Martin Lipset, 387–422. vol. 4. Boulder, Colo.: Lynne Rienner, 1989.

———. "Democracy and Citizen Action in Costa Rica: The Modes and Correlates of Popular Participation in Politics." Ph.D. diss., University of Texas at Austin, 1975.

———. "Representative Constitutional Democracy in Costa Rica: Adaptation to Crisis in the Turbulent 1980s." In *Central America: Crisis and Adaptation,* ed. Steve C. Ropp and James A. Morris, 153–88. Albuquerque: University of New Mexico Press, 1984.

Botey, Ana María, and Rodolfo Cisneros. *La crisis del 1929 y la fundacion del Partido Comunista de Costa Rica.* San José: Editorial Costa Rica, 1984.

Boucher, Phillip Paul. "U.S. Foreign Aid to Latin America: Hypothesis and Patterns in Historical Statistics, 1934–1974." Ph.D. diss., University of California, Berkeley, 1979.

Bourne, Kenneth. "The Clayton-Bulwer Treaty and the Decline of British Opposition to the Territorial Expansion of the United States, 1857–1860." *Journal of Modern History* 33 (Summer 1961): 281–97.

Brockett, Charles D. *Land, Power and Poverty: Agrarian Transformation and Political Conflict in Central America.* Boston: Unwin-Hyman, 1988.

Brumbaugh, Chalmers Sherfey. "Costa Rica: The Making of a Livable Society." Ph.D. diss., University of Wisconsin–Madison, 1985.

Bulmer-Thomas, Victor. "Economic Development Over the Long-Run: Central America since 1920." *Journal of Latin American Studies* 15 (November 1983): 269–94.

———. *The Political Economy of Central America since 1920.* New York: Cambridge University Press, 1987.

Busey, James L. "Foundations of Contrast: Costa Rica and Nicaragua." *Western Political Quarterly* 11 (September 1958): 627–59.

———. *Notes on Costa Rican Democracy.* Boulder: University of Colorado Press, 1962.

———. "The Presidents of Costa Rica." *The Americas* 18 (January 1961): 55–70.

Cabot, John Moors. *First Line of Defense: Forty Years' Experience of a Career Diplomat.* Washington, D.C.: Georgetown School of Foreign Service, 1979.

———. Interview with Philip A. Crowl, 15 November 1965. Transcript. John Foster Dulles Oral History Collection. Princeton University Library, Princeton, N.J.

———. *Toward Our Common American Destiny.* Medford, Mass.: Fletcher School of Law and Diplomacy, 1955.

Calderón-Guardia, Rafael Ángel. *El gobernante y el hombre frente al problema social costarricense.* San José: Privately published, 1942.

Callcott, Wilfrid Hardy. *The Caribbean Policy of the United States, 1890–1920.* New York: Octagon Books, 1942.

Calvert, Peter, and Susan Calvert. *Latin America in the Twentieth Century.* 2d ed. New York: St. Martin's Press, 1993.

Calvo-Gamboa, Carlos. *Costa Rica en la segunda guerra mundial, 1939–1945.* San José: Editorial Universidad Estatal a Distancia, 1985.

Calvo-Mora, Joaquín Bernardo. *La República de Costa Rica.* New York: Rand McNally, 1890.

Cañas, Alberto F. *Los ocho años.* San José: Editorial Liberación Nacional, 1955.

Carlson, Reynold E. "Economic Development in Central America." *Inter-American Economic Affairs* 2 (Autumn 1948): 27–28.

Carr, Albert Z. *The World and William Walker.* New York: Harper and Row, 1963.

Carvajal-Herrera, Mario. "Ideologías en la política costarricense y sus resultados electorales." *Revista de Ciencias Sociales* 7 (April 1973): 7–20.

———. "Political Attitudes and Political Change in Costa Rica: A Comparison of Attitudes of Leaders and Followers with Respect to Regime Values and Party Identification." Ph.D. diss., University of Kansas, 1972.

Castro-Esquivel, Arturo. *José Figueres-Ferrer.* San José: Imprenta Tormo, 1955.

Cerdas-Albertazzi, Ana Luisa. *La abolición del ejército en Costa Rica.* San José: Nacional de Conmemoraciones Históricas, 1988.

Cerdas-Cruz, Rodolfo. *Formación del estado en Costa Rica.* San José: Editorial Universidad de Costa Rica, 1967.

———. *La crisis de la democracia liberal en Costa Rica.* San José: Editorial Universitaria Centroamérica, 1972.

Cespedes, Victor Hugo. *Evolución de la distribución del ingreso en Costa Rica.* San José: Academia de Centroamérica, 1986.

Chase, Alfonso. *José Figueres: Escritos y discursos, 1942–1962.* San José: Editorial Costa Rica, 1989.

Child, Irving L. "The Background of Public Opinion in Costa Rica." *Public Opinion Quarterly* 7 (Summer 1943): 242–57.

Chinchilla, Norma Stolz. "Class Struggles in Central America: Background and Overview." *Latin American Perspectives* 7 (Spring–Summer 1980): 2–23.

Church, George Earl. "Costa Rica." *The Geographical Journal* 10 (July–December 1897): 56–84.

Clark, Paul Coe, Jr. *The United States and Somoza, 1933–1956: A Revisionist Look.* New York: Praeger, 1992.

Clays-Spoelder, Ivonne. *El otro Calderón Guardia.* San José: Casa Grafica, 1985.

Clifford, J. Garry. "Bureaucratic Politics." In *Explaining the History of American Foreign Relations,* ed. Michael J. Hogan and Thomas G. Patterson, 141–50. New York: Cambridge University Press, 1991.

Conn, Stetson, and Byron Fairchild. *The Framework of Hemispheric Defense.* Washington, D.C.: Government Printing Office, 1960.

Cortés, Carmen. "The Costa Rican Invasion-Revolt." *The Pan American* 9 (July 1949): 8–11.

"Costa Rica and the Invasion: Difficulties of a Central American Democracy." *World Today* 11 (March 1955): 129–38.

Costigliola, Frank. *Awkward Dominion: American Political, Economic, and Cultural Relations with Europe, 1919–1933.* Ithaca, N.Y.: Cornell University Press, 1984.

Crassweller, Robert. *The Caribbean Community: Changing Societies and U.S. Policy.* New York: Praeger, 1972.

Creedman, Theodore. "The Political Development of Costa Rica, 1936–1944: Politics of an Emerging Welfare State in a Patriarchal Society." Ph.D. diss., University of Maryland, 1971.

Crowe, Frederick. *The Gospel in Central America.* London: Charles Gilpin, 1850.

Crowther, Samuel. *The Romance and Rise of the American Tropics.* Garden City, N.Y.: Doubleday, Doran, 1929.

Cullather, Nick. *Illusions of Influence: The Political Economy of United States–Philippines Relations, 1942–1960.* Palo Alto, Calif.: Stanford University Press, 1994.

Curtis, William E. "The Smallest of the American Republics." *Harper's Magazine* 75 (October 1887): 668–82.

Daniels, Paul C. "Influence of Inter-American Relations on U.S. Foreign Policy." *Department of State Bulletin* 20 (10 April 1949): 460–63.

———. Interview with Richard D. McKinzie, 11 June 1974. Transcript. Harry S. Truman Library Oral History Collection. Harry S. Truman Library, Independence, Mo.

Darling, Arthur B. *The Central Intelligence Agency: An Instrument of Goverment to 1950.* University Park: Pennsylvania State University, 1990.

del Vayo, J. Alvarez. "Costa Rican Crisis." *Nation* 180 (22 January 1955): 63–64.

Denton, Charles F. "Bureaucracy in an Immobilist Society: The Case of Costa Rica." *Administrative Science Quarterly* 14 (September 1969): 418–26.

———. *Patterns of Costa Rican Politics.* Boston: Allyn & Bacon, 1971.

———. "The Politics of Development in Costa Rica." Ph.D. diss., University of Texas at Austin, 1969.

DeWalt, Billie R. "The Agrarian Bases of Conflict in Central America." In *The Central American Crisis,* ed. Kenneth Coleman and George C. Herring, 43–54. Wilmington, Del.: Scholarly Resources, Inc., 1985.

Dozer, Donald. *Are We Good Neighbors? Three Decades of Inter-American Relations, 1930–1960.* Gainesville: University of Florida Press, 1959.

Duggan, Laurence. *The Americas: The Search for Hemisphere Security.* New York: Henry Holt, 1949.

Duncan, Kenneth, and Ian Rutledge. *Land and Labor.* Cambridge: Cambridge University Press, 1977.

Duncan, Quince, and Carlos Meléndez-Chavarri. *El negro en Costa Rica.* San José: Editorial Costa Rica, 1972.

Dunkerly, James. *Power in the Isthmus: A Political History of Modern Central America.* New York: Verso, 1988.

Earley, Stephen. *Arms and Politics in Costa Rica and Nicaragua, 1948–1981.* Albuquerque: Latin American Institute, 1982.

Ebel, Roland H., and Raymond Taras. "Cultural Style and International Policy-making: The Latin American Tradition." In *Culture and International Relations,* ed. Jongsuk Chay, 191–206. New York: Praeger, 1990.

Eisenhower, Milton. Interview with John Luter, 21 June 1967. Dwight D. Eisenhower Oral History Collection. Dwight D. Eisenhower Library, Abilene, Kansas.

———. *The Wine Is Bitter.* New York: Doubleday, 1961.

English, Burt H. *Liberación Nacional in Costa Rica: The Development of a Political Party in a Transitional Society.* Gainesville: University of Florida Press, 1971.

Erb, Claude Curtis. "Nelson Rockefeller and United States–Latin American Relations, 1940–1945." Ph.D. diss., Clark University, 1982.

Espinosa, J. Manuel. *Inter-American Beginnings of U.S. Cultural Diplomacy, 1936–1948.* Washington, D.C.: Government Printing Office, 1976.

Facio-Brenes, Rodrigo. *Estudio sobre economía costarricense.* vol. 1. San José: Editorial Costa Rica, 1975.

Fernández-Guardia, Ricardo. *Cartilla histórica de Costa Rica.* San José: Imprenta Lehmann, 1967.

———, ed. *Costa Rica en el Siglo XIX*. San José: Editorial Universitaria Centroamérica, 1929.

Fernández-Vásquez, Rodrigo. "Costa Rica: Interpretación histórica sobre reforma social y acción ecelsiastica, 1940–1982." *Estudios Sociales Centroamericano* 33 (September–December 1982): 221–48.

Ferrero, Luis. *Costa Rica precolombina: Arqueología, etnología, tecnología, arte*. San José: Editorial Costa Rica, 1981.

Figueres-Ferrer, José. "Blunting Point Four." *Commonweal* 59 (1 January 1954): 322–25.

———. *Cartas a un cuidadano*. San José: Imprenta Nacional, 1956.

———. "Costa Rica Welcomes Foreign Investments." *Central America and Mexico* 2 (December 1954): 37–40.

———. *El espíritu del 48*. San José: Editorial Costa Rica, 1987.

———. Interview with Donald R. McCoy, 8 July 1970. Transcript. Harry S. Truman Oral History Collection. Harry S. Truman Library, Independence, Mo.

———. "Latin American Liberals Laud U.S. Labor Aims." *AFL-CIO Free Labor News* 16 (February 1961): 1.

———. "Not to Have Dreamed in Vain." *Congress Weekly* 19 (October 1953): 8–9.

———. *Palabras gastadas*. San José: Imprenta Española, Soley y Valverde, 1943.

———. "Point Four, a Latin American View." *Central America and Mexico* 1 (April 1953): 3–16.

———. "The Problems of Democracy in Latin America." *Journal of International Affairs* 9, no. 1 (1955): 17.

———. "We Don't Want Foreign Investments." *New Leader* 36 (31 August 1953): 2–4.

Findling, John E. *Close Neighbors, Distant Friends: Central American Relations*. Westport, Conn.: Greenwood Press, 1987.

Fischel-Volio, Astrid. *Consenso y represión: Una interpretatción socio política de la educación costarricense*. San José: Editorial Costa Rica, 1987.

Fitzgibbon, Russell H. "Executive Power in Central America." *Journal of Politics* 3 (August 1941): 297–308.

Flora, Jan, Douglas K. Benson, and Cornelia B. Flora. "Central America: Cultures in Conflict." In *Sociology of Developing Societies: Central America*, ed. Jan Flora and Edelberto Torres-Rivas, 17–31. New York: Monthly Review Press, 1989.

Fonseca-Corrales, Elizabeth. *Costa Rica colonial: La tierra y el hombre*. San José: Editorial Universidad Centroamérica, 1984.

Francis, Michael J. "The United States at Rio, 1942: The Strains of Pan Americanism." *Journal of Latin American Studies* 6 (May 1974): 77–95.

Freeland, Richard. *The Truman Doctrine and the Origins of McCarthyism*. New York: Knopf, 1972.

Froncek, Mary Zygmunta. "Diplomatic Relations between [the] United States and Costa Rica, 1823–1882." Ph.D. diss., Fordham University, 1959.

Fuerst, J. S. "Central America's Forgotten Democracy." *Commonweal* 110 (20 May 1983): 302–3.

Furbay, John. *Education in Costa Rica.* Washington, D.C.: U.S. Office of Education, 1946.

Furniss, Edgar S. "American Wartime Objectives in Latin America." *World Politics* 11 (April 1950): 373–88.

———. "The Inter-American System and Recent Caribbean Disputes." *International Organization* 4 (November 1950): 585–97.

Gaddis, John L. *The United States and the Origins of the Cold War.* New York: Columbia University Press, 1972.

Gardiner, C. Harvey. "The Japanese and Central America." *Journal of Interamerican Studies* 14 (February 1972): 15–49.

Gardner, John W. "The Costa Rican Junta of 1948–49." Ph.D. diss., St. John's University (New York), 1971.

Gardner, Lloyd. *Architects of Illusion: Men and Ideas in American Foreign Policy, 1941–1949.* Chicago: Quadrangle Books, 1970.

Garro, Joaquín. *Veinte años de historia chica.* San José: Imprenta Vargas, 1967.

Gilderhus, Mark T. "An Emerging Synthesis? U.S.–Latin American Relations since World War II." *Diplomatic History* 16 (Summer 1992): 429–52.

Gillon, Steven M. *Politics and Vision: The ADA and American Liberalism, 1947–1985.* New York: Oxford University Press, 1987.

Glade, William P. *The Latin American Economies.* New York: American Books, 1969.

González-Flores, Luis Felipe. *Evolución de la instrucción pública en Costa Rica.* San José: Editorial Costa Rica, 1978.

———. *Historia de la influencia extranjera en el desenvolvimiento educacional y cientifico de Costa Rica.* San José: Imprenta Nacional, 1921.

Green, David. *The Containment of Latin America: A History of the Myths and Realities of the Good Neighbor Policy.* Chicago: Quadrangle Books, 1971.

Grieb, Kenneth J. "The Myth of a Central American Dictators League." *Journal of Latin American Studies* 10 (November 1978): 329–45.

Gudmundson, Lowell. "Costa Rica before Coffee: Occupational Distribution, Wealth, Inequality, and Elite Society in the Village Economy of the 1840s." *Journal of Latin American Studies* 15 (November 1983): 427–52.

———. *Costa Rica before Coffee: Society and Economy on the Eve of the Export Boom.* Baton Rouge: Louisiana State University Press, 1986.

Guerra, Tomás. *José Figueres: Una vida por la justicia social.* San José: Centro de Estudios Democraticos de América Latina, 1987.

Gunther, John. "Costa Rica: A True Democracy." *Current History and Forum* 52 (24 December 1940): 11–13.

Gutiérrez, Carlos José. "Neutralidad e intervención: Dirección y problemas de la política internacional costarricense durante el primer tercio del siglo XX." *Revista de la Universidad de Costa Rica* 13 (July 1956): 2–61.

Hahn, Peter. *The United States, Great Britain, and Egypt, 1945–1956: Strategy and Diplomacy in the Early Cold War.* Chapel Hill: University of North Carolina, 1991.

Hall, Carolyn. *Costa Rica: A Geographical Interpretation in Historical Perspective.* Boulder, Colo.: Westview Press, 1985.

Hammond, Peter B. *An Introduction to Cultural and Social Anthropology.* New York: Macmillan, 1971.

Hansen, Alvin H. "Hemisphere Solidarity." *Foreign Affairs* 19 (October 1940): 12–21.

Harris, Marvin. *The Rise of Anthropological Theory: A History of Theories of Culture.* New York: Thomas Crowell, 1968.

Hathaway, Hanson. "Costa Rica's Bloodless Revolution." *The Pan American* 5 (May 1944): 13–16.

Healy, David. *Drive to Hegemony: The United States in the Caribbean, 1898–1917.* Madison: University of Wisconsin Press, 1988.

Heggy, Liane Llane. "The Development of Dependence in Costa Rica and the Role of the Soviet Union." Ph.D. diss., University of Maryland, 1990.

Hernández, Edward D. "Modernization and Dependency in Costa Rica During the Decade of the 1880s." Ph.D. diss., University of California, Los Angeles, 1980.

Herrera-Balharry, Eugencio. *Los alemanes y el estado cafetalero.* San José: Editorial Universidad Estatal a Distancia, 1988.

Herring, Hubert. *Good Neighbors: Argentina, Brazil, Chile and Seventeen Other Countries.* New Haven, Conn.: Yale University Press, 1941.

Hill, Robert C. Interview with John T. Mason, Jr., 19 October, 1972. Dwight D. Eisenhower Oral History Collection. Dwight D. Eisenhower Library, Abilene, Kansas.

Hobsbawm, Eric. "Peasants and Politics." *Journal of Peasant Studies* 1, no. 1 (1973): 3–22.

Holland, Henry. "OAS Action in the Costa Rican Conflict." *Department of State Bulletin* 32 (31 January 1955): 178–80.

Holmes, Olive. "Acheson Clarifies U.S. Policy in Latin America." *Foreign Policy Bulletin* 28 (7 October 1949): 3.

———. "Costa Rican Crisis Exposes Central American Feuds." *Foreign Policy Bulletin* 28 (24 December 1948): 2–3.

Howell, Henry M. "Western Hemisphere Accord." *The South Atlantic Quarterly* 41 (July 1942): 239–53.

Howland, Charles P. *American Relations in the Caribbean.* New Haven, Conn.: Yale University Press, 1929.

"How the Rio Treaty Works." *Americas* 1 (March 1949): 9–11.

Hunt, Michael H. "Internationalizing U.S. Diplomatic History: A Practical Agenda." *Diplomatic History* 15 (Winter 1991): 1–12.

Immerman, Richard. *The CIA in Guatemala: The Foreign Policy of Intervention.* Austin: University of Texas Press, 1982.

Inman, Samuel Guy. *Inter-American Conferences, 1826–1954.* Washington, D.C.: University Press of Washington, D.C., 1965.

International Bureau of the American Republics. *Commercial Directory of Costa Rica, Guatemala, Honduras, Nicaragua, Salvador.* Washington, D.C.: Government Printing Office, 1891.

———. *Costa Rica: A Handbook.* Washington, D.C.: Government Printing Office, 1892.

International Encyclopedia of the Social Sciences. New York: Macmillan and the Free Press, 1961.

Ireland, Gordon. *Boundaries, Possessions and Conflicts in Central and North America and the Caribbean.* New York: Octagon Books, 1971.

Iriye, Akira. "Culture." *Journal of American History* 77 (June 1990): 99–107.

———. *Power and Culture: The Japanese-American War, 1941–1945.* New York: Cambridge University Press, 1981.

Jacobstein, Helen L. *The Process of Economic Development in Costa Rica, 1948–1970: Some Political Factors.* New York: Garland Publishers, 1987.

James, Daniel. *Red Design for the Americas.* New York: John Day, 1954.

Jiménez, Manuel F. "Coffee in Costa Rica." *Bulletin of the Pan American Union* 74 (February 1945): 88–90.

Jinesta, Ricardo, and Carlos Jinesta. *La instrucción pública en Costa Rica.* San José: Imprenta Falco y Borrase, 1921.

Johnson, Robert E. "Facts Behind the Figueres-Somoza Feud." *American Mercury* 81 (September 1955): 91–95.

Jones, Chester Lloyd. *The Caribbean Policy of the United States, 1890–1920.* New York: Octagon Books, 1966.

———. *The Caribbean since 1900.* New York: Russell and Russell, 1936.

———. *Costa Rica and Civilization in the Caribbean.* Madison: University of Wisconsin Press, 1935.

———. "The Costa Rican Attitude Toward the United States." *World Affairs* 96 (March 1933): 41–43.

Jones, Clarence F., and Paul C. Morison. "Evolution of the Banana Industry in Costa Rica." *Economic Geography* 28 (January 1952): 12–19.

Kantor, Harry. *Bibliography of José Figueres.* Tempe: Center for Latin American Studies, Arizona State University, 1972.

———. *The Costa Rican Election of 1953: A Case Study.* Gainesville: University of Florida Press, 1958.

———. "A 'New Deal' Government for Costa Rica." *World Affairs* 117 (Spring 1954): 11–13.

———. "The Struggle for Democracy in Costa Rica." *The South Atlantic Quarterly* 55 (January 1956): 12–19.

Karnes, Thomas L. *The Failure of Union: Central America, 1824–1975.* Tempe: Center for Latin American Studies, Arizona State University, 1976.

———. "The Origins of Costa Rican Federalism." *The Americas* 15 (June 1959): 249–69.

Katz, Friedrich, ed. *Riot, Rebellion, and Revolution: Rural-Social Conflict in Mexico.* Princeton, N.J.: Princeton University Press, 1988.

Kaufman, Edy, Yoram Shapira, and Joel Barromi. *Israel-Latin American Relations.* New Brunswick, N.J.: Transaction Books, 1979.

Kepner, Charles D., Jr. *Social Aspects of the Banana Industry.* New York: AMS Press, 1967.

Kinzer, Stephen, and Stephen C. Schlesinger. *Bitter Fruit: The Untold Story of the American Coup in Guatemala.* Garden City: Doubleday, 1982.

Krehm, William. *Democracies and Tyrannies of the Caribbean.* Westport, Conn.: Lawrence Hill, 1984.

Kunz, Josef L. "The Idea of 'Collective Security' in Pan-American Developments." *Western Political Quarterly* 6 (December 1953): 658–79.

Kuper, Adam, and Jessica Kuper, eds. *The Social Science Encyclopedia.* Boston: Routledge and Kegan Paul, 1985.

LaFeber, Walter. *America, Russia, and the Cold War.* 7th ed. New York: McGraw-Hill, 1992.

———. *Inevitable Revolutions.* New York: W. W. Norton, 1983.

———. *The Panama Canal: The Crisis in Historical Perspective.* 2d ed. New York: Oxford University Press, 1989.

Lange, Frederick. "The Cultural Geography of Costa Rica." In *Prehistoric Settlement Patterns in Costa Rica,* ed. Frederick Lange and Lynette Norr. Urbana, Ill.: Journal of the Steward Anthropological Society, 1986.

Langley, Lester. *The United States and the Caribbean, 1900–1970.* Athens: University of Georgia Press, 1980.

Láscaris-Comneno, Constantino. *El costarricense.* San José: Editorial Universitaria Centroamérica, 1977.

Lee, Hal F. "Rio Conference." *The Pan American* 8 (October 1947): 5–8.

León, Jorge. "Land Utilization in Costa Rica." *The Geographical Review* 38 (July 1948): 444–56.

Leonard, Thomas M. *Central America and the United States: The Search for Stability.* Athens: University of Georgia Press, 1991.

———. *Central America and United States Policies, 1820s–1980s.* Claremont, Calif.: Regina Books, 1985.

———. "Costa Rica: The U.S. Perception of the Church and Communism, 1931–1948." In *The Church and Society in Latin America,* ed. Jeffrey A. Cole. New Orleans: Tulane University Press, 1984.

———. *The United States and Central America, 1944–1949.* Tuscaloosa: University of Alabama Press, 1984.

———. "The United States and Costa Rica, 1944–1949: Perceptions of Political Dynamics." *SECOLAS Annals* 13 (1982): 17–31.

Linden, Eugene. *The Alms Race: The Impact of American Voluntary Aid Abroad.* New York: Random House, 1976.

Lines, Jorge A. *Anthropological Bibliography of Aboriginal Costa Rica.* San José: Tropical Science Center, 1967.

Liss, Sheldon. *Radical Thought in Central America.* Boulder, Colo.: Westview Press, 1991.

Livezey, Lowell. *Nongovernmental Organizations and the Idea of Human Rights.* Princeton, N.J.: Princeton University Press, 1987.

Lleras-Camargo, Alberto. "The Bogotá Conference." *Bulletin of the Pan American Union* 82 (June 1948): 301–11.

Lommel, Anne W. "The United States' Efforts to Foster Peace and Stability in Central America, 1923–1954." Ph.D. diss., University of Minnesota, 1967.

Longley, Kyle. "Resisting Domination: The Relationship between the United States and José Figueres." *South Eastern Latin Americanist* 36 (Winter 1993): 6–18.

McAuliffe, Mary Sperling. *Crisis on the Left: Cold War Politics and American Liberals, 1947–1954.* Amherst: University of Massachusetts Press, 1978.

McBride-Stetson, Dorothy. "Elite Political Culture in Costa Rica." Ph.D. diss., Vanderbilt University, 1968.

McCamant, John. *Development Assistance in Central America.* New York: Praeger, 1968.

McCormick, Thomas J. "World Systems." In *Explaining the History of American Foreign Relations,* ed. Michael J. Hogan and Thomas G. Paterson, 89–98. New York: Cambridge University Press, 1991.

McGovern, Joseph J. "The Costa Rican Labor Movement: A Study in Political Unionism." *Public and International Affairs* 4 (Spring 1966): 88–116.

MacLeod, Murdo. *Spanish Central America: A Socioeconomic History, 1520–1720.* Berkeley: University of California Press, 1973.

MacMahon, Robert J. *The Cold War on the Periphery: The United States, India and Pakistan.* New York: Columbia University Press, 1994.

Mallon, Florencia E. *The Defense of Community in Peru's Central Highlands: Peasant Struggle and Capitalist Transition, 1860–1940.* Princeton, N.J.: Princeton University Press, 1983.

Mann, Thomas C. Interview with Maclyn P. Burg, 17 December 1975. Dwight D. Eisenhower Oral History Collection. Dwight D. Eisenhower Library, Abilene, Kansas.

Martin, Lawrence, and Sylvia Martin. "Four Strong Men and a President." *Harper's Magazine* 185 (September 1942): 418–27.

Martz, John D. *Central America: The Crisis and the Challenge.* Chapel Hill: University of North Carolina Press, 1959.

———. "Costa Rican Electoral Trends, 1953–1966." *Western Political Quarterly* 20 (December 1967): 888–909.

Mathews, John. "Roosevelt's Latin American Policy." *American Political Science Review* 29 (October 1935): 805–21.

May, Stacy, and Galo Plaza-Lasso. *The United Fruit Company in Latin America.* New York: Arno Press, 1976.

Meagher, Thomas Francis. "Holidays in Costa Rica." *Harper's Magazine* 20 (December 1859–May 1860): 18, 145, 304.

Mecham, Lloyd. *The United States and Inter-American Security, 1889–1960.* Austin: University of Texas Press, 1961.

Meléndez-Chaverri, Carlos. *Conquistadores y Pobladores: Orígenes histórico-sociales de los costarricense.* San José: Editorial Universidad Estatal a Distancia, 1982.

Merrill, Dennis. *Bread and the Ballot: The United States and India's Economic Development, 1947–1963.* Chapel Hill: University of North Carolina Press, 1990.

Mijeski, Kenneth J. "The Executive-Legislative Policy Process in Costa Rica." Ph.D. diss., University of North Carolina, 1971.

Miller, Eugene Willard. *The Third World: Guatemala, Honduras, Belize, Costa Rica, Panama: A Bibliography.* Monticello, Ill.: Vance Bibliography, 1990.

Monge-Alfaro, Carlos. *Geografía social y humana de Costa Rica.* San José: Imprenta y Libreria Universal, 1942.

———. *Historia de Costa Rica.* San José: Libreria Trejos, 1976.

Montero-Barrantes, Francisco. *Historia de Costa Rica.* San José: Tipografía Nacional, 1892.

Morgan, John Charles. "The Partido Nacional of Costa Rica: A Case Study of Political Myth and Political Culture." Ph.D. diss., Louisiana State University, 1979.

Muñoz-Guillén, Mercedes. *El estado y la abolición del ejército, 1914–1949.* San José: Editorial Porvenir, 1990.

Munro, Dana. *The Five Republics of Central America.* New York: Oxford University Press, 1918.

Murillo-Jiménez, Hugo. *Tinoco y los Estados Unidos: Génesis y caída de un régimen.* San José: Editorial Universidad Estatal a Distancia, 1981.

———. "Wilson and Tinoco: The U.S. and the Policy of Non-Recognition in Costa Rica, 1917–1919." Ph.D. diss., University of California, San Diego, 1978.

Murillo-Visquez, Jaime, ed. *Historia de Costa Rica en el Siglo XX.* San José: Editorial Provenir, 1989.

Murkland, Harry B. "The Complicated Caribbean." *Current History* 18 (January 1950): 8–12.

———. "Costa Rica: Fortunate Society." *Current History* 22 (March 1952): 141–44.

Murphy, Dana Winthrop. "Costa Rica, 1953–1970: The Evolution of a Working Multiparty System in the Post-Revolutionary Era." Ph.D. diss., University of Washington, 1976.

Navarro-Bolandi, Hugo. *José Figueres en la evolución de Costa Rica.* Mexico City: Imprenta Quirós, 1953.

———. *La generación del 48: Jucio histórico-político sobre la democracia costarricense.* Mexico City: Ediciones Humanismo, 1957.

Nelson, Wilton M. *A History of Protestantism in Costa Rica*. Lucknow, England: Lucknow Publishing House, 1963.

Ninkovich, Frank A. *The Diplomacy of Ideas: United States Foreign Policy and Cultural Relations, 1938–1950*. New York: Cambridge University Press, 1981.

Obregón-Loría, Rafael. *Conflictos militares y políticos de Costa Rica*. San José: Imprenta Nacional, 1966.

———. *Hechos militares y políticos*. Alajuela, Costa Rica: Museo Histórico Cultural Juan Santamaría, 1981.

———. "Nuestras relaciones internacionales a mediados del siglo XIX." *Revista de la Universidad de Costa Rica* 14 (November 1956): 63–140.

Oconitrillo-García, Eduardo. *Un siglo de política costarricense: Crónica de 32 campañas presidenciales*. San José: Editorial Universidad Estatal a Distancia, 1981.

O'Connor, Suzanne. "Costa Rica in the World Community of Nations, 1919–1939: A Case Study in Latin American Internationalism." Ph.D. diss., Loyola University of Chicago, 1976.

Olien, Michael D. "The Negro in Costa Rica: The Ethnohistory of an Ethnic Minority in a Complex Society." Ph.D. diss., University of Oregon, 1967.

Oliver, Judy. "Twelve Who Ruled Costa Rica: The Junta of 1948–1949." Master's thesis, Louisiana State University, 1968.

Oliver-Milner, Judy. "Otílio Ulate and the Traditional Response to Contemporary Change in Costa Rica." Ph.D. diss., Louisiana State University, 1977.

———. "Political Thought of José Figueres." *South Eastern Latin Americanist* 17 (June 1973): 1–4.

Pan American Union. "The Ambassador of Costa Rica to the United States." *Bulletin of the Pan American Union* 77 (August 1943): 438–39.

———. "Amendment to the Constitution of Costa Rica." *Bulletin of the Pan American Union* 80 (November 1946): 53.

———. "Boundary between Costa Rica and Panama." *Bulletin of the Pan American Union* 79 (May 1945): 165.

———. "Boundary Treaty between Costa Rica and Panama." *Bulletin of the Pan American Union* 75 (July 1941): 430–31.

———. "Costa Rican Election Law." *Bulletin of the Pan American Union* 81 (January 1947): 49–50.

———. "Costa Rican Housing Board." *Bulletin of the Pan American Union* 75 (May 1941): 314–15.

———. "Costa Rican National University Established." *Bulletin of the Pan American Union* 74 (December 1940): 844–45.

———. "The Inter-American Conference for the Maintenance of Continental Peace and Security." *Bulletin of the Pan American Union* 81 (October 1947): 527–42.

———. "Message of the President of Costa Rica." *Bulletin of the Pan American Union* 77 (December 1943): 706–9.

———. "Message of the President of Costa Rica." *Bulletin of the Pan American Union* 78 (September 1944): 526–28.

———. "Message of the President of Costa Rica." *Bulletin of the Pan American Union* 79 (August 1945): 470–71.

———. "Message of the President of Costa Rica." *Bulletin of the Pan American Union* 80 (September 1946): 524–25.

———. "The President Reports to the Costa Rican Congress." *Bulletin of the Pan American Union* 81 (September 1947): 510–11.

———. "Visit of the President-Elect of Costa Rica to Washington." *Bulletin of the Pan American Union* 78 (July 1944): 363–64.

———. "The Washington Visit of the President-Elect of Costa Rica." *Bulletin of the Pan American Union* 14 (May 1940): 372–75.

Parker, Franklin. *Travels in Central America, 1821–1840.* Gainesville: University of Florida Press, 1970.

Parker-Wallace, Lillian. *Leo XIII and the Rise of Socialism.* Durham, N.C.: Duke University Press, 1966.

Pastor, Robert A. *Whirlpool: U.S. Foreign Policy toward Latin America and the Caribbean.* Princeton, N.J.: Princeton University Press, 1992.

Paterson, Thomas G. "Introduction: Explaining the History of American Foreign Relations." *Journal of American History* 77 (June 1990): 93–98.

———. *On Every Front: The Making of the Cold War.* New York: W. W. Norton, 1979.

———. *Soviet-American Confrontation.* Baltimore: Johns Hopkins University Press, 1973.

Peeler, John A. *Latin American Democracies: Colombia, Costa Rica, Venezuela.* Chapel Hill: University of North Carolina Press, 1985.

Peralta, Hernan G. *Augustín de Iturbide y Costa Rica.* San José: Editorial Costa Rica, 1968.

Pérez, Louis A., Jr. "Dependency." In *Explaining the History of American Foreign Relations,* ed. Michael J. Hogan and Thomas G. Paterson, 99–110. New York: Cambridge University Press, 1991.

Perkins, Dexter. *The United States and the Caribbean.* 2d ed. New York: Cambridge University Press, 1966.

Perry, Elizabeth J. "Introduction: Chinese Political Culture Revisited." In *Popular Protest and Political Culture in Modern China,* ed. Elizabeth J. Perry and Jeffery N. Wasserstrom, 1–13. Boulder, Colo.: Westview Press, 1992.

Petersen, Juan Andres. "Somoza Versus the Americas." *Nation* 168 (15 January 1949): 63–66.

Picado-Michalski, Teodoro. *El pacto de la Embajada de Mexico, su incumplimiento.* Managua: Privately published, 1949.

Pike, Frederick B. *The United States and Latin America: Myths and Stereotypes of Civilization and Nature.* Austin: University of Texas Press, 1992.

Poitras, Guy. *The Ordeal of Hegemony: The United States and Latin America.* Boulder, Colo.: Westview Press, 1990.

Pollan, Arthur A. *The United Fruit Company in Middle America.* New York: Privately published, 1944.

Popkin, Samuel L. *The Rational Peasant: The Political Economy of Rural Society in Vietnam.* Berkeley: University of California Press, 1979.

Proctor, Charles. "Political Systems." In *Turrialba: Social Systems and the Introduction of Change,* ed. Charles P. Loomis, Julio O. Morales, Roy A. Clifford, and Olen E. Leonard, 215–30. Glencoe, Ill.: Free Press, 1953.

Pye, Lucian W. "Culture and Political Science: Problems in the Evolution of Political Culture." *Social Science Quarterly* 53 (September 1972): 285–96.

Quién es quién en política: Relación circunstanciada de los más connotados hombres públicos de nuestra patria en quiénes decansa la responsabilidad del futuro nacional. San José: Publicadad Roala, 1985.

Rabe, Stephen. *Eisenhower and Latin America: The Foreign Policy of Anticommunism.* Chapel Hill: University of North Carolina Press, 1988.

———. "Marching Ahead (Slowly): The Historiography of Inter-American Relations." *Diplomatic History* 16 (Summer 1989): 297–316.

Rippy, James F. *The Caribbean Danger Zone.* New York: Putnam's, 1940.

Rippy, J. Fred. "Relations of the United States and Costa Rica during the Guardia Era." *Bulletin of the Pan American Union* 77 (February 1943): 61–68.

Robinson, Ronald. "Non-European Foundations of European Imperialism: Sketch for a Theory of Collaboration." In *Imperialism: The Robinson and Gallagher Controversy,* ed. William Roger Louis, 128–52. New York: New Viewpoints, 1976.

Rodríguez, Mario. *Central America.* Englewood Cliffs, N.J.: Prentice-Hall, 1965.

Rodríguez-Porras, Armando. *Juan Rafael Mora-Porras y la guerra contra los filibusteros.* San José: Imprenta Las Americas, 1955.

Rodríguez-Stein, Rosa Emilia. "Collective Actions in Peripheral Nations: A Comparative Analysis of Five Central American Countries." Ph.D. diss., University of Arizona, 1989.

Rodríguez-Vega, Eugenio. *De Calderón a Figueres.* San José: Editorial Universidad Estatal a Distancia, 1981.

Rojas-Bolanos, Manuel. *Lucha social y guerra civil en Costa Rica, 1940–1948.* San José: Editorial Porvenir, 1980.

Rolbein, Seth. *Nobel Costa Rica: A Timely Report on Our Peaceful, Pro-Yankee Central American Neighbor.* New York: St. Martin's Press, 1989.

Romualdi, Serafino. *Presidents and Peons: Recollections of a Labor Ambassador in Latin America.* New York: Funk and Wagnalls, 1967.

Ronning, Neale. "Intervention, International Law, and the Inter-American System." *Journal of Interamerican Affairs* 3 (April 1961): 250–54.

Rosenberg, Emily. *Spreading the American Dream: American Cultural Expansion, 1890–1945.* New York: Hill and Wang, 1982.

Rosenberg, Mark. "The Politics of Health Care in Costa Rica, 1941–1975." Ph.D. diss., University of Pittsburgh, 1976.

———. "Social Reform in Costa Rica: Social Security and the Presidency of Rafael Angel Calderón." *Hispanic American Historical Review* 62 (May 1981): 278–96.

———. "Social Security Policymaking in Costa Rica: A Research Report." *Latin American Research Review* 14 (1979): 116–33.

———. "State Intervention and Presidential Control in Costa Rica: The Role of the Partido Liberación Nacional." *SECOLAS Annals* 10 (March 1979): 95–108.

Ross, Thomas, and David Wise. *The Invisible Government.* New York: Random House, 1969.

Rovinski, Samuel. *Cultural Policy in Costa Rica.* Vendôme: Imprimerie des Presses Universitaires de France, 1977.

Rubio-Orbe, Gonzalo, ed. *América Indígena* 43 (April–June 1974): 291–559.

Rubottom, Roy R. Interview with Richard D. Challener, 12 June 1966. Transcript. John Foster Dulles Oral History Collection. Princeton University Library, Princeton, N.J.

Salazar-Mora, Jorge Mario. *Calderón-Guardia.* San José: Ministerio de Cultura, Juventud y Desportes, Direción de Publiciones, 1980.

———. "Rafael Angel Calderón-Guardia, el funador." *Revista de Ciencias Sociales* 49–50 (September–December 1990): 7–11.

Salazar-Mora, Orlando. *El apogeo de la república liberal en Costa Rica, 1870–1914.* San José: Editorial de la Universidad de Costa Rica, 1990.

Salisbury, Richard V. *Anti-Imperialism and International Competition in Central America, 1920–1929.* Wilmington, Del.: Scholarly Resources, 1989.

———. "The Anti-Imperialist Career of Alejandro Alvarado Quirós." *Hispanic American Historical Review* 57 (November 1977): 587–612.

———. "Costa Rica and the 1920–1921 Union Movement: A Reassessment." *Journal of Interamerican Studies and World Affairs* 19 (August 1977): 393–418.

———. *Costa Rican Relations with Central America, 1900–1934.* Buffalo: Council on International Studies, 1975.

———. "Costa Rica's Stand on Recognition, 1923–1934." *Hispanic American Historical Review* 54 (August 1974): 453–78.

Sancho, Mario. *Costa Rica: Suiza Centroamérica.* San José: Talleoces Tipográficos "La Tribuna," 1935.

Sancho-Riba, Eugenio. "Merchant-Planters and Modernization: Early Liberal Experiments in Costa Rica, 1849–1870." Ph.D. diss., University of California, San Diego, 1982.

Schifter-Sikora, Jacobo. *La fase oculta de la guerra civil en Costa Rica.* San José: EDUCA, 1981.

———. *Las alianzas conflictivas: Las relaciones de Costa Rica y Estados Unidos de la Segunda Guerra Mundial a los inicios de la Guerra Civil.* San José: Libro Libre, 1986.

———. "Origins of the Cold War in Central America: A Study of Diplomatic Relations between Costa Rica and the United States, 1940–1949." Ph.D. diss., Columbia University, 1983.

Schlesinger, Arthur M., Jr. *A Thousand Days: John F. Kennedy in the White House.* Boston: Houghton Mifflin, 1965.

Schoonover, Thomas. *The United States in Central America, 1860–1911: Episodes of Social Imperialism and Imperial Rivalry in the World System.* Durham, N.C.: Duke University Press, 1991.

Schwarz, Jordan A. *Liberal: Adolf A. Berle and the Vision of an American Era.* New York: Free Press, 1987.

Scott, James C. *Weapons of the Weak: Everyday Forms of Peasant Resistance.* New Haven, Conn.: Yale University Press, 1985.

Scully, Michael. "Don Pepe's Private War against Communism." *Reader's Digest* 56 (June 1950): 311–15.

Seligson, Mitchell. "Agrarian Policies in Dependent Societies: Costa Rica." *Journal of Interamerican Studies and World Affairs* 19 (May 1977): 201–32.

———. "La tesis de la 'sociedad dual': Una reexaminación del caso de Costa Rica." *Revista de Ciencias Sociales* (Universidad de Costa Rica) 10 (1977): 33–47.

———. *Peasants of Costa Rica and the Development of Agrarian Capitalism.* Madison: University of Wisconsin Press, 1980.

Shaw, Paul. *Land Tenure and the Rural Exodus in Chile, Colombia, Costa Rica and Peru.* Gainesville: University of Florida Press, 1976.

Slade, William F. "The Federation of Central America." Ph.D. diss., Clark University, 1917.

Slater, Jerome. *The OAS and United States Foreign Policy.* Columbus: Ohio State University Press, 1967.

Solera-Castro, Mario, Lowell Gudmundson, and Jacobo Schifter-Sikora. *El judío en Costa Rica.* San José: Editorial Estatal a Distancia, 1979.

Squier, Ephraim. *Notes on Central America.* New York: Harper, 1855.

———. *The States of Central America.* New York: Harper, 1858.

Stansifer, Charles L. "Application of the Tobar Doctrine to Central America." *The Americas* 23 (January 1967): 251–72.

Stephens, John L. *Incidents of Travel in Central America, Chiapas and Yucatan.* New Brunswick, N.J.: Rutgers University Press, 1949.

Stephenson, Paul G. "Costa Rican Government and Politics." Ph.D. diss., Emory University, 1965.

Stern, Steve J. "Feudalism, Capitalism, and the World-System in the Perspective of Latin America and the Caribbean." *American Historical Review* 93 (October 1988): 829–72.

———, ed. *Resistance, Rebellion, and Consciousness in the Andean Peasant World.* Madison: University of Wisconsin Press, 1987.

Stetson, Dorothy. "Social Characteristics of Costa Rican Decision Makers." *Journal of Politics* 31 (August 1969): 799–804.

Stone, Samuel Z. *The Heritage of the Conquistadors: Ruling Classes in Central America from Conquest to the Sandinistas.* Lincoln: University of Nebraska Press, 1990.

———. *La dinastía de los conquistadores: La crisis del poder en la Costa Rica contemporánea.* San José: Editorial Universitaria Centroamérica, 1982.

———. "Production and Politics in Central America's Convulsions." *Journal of Latin American Studies* 15 (November 1983): 453–69.

Tavares de Sá, H. "Test Tube for Peace: Costa Rica and Nicaragua." *Américas* 1 (March 1949): 2–8.

Thompson, Wallace. *Rainbow Countries of Central America.* New York: E. P. Dutton, 1926.

Thorning, Joseph F. "Costa Rica: A Rural Democracy." *World Affairs* 108 (September 1945): 171–80.

———. "The Costa Rican Story." *World Affairs* 112 (Summer 1949): 49–50.

Tillapaugh, J. "Closed Hemisphere and Open World? The Dispute Over Regional Security at the U.N. Conference, 1945." *Diplomatic History* 2 (Winter 1977): 25–42.

Tomasek, Robert D. "Costa Rica." In *Political Forces in Latin America: Dimensions of the Quest for Stability,* ed. Ben G. Burnett and Kenneth Johnson, 91–114. Belmont, Calif.: Wadsworth Publishing, 1968.

Torres-Rodríguez, José Luis. *Otílio Ulate: Su partido y sus luchas.* San José: Editorial Costa Rica, 1985.

Torres-Vincenzi, Fernando. *Doctor Rafael Calderón-Guardia—esbozos biográfico.* San José: Imprenta Lehmann, 1940.

Trask, Roger. "The Impact of the Cold War on U.S.–Latin American Relations, 1945–1949." *Diplomatic History* 1 (Summer 1977): 271–79.

Trejos, José Francisco. *Origen y desarrollo de la democracia en Costa Rica.* San José: Editorial Trejos Hermanos, 1939.

Triska, Jan R., ed. *Dominant Powers and Subordinate States: The United States in Latin America and the Soviet Union in Eastern Europe.* Durham, N.C.: Duke University Press, 1986.

Ulam, Adam. *The Rivals: American and Russia since World War II.* New York: Viking Press, 1971.

Ulate-Blanco, Otílio. *Hacia dónde lleva a Costa Rica el Señor Presidente Figueres?* San José: Imprenta Universal, 1955.

———. "Responsible Freedom in the Americas: The Individual and the States." *Vital Speeches* 21 (15 January 1955): 969–71.

United Nations. "Costa Rican–Nicaraguan Incident." *United Nations Bulletin* 6 (15 April 1949): 384.

U.S. Congress. *Congressional Record,* 83rd Cong., 2d sess., 1 February 1954. Vol. 100, pt. 1:1073.

———. *Congressional Record,* 84th Cong., 1st sess., 13 January 1955. Vol. 101, pt. 1:329–30.

U.S. Department of State. "Action Under Rio Treaty in Costa Rican–Nicaraguan Case Terminated: OAS Council Resolution." *Department of State Bulletin* 33 (3 October 1955): 546–48.

———. "Costa Rica and Nicaragua Sign Friendship Agreements." *Department of State Bulletin* 34 (27 February 1956): 339–40.

———. "Eximbank Extends Credit to Costa Rican Power Company." *Department of State Bulletin* 31 (11 April 1955): 604.

———. "Point 4 Agreement with Costa Rica." *Department of State Bulletin* 24 (22 January 1951): 151.

———. "Sale of Four U.S. Aircraft to Government of Costa Rica." *Department of State Bulletin* 32 (31 January 1955): 182.

———. "$3 Million World Bank Loan to Costa Rica." *Department of State Bulletin* 35 (8 October 1956): 559–60.

Van Alystne, Richard. "British Diplomacy and the Clayton-Bulwer Treaty." *Journal of Modern History* 11 (Spring 1939): 149–83.

Vargas, Frederico Gonzalo. "The Income Tax in a Developing Nation: The Costa Rican Case." Ph.D. diss., University of Colorado, 1973.

Vega-Carballo, José Luís. "Parties, Political Development and Social Conflict in Honduras and Costa Rica: A Comparative Analysis." In *Sociology of Developing Nations: Central America,* ed. Jan L. Flora and Edelberto Torres-Rivas, 92–111. New York: Monthly Review, 1989.

Verba, Sidney, and Gabriel Almond, eds. *The Civic Culture.* Princeton, N.J.: Princeton University Press, 1963.

Verba, Sidney, and Lucien Pye, eds. *Political Culture and Political Development.* Princeton, N.J.: Princeton University Press, 1965.

Villafranca-Carazo, Richard. *Costa Rica: The Gem of the American Republics: The Land, Its Resources and Its People.* New York: Sackett & Wilhems, 1895.

Volio-Mata, A. "Lighting the Path to a Better World." *United Nations Bulletin* 13 (1 December 1952): 504–6.

Waibel, Leo. "White Settlement in Costa Rica." *Geographical Review* 24 (October 1939): 529–60.

Wallerstein, Immanuel. *The Modern World-System: Capitalist Agriculture and the Origins of the European World-Economy in the Sixteenth Century.* New York: Academic Press, 1976.

Watt, Stewart. *Keith and Costa Rica.* Albuquerque: University of New Mexico Press, 1964.

Webb, J. E. "U.S. Expresses Gratification With New Costa Rican Government." *Department of State Bulletin* 21 (28 November 1949): 833.

Weinrub, Al. *The AFL-CIO in Central America: A Look at the American Institute for Free Labor Development.* Oakland, Calif.: Labor Network on Central America, 1987.

White, Leslie A. *The Concept of Cultural Systems: A Key to Understanding Tribes and Nations.* New York: Columbia University Press, 1975.

Wilcox, Francis. "The Monroe Doctrine and World War II." *American Political Science Review* 36 (June 1942): 433–53.

Williams, Philip J. *The Catholic Church and Politics in Nicaragua and Costa Rica.* Pittsburgh: University of Pittsburgh Press, 1989.

Williams, Robert G. *Export-Agriculture and the Crisis in Central America.* Chapel Hill: University of North Carolina Press, 1986.

Wilson, Charles Morrow. *Challenge and Opportunity: Central America.* New York: Henry Holt, 1941.

Winson, Anthony. *Coffee and Democracy in Modern Costa Rica.* Toronto: Between the Lines, 1989.

———. "One Road to Democracy with Development: José Figueres and the Social Democratic Project after 1948." In *Central America: Democracy, Development, and Change,* ed. John M. Kirk and George W. Schuyler, 89–100. New York: Praeger, 1988.

Wolf, Eric R. *Peasants.* Englewood Cliffs, N.J.: Prentice-Hall, 1966.

Wood, Bryce. *The Dismantling of the Good Neighbor Policy.* Austin: University of Texas Press, 1985.

———. *The Making of the Good Neighbor Policy.* New York: Columbia University Press, 1961.

———. *The United States and the Latin American Wars, 1932–1942.* New York: Columbia University Press, 1966.

Woods, Lawrence T. *Asia-Pacific Diplomacy: Nongovernmental Organizations and International Relations.* Vancouver: UBC Press, 1993.

Woods, Randall B. "Decision-making in Diplomacy: The Rio Conference of 1942." *Social Science Quarterly* 55 (1975): 901–18.

Woodward, Ralph Lee, Jr. *Central America.* New York: Oxford University Press, 1985.

Wortman, Miles L. *Government and Society in Central America, 1680–1840.* New York: Columbia University Press, 1982.

Young, Allen M. *Costa Rica: Nature, Prosperity and Peace on the Rich Coast.* Milwaukee: Interamerican Research Corporation, 1984.

Zahniser, Marvin R., and W. Michael Weis. "A Diplomatic Pearl Harbor? Richard Nixon's Goodwill Mission to Latin America in 1958." *Diplomatic History* 13 (Spring 1989): 163–90.

Zamora-Acosta, Elias. *Etnografía histórica de Costa Rica, 1561–1615.* Seville: Imprenta Raimundo, 1980.

Zelaya C., Antonio. *Cien años de libertad de prensa en Costa Rica: 1843–1943.* San José: Edicion en homenaje al periodísmo nacional, 1943.

Zeledón, Marco Tulio. *Historia constitucional de Costa Rica en el bienio, 1948–1949.* San José: Franklin Aguilar, 1950.

Zemurray-Stone, Doris. "Indians and Costa Rica." *Bulletin of the Pan American Union* 82 (February 1948): 61–69.

———. *Pre-Colombian Man in Costa Rica.* Cambridge, Mass.: Peabody Museum Press, 1977.

INDEX